WHY PERÓN
CAME TO POWER

Borzoi Books on LATIN AMERICA

General Editor
LEWIS HANKE

UNIVERSITY OF CALIFORNIA, IRVINE

WHY PERÓN CAME TO POWER

❄ ❄ ❄

The Background to Peronism in Argentina

EDITED WITH AN INTRODUCTION BY

JOSEPH R. BARAGER
The Catholic University of America

❄ ❄ ❄

Alfred · A · Knopf / New York

Acknowledgments

I am particularly indebted to Lewis Hanke for his advice and for his patience during the delays encountered in preparing this manuscript; and to Professor Arthur P. Whitaker for much of my training in the discipline of history and for his counsel as a friend over the past two decades. My wife, Jane Barager, made many valuable suggestions while typing the manuscript.

My interest in the Peronist Revolution owes much to a Doherty Foundation Fellowship, and to a Penfield Traveling Scholarship from the University of Pennsylvania, which enabled me to visit, live, and travel in Argentina during 1949-1950. A complete listing of the Argentines who contributed to my understanding of and deep admiration for their troubled nation would be too extensive to be cited here, but I must single out Arturo Frondizi, the late Alberto Palcos, and Mario Rey for their aid and friendship. I also wish to acknowledge the assistance of Mrs. David Peterson in translating the selections by Gino Germani and Alejandro Ruiz-Guiñazú.

The translations, the choice of documents, interpretations, and any errors are my sole responsibility.

McLean, Virginia
November 1967

JOSEPH R. BARAGER

Contents

WHY PERÓN
CAME TO POWER

Introduction

Juan Domingo Perón is far and away the most controversial Argentine figure of the post-World War II period. There are those who maintain that he is personally responsible for virtually all the ills and misfortunes that have beset Argentina during the last two decades. Some of this group owe their fervor to their own experiences in opposing the Peronist Revolution, while others have accepted the judgments expressed in the great mass of publications critical of Perón, which have appeared since he began his ascent to power.[1]

Another group, about a third of the Argentine electorate, remembers Perón as its champion against those who would keep the lower classes in their "proper place," and as the leader who brought hope, status, and a sense of security to Argentina's forgotten ones, the *descamisados* (shirtless ones).

Justice would indeed be blind if the scales were tilted completely to either side in this controversy. The purpose of this study, however, is not to estimate Clio's ultimate judgment on Perón, but to present the conditions that enabled Perón, and Peronism, to come to power. In so doing the weight of evidence has necessitated giving short shrift to the myth that Perón alone is responsible for Argentina's time of troubles. At the same time, even the most cursory examination of Perón in power indicates that the other myth, that Perón consciously and selflessly dedicated himself to the welfare of the descamisados, should receive

---

[1] Fritz L. Hoffmann has reviewed a considerable number of these publications in *The Hispanic American Historical Review*, XXXVI (November 1956), 510–528, and XXXIX (May 1959), 213–233.

similar treatment. That, however, is more properly the theme of another study.

One of the most astute and experienced politicians of the Perón era insists that Perón was created by the actions and policies of the government in power after the overthrow of President Hipólito Yrigoyen[2] in September 1930. "This act made the feet, that policy provided the legs, this one created his chest, etc., etc." [3] One can agree that the events of the post-September 1930 period are the ones that stand out most sharply as answers to the question, "Why Perón?" but the evidence indicates that the way for Perón was also being prepared during a much earlier period in Argentine history.

As Domingo F. Sarmiento (document 1) makes clear, an Argentine nation was not formed as an immediate result of the area's achieving independence from Spain. The liberal leadership of the independence movement distrusted the masses, who in turn opposed the liberals' efforts to introduce foreign ideas and customs. Ricardo Levene, one of Argentina's leading historians, has described (document 2) how the people in the provinces and their local leaders, the *caudillos,* reacted to protect their local autonomy, regional interests, and way of life against the centralizing efforts of the liberal leadership in Buenos Aires.[4]

---

[2] Irigoyen is the standard spelling, but Hipólito wrote his name with an initial Y. In official government documents, however, it is Irigoyen. Some authors use the Y, others the I.

[3] Conversation with former President Arturo Frondizi during February 1966. In 1930 Frondizi entered politics to oppose the military regime that succeeded Yrigoyen. Frondizi was the minority (Radical Party) opposition leader in the Argentine Chamber of Deputies (1948–1951), and the Radical Party vice-presidential candidate in the 1951 elections. He won the presidential election of 1958 but was ousted by a military coup in March 1962.

[4] For a useful analysis of *caudillismo* see Hugh M. Hamill, Jr., ed., *Dictatorship in Spanish America* (New York: Alfred A. Knopf, 1965).

This tendency of the provincial masses to follow leaders who promised and provided protection against alien ideas became even more deeply rooted in the chaotic years of the post-revolutionary period and has persisted down to the present. When the migrants from the provinces poured into Buenos Aires in ever-increasing numbers during the second third of this century, Col. Juan D. Perón was the caudillo figure around whom they rallied in return for his assurance that he was their protector against "the oligarchs."

Order was more or less restored during the lengthy reign (1829–1831, 1835–1852) of Juan Manuel de Rosas, the gaucho caudillo par excellence, who successfully exploited the xenophobic cast of *criollo* nationalism among the country's illiterate masses and the provincial outlook of the regional caudillos for his own purposes (document 3). This experience further strengthened the conviction of the Argentine liberals that the masses had to be—as one of them, Domingo F. Sarmiento, put it—"educated to the use of sovereignty." Yet Rosas did restore order, and the efforts of two world powers, Great Britain and France, to coerce his government with a naval blockade and assistance for his enemies enabled him to play the role of defender of Argentine sovereignty. Thus it is not surprising that a century later ardent nationalists, looking back to the Rosas era as a "golden age," would look forward to the coming of a second Rosas and find him in a career military officer, a nationalist champion with a charismatic appeal to the lower classes.

When Rosas was overthrown, the constitution adopted, in order to mollify regional interests (including those of the caudillo of Santa Fe, Juan José de Urquiza, who had been instrumental in the overthrow of Rosas), followed the United States Constitution in establishing a federal system. The Constitution of 1853 provided the national government with powers for intervening in the provinces which were, in written form, somewhat similar to those included in its North American model. As a neutral observer has noted, however, these powers were used quite differently in Argentina (document 3). There the power to intervene not only enabled the national government to restore order disrupted by local political struggles but also ensured that the provincial government was controlled by the party in power in Buenos Aires. Indirect elections for president, vice president, and national senators (as in the United States), along with restrictions on suffrage, further reflected the Argentine liberals' lack of confidence in the masses in general and in the gaucho followers of the provincial caudillos in particular.

The Constitution of 1853 also contained many of the checks and balances which, in its North American model, were designed to retain a balance among the executive, legislative, and judicial branches of government. The drafters of the Argentine constitution, however, adapted their fundamental charter to the physical and political realities of mid-nineteenth century Argentina, and the constitutional powers accorded the Argentine president were considerably greater than those of his North American counterpart (document 3). Even though weak presidents might not exercise them to their fullest extent, those powers would be consistently expanded under the administrations of strong political leaders. The tradition of a dominant executive branch would be established long before Perón came to power nearly a century later, thus preparing the way for his almost complete domination of the other two branches of government for nearly a decade.

Nevertheless, the Generation of 1837, which sought to consolidate the Argentine nation after Rosas' overthrow in 1852, did try to prepare the masses for intelligent use of suffrage by greatly expanding public education. They also sought to introduce a new leavening agent by encouraging European immigrants to populate Argentina's empty spaces and to help speed economic progress. The first four presidents to serve full terms under the Constitution of 1853—the post-Rosas leaders Urquiza, Bartolomé Mitre, Sarmiento, and Nicolás Avellaneda—devoted their efforts to the material progress of the nation and believed that they were firmly linked to the mass of the people. Yet, as an Argentine historian points out, these men, together with the other leading intellectual and political figures of their time, constituted an elite.[5] Contests for, and transfers of, political power occurred within that elite.

The majority of Argentine lower class rural inhabitants, the *gauchaje,* had little part in the political scene except when it followed a gaucho caudillo in revolt against the alien way of life being introduced by the post-Rosas leaders. The unfortunate alienation of Argentine intellectuals from the Argentine masses, which was so clearly evident during the Rosas period, was merely less marked during the post-Rosas period. After 1880 the two groups drifted further and further apart until by the time of Perón they were separated by an almost unbridgeable abyss. The depth and width of that abyss is indicated by the Argentine historian José Luis Romero who wrote that:

> Below [the members of the liberal elite] were the popular masses, the *gauchaje,* which felt itself oppressed by the new ways of life and voiced its complaint, comparing the past with the present, in the poetry of José Hernández in the gaucho epic, *Martín Fierro*:

[5] José Luis Romero, *Las ideas políticas en Argentina* (Mexico, D.F.: Fondo de Cultura Económica, 1946), pp. 163–164.

> The gaucho was there in his stomping grounds
> feeling quite safe and at ease;
> but now . . . damn it all!
> things are so messed up
> that the poor guy spends all his time
> running from the authorities.

And Martín Fierro ended by expressing this hope:

> And I let the ball of fate roll on
> for it has to stop some day.
> The gaucho just has to grin and bear it
> until death comes to swallow him up
> or we get a criollo chap to rule
> this land in the gaucho's way.[6]

This was a theme that Perón would pick up and use to good advantage in his drive for power.

The year 1880 was a bench mark in Argentine history. The end of Avellaneda's presidency represented the high tide of the nineteenth-century liberal influence. The work of the liberals continued to bear fruit in the material prosperity that followed and in the flood of foreign immigrants that came to Argentina between 1880 and 1914. But the old elite liberal leadership, which had devoted its efforts to the service of the nation and had tried to maintain touch with the masses, was replaced by a new elite. The succeeding governments were closely identified with those groups that profited most from the economic expansion: "the oligarchy," the great landowners (many of whom had secured their enormous holdings under Rosas), and the commercial interests thriving on the export and import trade that was largely funneled through the port of Buenos Aires. As Thomas F. McGann points out (document 4), this elite held and manipulated political power

---

[6] Quoted from José Luis Romero, *A History of Argentine Political Ideas,* translated and with an Introduction by Thomas F. McGann (Stanford, Calif.: Stanford University Press, 1963), p. 163.

for the protection and advancement of its own and allied interests. For decades the political domination by the elite was facilitated by the failure of the immigrants to become naturalized and vote. This lack of interest on the part of the immigrants was encouraged by laws which gave the foreigner virtually all the rights of a citizen, except voting, and did not require the foreigner to perform military service (document 4).

The post-1880 elite groups were not much concerned with preparing the country's masses, whose numbers were being augmented by the increasing flow of immigrants from southern Europe, for participation in elections. Nor did they have any intention of sharing power with the growing middle class, which was casting about for a political movement to represent its interests and aspirations. The technique of official control of elections became even more highly refined after 1880. The increasingly conservative and elite groups fought among themselves but closed ranks whenever their interests were threatened by middle and lower class attempts to win power. The efforts of the middle class were also aborted by the inability of its diverse elements to achieve the unity of its opponents and to secure wide popular support in the provinces. In Buenos Aires, the Federal Capital, and in adjacent heavily populated parts of the province of Buenos Aires the rapid increase in population should have been accompanied by a substantial increase in the size of the electorate. However, as James Scobie indicates (document 5), there was considerable voter apathy, and the manipulation of elections only required the use of methods that were slightly more sophisticated than those employed a half century earlier. Elsewhere in the nation, election results frequently reflected agreements reached between the local political leaders and the groups in power in the Federal Capital. When elections did not re-

flect such ententes, intervention by the national government often followed to correct the provincial political
aberration.

In sum, liberalism came to have a quite different role
after 1880 than it had had in the previous half century or
so. It was no longer a radical doctrine, and to many
Argentines, particularly those denied access to political
power, liberalism became little more than a shield for the
privileges of an aristocracy (document 4).

While the elite managed elections with ease, it did not
display the same sure hand in economic matters, particularly fiscal ones. By 1889 an inflationary cycle was undermining Argentine credit abroad and ruining the small
merchants and other middle class urban groups (document 5). Since these groups were not represented by any
political party, they set about creating one. The Unión
Cívica, formed in protest against the policies of President
Miguel Juárez Celman, quickly gained the support of such
notable figures as the elder statesman Bartolomé Mitre, the
influential politician Leandro N. Alem, and Senator Aris-
tóbulo del Valle. Younger army officers also rallied to the
cause, but a revolution organized for July 1890 was
betrayed and quickly suppressed by the government.
Within a few days, however, President Juárez Celman was
forced to resign.

That victory should have marked the beginning of a
new era in Argentine politics, but, as Professor Scobie
writes, "The reformers emerged from the 1890 revolution as divided as they had entered it" (document 5).
Within a year the Unión Cívica was split, one group of
its leaders joining with the conservative elite while another formed what became Argentina's great middle
class party, the Unión Cívica Radical (UCR). The Radicals, as the party was usually called, campaigned for

open and honest elections. The party, however, suffered defeat after defeat as the conservative aristocrats monopolized political power through fraudulent elections and federal intervention in the provinces.

Against this background, Hipólito Yrigoyen became the dominant Radical caudillo and decreed that the party would shun elections and seek power by force of arms. For nearly two decades the new strategy was no more successful than the old in loosening the grip of the conservatives who were in power. Some of those who disagreed with Yrigoyen's tactics left the UCR to found other parties: Juan B. Justo to establish the Argentine Socialist Party and Lisandro de la Torre to form an agrarian party in the province of Santa Fe which later became the base of the Progressive Democratic movement. Both groups challenged the Radicals' claim to represent the disfranchised Argentine masses.

In 1904, with the Radicals abstaining from elections, the Socialists were able to elect their first deputy to Congress, Dr. Alfredo L. Palacios from the Federal Capital. Nevertheless, the political prospect for the "outs" was a bleak one. As an acute observer sums it up:

> The landed aristocracy had the country's economic wealth, and the government represented them and their interests. The small tenant farmers of Santa Fe, the importers and small-businessmen of Buenos Aires, the working class of city and country might have other interests; but their voice was not heard, nor was there the legal mechanism to make it heard. Labor meetings and strikes were broken up by the police. The Radicals, by their own free choice, abstained from voting. The provinces, which nominally had their own governments, were in fact ruled from Buenos Aires by intervention. The government was conservative and aristocratic, and was determined

to hold on to present advantage. Yrigoyen, survey-
ing the scene, calculated that successful revolution
was the only solution. Juan B. Justo wryly estimated
that if the present [late nineteenth-century] trend continued, he would be elected to the Chamber of Deputies in 1940.[7]

In 1912 the political scene was changed as the result
of an electoral reform sponsored by President Roque
Saenz Peña,[8] the distinguished Argentine diplomat who
had assumed office in 1910. The new President and a
group of his fellow aristocrats were convinced that electoral reform was essential. Even some of Saenz Peña's
predecessors in office had consulted with Yrigoyen on the
subject. As Professor Scobie points out (document 5),
however: "Behind such proposed changes lay no romantic concept of surrender to Jacksonian democracy but
rather the realistic expectation that the oligarchy might
steal the mantle of reform and deprive the Radicals of
their only popular appeal or unifying purpose."

The Saenz Peña Law (passed by Congress in 1911)
coupled voting and military service in providing for universal, secret, and compulsory suffrage for all males over
eighteen. When an Argentine male registered for military
service at the age of eighteen, he was given an enlist-
ment book (*libreta de enrolamiento*) which admitted him
to the polls and his name was placed on the election
register. Closed booths and sealed urns replaced the
former practice of marking the distinctively colored party
ballots in public. The law also established the "incomplete
list," which reserved two thirds of each electoral district's
seats in the national Chamber of Deputies for the major-

---

[7] Ysabel F. Rennie, *The Argentine Republic* (New York: Mac-
millan, 1945), p. 202.

[8] The surname Saenz is usually written with an accent on the *a*
(Sáenz). Roque, however, did not use the accent. See McGann's
text (from which document 4 was taken), p. 76.

ity party and the remaining one third for the ranking minority party.[9]

Despite Yrigoyen's reluctance to abandon the Radicals' policy of abstaining from elections until guaranteed by the elite that the Saenz Peña Law would be enforced, the Radicals contested the elections of April 1912. In the Federal Capital and the province of Santa Fe the Radicals won their first seats in the Congress in spite of considerable violence and electoral fraud. In 1916 the taciturn Yrigoyen was the Radical Party's reluctant candidate for the presidency.

The 1916 presidential elections were the focus of attention. For the first time in its history the nation was going to have a President that represented the popular majority. In their hearts, all parties—Conservatives, Radicals, Socialists, even the Partido Demócratico Progresista—knew what that meant: the next President would be the caudillo, the political boss, the conspirator from Buenos Aires, Hipólito Yrigoyen. For years Yrigoyen had been building his machine all over the country. For years he had worked as a backroom politician who was seldom seen and seldom heard, but always felt. Yrigoyen said that he had no personal ambitions, and refused to discuss his candidacy. His enemies believed that he was a hypocrite and that only a miracle could prevent his being the next President of Argentina. The great middle class adored him. Lisandro de la Torre said that he represented the *reacción gauchesca*—the gauchesque reaction. The Conservatives did not care what he represented, but trembled for their lost power.[1]

Although Yrigoyen received a clear majority of the popular vote, he did not have a majority in the electoral

---

[9] Each province and the Federal Capital constitute separate electoral districts in national elections.

[1] Rennie, *op. cit.,* pp. 203–204.

college, where the balance of power was held by a group
of anti-Yrigoyen Radicals from Santa Fe. This group
finally supported Yrigoyen only because its members disliked him less than they did his conservative opponents.
After he had taken the oath of office on October 12,
1916, the crowds outside the Congress unhitched the
horses from Yrigoyen's carriage and triumphantly pulled
it through the streets of Buenos Aires. Seemingly, the age
of the "common man" was finally at hand.

The tragedy of Yrigoyen for Argentina was that the
promise of the election of 1916 and the hopes of those
who celebrated his inauguration were not realized. His
firm insistence on neutrality kept Argentina out of World
War I, and the nation prospered by supplying materials to
the belligerents on both sides. Furthermore, the sharp
reduction of imports gave an impetus to the manufacture
of light consumer goods. But despite Argentina's prosperity, the wealth of the nation was not much more evenly
distributed than before Yrigoyen assumed power.

Under Yrigoyen numerous measures for the benefit of
labor were passed in spite of conservative control of the
Senate. However, as Gino Germani indicates (document
6), "the legislation was not only rather moderate, but
it also often had no practical application." Labor unions
did have more freedom to operate than before, but the
Yrigoyen administration's laissez-faire policy toward the
economy did not extend to a hands-off policy regarding
labor's strike powers—let alone supporting such strikes.
Any illusions Argentine labor may have had on that
score were shattered by the events of January 1919.

Early in January 1919 a minor strike by metal workers
was exacerbated by pickets firing on policemen escorting
metal shipments into the struck plant. When one of the
policemen died, the police forces escorting another ship-
ment laid a trap in which five workers were killed and

twenty wounded. That same day, a Tuesday, the maritime
workers had voted a general strike for better hours and
wages. The following day was quiet as the general maritime strike began, but the rest of the week justified its
designation as the Tragic Week (*Semana Trágica*). As
workers marched in a funeral procession for their fellow
workers killed earlier in the week, they clashed with the
police and turned their fury on whatever they encountered; mobs roamed the city plundering and burning; the
police fired on bystanders as well as demonstrators; and
sailors and soldiers had to be brought in to restore order.
Many of the mobs were not made up of workers but
rather of groups intent on invading Russian Jewish sections of the city in order to seize, beat, and kill anyone
suspected of being a Jew and therefore—to those groups
—a Bolshevik or anarchist. By the week's end the proud
city of Buenos Aires was a desolate scene with wrecked
vehicles and refuse cluttering the streets. The fighting and
looting and the persecution of Jews were over, but the
memory of the events of the Tragic Week would linger
long in the memory of Argentine labor. Yrigoyen should
not bear the entire blame for the Tragic Week, but there
can be no doubt that his administration badly mishandled
the entire affair.

By the end of World War I Argentina had changed considerably since Yrigoyen had taken over control of the
Unión Cívica Radical in the 1890's. Buenos Aires had
been transformed even more than had the rest of the
country during those three decades. While the nation's
great landowners were native Argentines, the management of industrial and commercial enterprises and the industrial workers concentrated in and about the nation's
capital were mainly foreigners who had arrived during
the pre-World War I period. Although these groups had
supported the Radicals in the election of 1916 (and would

again in 1922 and 1928), neither Yrigoyen nor his successor, Marcelo T. de Alvear, did much either to advance their interests or to reduce the influence of the great landholders on economic policies. As Professor Germani acutely observes (document 6), the Radicals should have represented the new forces that emerged during the 1916–1930 period when they governed the country, but they did little or nothing to prepare the way for the integration of those forces into the national society. They did little, if anything, to solve the country's agrarian problem and did not remove the repressive legislation enacted by conservative governments at the turn of the century to contain the labor movement.

The Radical Party's leadership and much of its support came from those groups which Professor John J. Johnson describes (document 7) as the middle sector of Argentine society. As he indicates, no middle sector leadership in Latin America, upon coming to power, ever had a greater opportunity. The Radicals inherited a government that was financially sound and an economy whose agricultural exports were eagerly sought by the European powers engaged in World War I. Its railroad system was without a rival in Latin America and one of the best in the world. The Argentine workers were healthier and had a lower illiteracy rate and a higher standard of living than their counterparts in any other Latin American country. In view of the number of immigrants that came swarming in, life in the Argentine must also have compared well with conditions in southern and eastern Europe.

If much of the credit for the victory of the Radicals after a prolonged struggle must go to Yrigoyen, so must much of the onus for the party's failures during its fourteen years in power. Despite the success of the Radicals in broadening the electoral base and maintaining an atmos-

phere of freedom, Yrigoyen increased the centralization
of authority in the national government at the expense of
the provinces (document 7). For more than two decades
Yrigoyen had campaigned against federal intervention in
the provinces. But once he was in power it was difficult to
distinguish his conduct in these matters from that of his
predecessors. Elections were still manipulated, and provincial governments were still subject to intervention. The
only change was that the Radicals and not the Conservatives were the manipulators and the interveners!

Perhaps the most disastrous aspect of Yrigoyen's leadership, as far as the future of the Radical Party was concerned, was his insistence upon treating the party as a personal vehicle. The result was a continuing fragmentation
of the party as important leaders revolted against Yrigoyen's capricious and tyrannical role as party chief (document 7).

This tendency was demonstrated in 1922 when Yrigoyen's chosen successor, Marcelo T. de Alvear, a wealthy
aristocrat, assumed office. The aging Radical caudillo evidently expected to continue his domination of both the
party and the government. Alvear, however, soon demonstrated his independence and in so doing again split the
Radicals. The group supporting Alvear become known as
the Anti-Personalistas, a title indicative of their resistance
to Yrigoyen's personal rule. The Anti-Personalistas were
the more conservative element of the UCR. They were
apathetic to, if not adamantly opposed to, social welfare
and pro-labor measures. Thus they readily joined in an
informal coalition with the Conservatives in the Congress,
and the Alvear administration moved to the right with a
"business as usual" attitude. As one scholar concluded:
"Notwithstanding the nearness of social and constitutional
changes in Argentina's neighbors—Uruguay and Chile—

the administration of Alvear took up no basic economic or social problems." [2]

In 1928, to the dismay of the Conservatives, the Alvear government conducted what was probably the second freely contested presidential election in Argentine history. Despite Yrigoyen's advanced age (he was born in 1852), he was elected in a landslide. If Yrigoyen's first term had disappointed the expectations of his supporters, his second term was a disaster for the entire nation. The Yrigoyen of 1928–1930 was an old man, at times senile and unable to make decisions but consistently obstinate in refusing to delegate authority, and surrounded by sycophants and quite a few scoundrels. In the best of times his second administration would have had trouble surviving; with the advent of the world depression and its paralyzing effect on world trade, the days of his administration were numbered. Argentina could still afford corruption but not the almost complete incompetence that marked Yrigoyen's second administration.

On September 6, 1930, when an army column entered Buenos Aires to depose Yrigoyen it met scant resistance.[3] General José F. Uriburu assumed control with the open support of the country's major economic interests and with the acquiescence, if not the support, of most political groups. Among the many minor figures involved in ending Argentina's first attempt at middle class government was army captain Juan Domingo Perón, one month short of celebrating his thirty-fifth birthday.

In summing up the Radicals' fourteen years in power, one must acknowledge their contribution to the broadening of the electoral base, to the growth of more represen-

---

[2] Harry Bernstein, *Modern and Contemporary Latin America* (Philadelphia: J. B. Lippincott, 1952), p. 266.

[3] Yet, when Yrigoyen died less than three years later (July 1922), 100,000 Argentines followed the funeral procession.

tative government, and to the development of education. At the same time, however, it is clear that their efforts in promoting the welfare of the lower class, of the neglected elements of society, left much to be desired. Although labor legislation was passed, it often was not enforced, and Radical administrations sometimes used their powers to prevent or to break strikes. As Professor Johnson concludes (document 7): "The over-all view of labor's status under the Radicals revealed that the leadership's thinking had not been affected by the Mexican Revolution or the world trade union movement."

Thus it is not surprising that there was so little popular resistance to the September 1930 military coup, which marked the end of a lengthy period in which Argentina's military leaders had largely abstained from direct intervention in national and local politics. It also marked the end of the era of governments that were, if not benevolent, at least not openly hostile toward labor. The return of conservative rule was accompanied by an authoritarian military attitude not inclined to tolerate strikes or demonstrations, particularly in key industries or services.

As a result, labor leadership also changed its attitude, from the political tendencies of the old anarchists to the new career union leadership's emphasis on social security and social service for their memberships. As Robert J. Alexander indicates, however, there was considerable evidence of a growing gap between the leaders and regular members of many labor unions, which was exploited by the Communists in the late 1930's and early 1940's (document 12).

The character of labor union membership was also changing as a result of the restrictions on immigration imposed by the post-Yrigoyen governments. Union organization was still almost completely limited to the larger urban areas, and urban labor increasingly consisted of second-generation Argentines and migrants from the country-side.

In 1936 some 49 per cent of the population of the Federal Capital had been born there, 36 per cent were foreign-born, and only 15 per cent had been born in the interior of the country. By 1947, however, the foreign-born constituted only 28 per cent of the residents of the nation's capital, and the number of inhabitants from the interior had grown to 32 per cent of its population.[4] These largely politically illiterate migrants and the second-generation Argentines were "good tinder for the fire which Perón was soon going to light." (See document 12.)

The new governors of Argentina, the country's armed forces, were not united when they assumed power in 1930. One group, led by General Uriburu and supported by certain civilian elements deeply mistrustful of representative governments, wanted to hold power for an extended period during which all vestiges of Radicalism would be rooted out and a "new order" established. The other main military group, led by General Agustín P. Justo, Uriburu's military rival, was opposed to the totalitarian ideas favored by the Uriburu regime. They preferred a return to the pre-Yrigoyen *status quo* in which the form, if not the substance, of representative institutions would be followed. This splitting of the military, particularly of its key service, the Army, was to occur again and again in the coming decades, facilitating Perón's rise to power and the consolidation of his position, but then also becoming a factor in his downfall in 1955.

Uriburu's plans for converting Argentina into a corporate state under elite control also met widespread resistance from the leadership of the political parties that Uriburu planned to eradicate. Arthur P. Whitaker (docu-

---

[4] Eduardo Zalduendo, *Geografía electoral de la Argentina* (Buenos Aires: Ediciones Ancora, 1958), p. 63.

ment 8) concludes that: "As for mass support, Uriburu made no effort to build it up until too late, and in any case it was in all probability ruled out by the elitist character of the plan; this was a sobering lesson that was not lost on one of Uriburu's junior associates, Captain Juan Perón."

Within a year Uriburu's design for Argentina was collapsing under joint civilian-military pressure for elections. When the elections were held, in November 1931, a coalition of conservatives, Anti-Personalista Radicals and a group of conservative Socialists (Independent Socialists) joined to elect General Justo to the presidency. The elections had been carefully controlled to prevent a Radical victory.

The years 1930–1943 have been called the Era of Infamy in Argentina. Elections were tightly controlled by fraud, intimidation, or whatever other means were necessary to ensure keeping the reins of government in the hands of the conservative-military coalition. State intervention in the economy was facilitated by centralization of controls over currency, commercial credit, and foreign exchange. The Banco Central Argentino, a private institution operated under government supervision, was given control in those vital fields. Provincial autonomy became more and more a fiction as the federal government repeatedly intervened in provincial politics and many of the provinces became increasingly dependent on the federal treasury for funds.

In 1933 the Justo administration concluded a trade agreement, the Roca-Runciman pact, with Great Britain. The government's acceptance of the very short end of the agreement raised the hackles of Argentine nationalists, many of whom were fervent Anglophobes. Argentine nationalism became even more extreme as Argentine governments under Justo and his successors, Roberto M. Ortiz and Ramón S. Castillo, continued their close economic alignment with Great Britain. Extreme nationalists of the right and of the left denounced what they referred to as Argentine subservience before British tradesmen. Among the military, particularly the Army with its German advisers and pro-German traditions, disgust with Argentina's international orientation was growing.

The advent of World War II added still another divisive factor to the Argentine scene. Many Argentines, possibly a majority, were apathetic and tended to regard the war as another great-power struggle that was not their affair. A vocal minority, however, were intensely pro-Allied, either because of a deep repugnance to the totalitarian Axis dictatorships or because support of the democratic powers became equated with opposition to the reactionary regime of Ramón S. Castillo.[5] Another minority was adamantly anti-Allied and hopeful of an Axis victory. Both groups had partisans in the military, where the Navy was traditionally pro-British and the Army, reflecting the influence of its German instructors, had many pro-Axis adherents.

In December 1941, Castillo, acting president at the time, used the Japanese attack on Pearl Harbor as a pretext for imposing a state of siege to stifle the increasing criticism of his domestic and foreign policies. His obvious pro-Axis attitude made him anathema to the Argentine liberals but bearable to the pro-Axis groups despite his regime's continued close economic ties with the British.

Castillo, one of the most unpopular of Argentine presidents, was maintained in office by the support of the oligarchy and the military. By mid-1943 he had offended

---

[5] Roberto M. Ortiz had assumed office in 1937 after one of the most blatantly fraudulent elections in Argentine history. His efforts to redeem the manner of his election, by carrying further the relaxation of controls begun under Justo, were aborted by his declining health. By 1939 Vice President Castillo was acting as president and was in control much of the time. Ortiz finally resigned in 1942.

both groups. The oligarchs resented his clear intention to impose his own choice as his successor in the elections scheduled for September 1943. The armed forces were becoming increasingly uneasy as Brazil, Argentina's principal Latin American rival, received arms and other military supplies from the United States. Since Argentina, as a neutral with a government that had obvious pro-Axis leanings, received no such aid and had no other ready source of supply, the balance of power in southern Latin America was being rapidly shifted in Brazil's favor. When it became apparent that Castillo intended to elect a wealthy crony, the pro-Axis military faction joined with pro-Allied elements to depose the government. The coup of June 4, 1943, met with no resistance. In fact, the fall of Castillo was hailed in all political circles, with only a few voices raised in apprehension over what might follow. Juan D. Perón was then still a colonel and was overshadowed by the generals and admirals headlined in the immediate post-coup maneuvering for power.

The June 4, 1943, coup provides an occasion to take stock of the situation in Argentina on the eve of the period in which Perón would manipulate events and people in his drive for power. There had been significant changes in Argentina since the 1930 coup had restored the conservatives to power. Economic power was moving from the great landowners to a different group—the operators of service industries and the industrial interests manufacturing consumer goods that could no longer be imported in needed quantities once World War II had erupted. Although exports of agricultural products continued to be the principal source of foreign exchange, more Argentines were employed in industry than in cattle-raising and farming. Moreover, the individuals making the profits from the agrarian sector of the economy were not the ones who produced the beef, grapes, sugar, and other raw materials, but the ones who operated industries utilizing those materials. "Nevertheless, the landowning minority continued to behave as though nothing had altered, as though Irigoyen had never existed, and as though the new industries —whose development was so vitally important during the second world war—were of no account." [6]

Other elements of Argentine society had experienced equally significant changes. The sharp curtailment of foreign immigration in the early 1930's was followed by mass migrations from the country's interior provinces to the urban areas, particularly to the metropolitan zone of Buenos Aires (see Table 2 of document 6). Professor Germani underlines the significance of transplanting great masses of rural labor to the nation's capital without providing the institutional channels necessary for integrating them into the normal functioning of democracy (document 6). The general disillusionment caused by the failures of the Radical governments, the skepticism produced by the actions of their successors, and the lack of political parties able and willing to administer to the needs and aspirations of those transplanted rural masses all served to ready these masses for exploitation by whoever could provide the security of the *patrón* figure they had left behind and for a movement in which they could participate with a sense of belonging.

Although the 1853 Constitution (the longest-lived of Latin American constitutions) was still in force, its provisions establishing the separation of powers and checks and balances to prevent the predomination of one branch of government had been effectively negated by the course of events. As Carlos Sánchez Viamonte makes clear (document 9), one Argentine president after another had enlarged the powers of his office at the expense of both

---

[6] Pendle, *op. cit.*, p. 89.

the legislative and judicial powers. Yrigoyen had made his contribution to the domination of the executive branch and of the national government but had been constrained by his inability to keep unity among the forces that had brought him to power. By and large Argentine society had long become reconciled to the enlargement of presidential powers, and opponents could raise little effective resistance to skillful exploitation of those powers as long as the forms of constitutionalism were maintained.

These, then, were the components of the situation that Perón exploited: a constitutional system tailored to exploitation by a dynamic leader; a new class of economic interest groups and entrepreneurs whose needs were ignored by the old power elite representing the great landholders; an amorphous lower class neglected by the existing labor organizations and political parties; a military establishment divided over its attitude toward the world conflict whose final outcome was still in doubt; and a middle class, the largest in Latin America, which was resentful of more than a decade of corrupt, reactionary rule, but whose elements showed little ability to subordinate their individual group interests in a common effort. Individuals such as Alejandro Ruiz-Guiñazú (document 10) were urging a national rejuvenation and were looking for the provident leader to show the way. In other words, there was a political vacuum, and the man who would more than fill it was about to emerge on the center stage of Argentine politics.

Who was Juan Perón? What sort of man was this who in the short space of less than a year would be the most widely discussed figure in Argentina, would dominate the political scene in less than two years, and in less than three would be constitutional president and head of the most powerful political machine Argentina has ever known?

Juan D. Perón was born on October 8, 1895, in Lobos,

a town in the province of Buenos Aires. His parents, who were members of the growing Argentine middle class, were of predominantly Italian and Spanish background. Young Juan soon became familiar with gaucho lore as the area around Lobos had been the stamping ground of one of the famous gaucho outlaws, Juan Moreira. The outlaw had been a friend of Perón's grandparents before the authorities put an end to his exploits.[7] When the Perón family moved to the capital, Juan attended schools there. In early 1911, the youth entered the Colegio Militar. The die was cast; the young Perón would be an army officer.

In 1930, the Argentine Army was still relatively small, and Perón, after nineteen years of training and service, was still only a captain. During the next decade his horizons were considerably broadened by teaching assignments at the Army War College and service as an aide to the Army Chief of Staff and to the Minister of War. In the latter assignments he learned the workings of army politics and the value of controlling personnel assignments.

Then, in 1936–1938, Lieutenant Colonel Perón was sent to Chile as military attaché. In that assignment he revealed his taste for intrigue. As the Argentine expression aptly puts it, he was caught *con las manos en la masa* (red-handed) trying to secure Chile's national defense plans and was declared *persona non grata*.[8]

In early 1939 Perón received the assignment that was

---

[7] Arthur P. Whitaker, *The United States and Argentina* (Cambridge, Mass.: Harvard University Press, 1954), p. 116.

[8] During that tour of duty Perón formed a friendship with Arturo Alessandri, then concluding his second term as President of Chile. When Perón's espionage efforts were uncovered, Alessandri chided him for trying to buy Chile's defense plans from a minor Chilean official. "I took him to the window," Don Arturo later related, "and said, 'Look, amigo, there's Chile's defense,' and pointed to the cordillera real of the Andes." (Conversation of the editor with Alessandri in Santiago, Chile, during late November 1949.)

to have a lasting influence on his subsequent career. He was sent to Italy for military training, spending nearly two years in study there and in visits to Germany, France, Hungary, Albania, Spain, and Portugal. He came back to Argentina an admirer of Mussolini and the Fascist state, determined to emulate Il Duce's success—but without the latter's mistakes. Perón may also have been influenced by what he saw of Hitler's and Franco's regimes. Finally, the New State of Getúlio Vargas, in Brazil, with its authoritarian trappings, probably contributed something to the preparation of Argentina's "Caesar to be."

One must be very careful, however, not to overemphasize the effect of any single influence on Perón. True, he was willing to use anything that he could turn to advantage, regardless of the source, but what he borrowed from abroad he adapted to his needs. At the same time there has been too much emphasis on his foreign borrowings and not enough on what was indigenous in the Perón system. Those borrowings were, as one expert succinctly summarizes:

> . . . heavy in matters of technique and organization, particularly in the fields of propaganda and control of labor; but he used them to strengthen a system deeply rooted in his own understanding of the history of his own country and in his own observations of the successive regimes of Irigoyen, Uriburu, and the Conservative Restoration. He found in Rosas his slogan of discipline and order, and strong-arm squads of the Mazorca to support it, in Rosas and Irigoyen a fervent nationalism spiced with anti-imperialism; in Irigoyen the popularity of attacks on the oligarchy; in Uriburu the Army's mission of national regeneration; and in the Conservative Restoration the demoralization of the chief political parties and the abandonment of laissez faire in favor of economic controls.[9]

---

[9] Whitaker, *op. cit.*, p. 120.

When the June 4, 1943, coup took place Perón was not one of the prominent figures. He was, however, on intimate terms with General Edelmiro Farrell, who became minister of war and vice president in the military government headed by General Pedro Ramírez. Farrell immediately chose Perón to head the war ministry's secretariat, a key position because of its control over army personnel assignments. While that assignment gave him an edge over other ambitious colonels bidding for a military following, he was still overshadowed by higher ranking military figures. Within the secret military lodge (the Grupo de Oficiales Unidos or GOU), Perón was still only one of several officers contending for power and place in mid-1943.

The factionalism within the Army and its expansion under the post-Castillo governments enabled Perón to capitalize on his control over choice assignments. Soon he would be able to boast of the number of undated resignations in his possession that had been signed by army officers. When Ramírez was ousted in February 1944 and Farrell assumed the presidency, Perón also moved up to become minister of war and later (July 1944) vice president. When Perón was promoted from the ministry's secretariat he was very careful to ensure that his successor was someone in whom he had complete confidence (document 11).

If Perón had depended upon military support alone, he might still have won power. In that event his reign probably would have been measured in months rather than years. Unlike his fellow officers, however, Perón looked further than the existing political parties for additional support. He alone appears to have recognized the political potential in the country's discontented labor groups.

While other colonels were bidding for choice commands and political posts, Perón sought and received (October 27, 1943) appointment as head of the Department of

Labor and Social Security. The department was then under the Ministry of Interior but within a short time Perón was able to have it made an independent secretariat, thus securing cabinet rank. As Professor Alexander makes clear (document 12), the disunity within organized labor and the presence of great numbers of laborers outside the existing unions provided a fertile field for exploitation.

Perón made the most of his opportunity. By mid-1945 he had largely destroyed the independent labor-union leadership and had reorganized the trade union movement, making it his own powerful political ally. In October 1945, when Perón's military rivals secured his arrest, removal from his government posts, and imprisonment, the rank and file of Argentine labor realized that its newly won benefits were in danger (document 13). Consequently, labor rallied to the support of "the Colonel" to whom it owed virtually all the material gains that labor had made during the previous two years.

Perón's opponents mishandled their opportunity badly (documents 14 and 15), and he did have some military support during the crucial October 10–17 period. Had his military rivals chosen to use their troops against the Peronist mobs, Perón's return might have been prevented —albeit at a high cost in lives and property damage. But while his opponents wavered, Perón's supporters acted and their idol emerged from the events of that hectic week in an even stronger position.

After October 17, 1945, Perón dominated the Argentine scene so completely that he did not need an official position. The President, General Farrell, was his creature.[1] The cabinet and key military posts were filled with his

---

[1] An anecdote popular in Buenos Aires at the time reflected the position of the two men. Farrell was pictured as saying he looked forward to putting the wreath around the neck of the champion steer at the annual Palermo livestock show, because—the story went—"It's the only thing Perón lets me do on my own."

supporters. He had *de facto* power as the country's strong man but he wanted more—the sanctification of election as constitutional president of Argentina.

The ineptitude displayed by Perón's opponents in the October 1945 crisis was matched by their performance in the period preceding the February 24, 1946, election (document 16). After much infighting the anti-Perón political parties managed to form an electoral coalition, the Unión Democrática, and to produce a platform that had little, if any, appeal to the mass labor vote. The Unión Democrática's presidential candidate, José Tamborini, was an aging physician with a respectable but hardly notable political record. He was scarcely a match for the dynamic Perón, then a strikingly handsome physical specimen with considerable skill as either a polished urban orator or a rabble-rousing demagogue.

Perón not only was handed the labor vote by his opponents; they also allowed him to pre-empt the role of nationalist champion (document 17). In addition, he received an unexpected boon when the United States Department of State published its "Blue Book on Argentina" in the closing days of the campaign. The appearance of the Blue Book enabled Perón to capitalize on his much publicized feud with the former United States Ambassador to Argentina, Spruille Braden, who had returned to Washington to become assistant secretary of state for Latin America. Perón promptly seized on the publication as evidence to support his contention that the real choice for the Argentine vote was not "Tamborini or Perón" but "Braden or Perón" (document 16).

While the casting and counting of ballots was conducted openly and fairly—under army supervision—the Unión Democrática's candidates were subjected to harassment and physical attack during the campaign. The anti-Peronist forces had the support of a clear majority of the country's newspapers, but Perón benefited from the Farrell regime's controls over radio broadcasts and public assemblies. The opposition leaders, however, were so confident that victory was certain that they did not complain about the harassment they had undergone until after they had been soundly defeated.

The election results gave Perón the mandate he sought. He received some 56 per cent of the popular vote. In the electoral college his margin was even more convincing: 304 votes to 72 for Tamborini. In the congressional elections Perón's supporters secured a sizable majority in the Chamber of Deputies and all but two seats in the Senate.[2] They also dominated the elections for provincial governors and legislators and for municipal authorities. It was an election sweep without parallel in Argentine history.

Few men in history have had the opportunity presented Perón when he assumed office in June 1946. Argentina had prospered during the war, building up huge reserves of foreign exchange abroad. The country's railroads, roads, ports, and communications media needed modernization but were still serviceable. There were few, if any, soils in the world that could equal the fertility of the Argentine pampa, and a Europe devastated by war provided a ready market for Argentine foodstuffs. The Argentine population, one of the most literate in Latin America, was not split by racial or religious discord. Finally, the magnitude of Perón's electoral triumph afforded him ample margin to undertake the task of building a "new Argentina" and still respect the substance as well as the form of representative government. He could have been magnanimous in victory, assuming a conciliatory attitude toward the shat-

---

[2] The Peronist senators subsequently refused to seat the two opposition senators and the Senate became 100 per cent Peronist.

tered opposition and offering it a chance to play the role
—admittedly an innovation in Argentine politics—of a
"loyal opposition."

Unfortunately for Argentina, that was not the course
Perón chose. He concentrated on consolidating his own
political power and destroying the opposition with equal
fervor. The heterogeneous groups that had jointly supported his candidacy were merged into one organization
despite any objections their leaders might have had. There
was only one leader, Perón, whose authority was above
questioning in the Peronist Party.

In his relationship with each of the other two branches
of government, President Perón also brooked no opposition. The theory of a separation of powers was given little
more than lip service since, in practice, the presidential
powers were greatly expanded at the expense of the legislature and the judiciary. In that process Perón was aided
by the traditional weakness of the Argentine Congress
and of the Supreme Court whenever confronted by a
strong and popular chief executive (document 9). His
domination of all levels and branches of Argentine government was also facilitated by his party's obedient majorities in the national and provincial legislatures. For nearly
a decade after the 1946 election, there was little political
future in Argentina for anyone who dared to oppose
Perón's dictum. Whatever methods were necessary to stifle
the opposition were usually given a gloss of legality, but
whenever the bounds of constitutionality were exceeded
the victims found little, if any, relief in a judiciary which
had been purged and brought to heel by Perón.

The "new look" in Argentine politics, introduced by the
Peronist Revolution, was based on a shift in the traditional
combination of ruling forces. The military establishment,
which since 1930 had again become accustomed to having

the final say in Argentine politics, found itself sharing power with a rank newcomer—organized labor. Military figures still held cabinet posts, served in Congress, and held positions as provincial governors, as the agents of federal intervention in the provinces, and as directors of state enterprises. For the first time in Argentine history, however, labor was not only represented in the government but was also acknowledged as a full partner by the constitutional president of Argentina, who boasted of being the nation's "Number One Worker."

The organization of workers under Peronist labor leadership continued apace until the Confederación General de Trabajo (CGT), which in early 1943 had some 300,000 members, would boast that its membership was past the 5 million mark. Labor, which before Perón had usually found scant official sympathy for its legitimate grievances, now found its every wish quickly granted, as long as it accepted Peronist direction without question.

Perón's manipulation of labor was greatly facilitated by his principal collaborator after the events of mid-October 1945. During that crisis María Eva Duarte (documents 11 and 12) had been active in his behalf, providing money to rally labor support and exhorting her Peronist cohorts to greater efforts.[3] Shortly after Perón's restoration to power the two were married. When he assumed the presidency Perón turned over the direction of his labor following to his wife, "Evita" or "La Señora" as she was called by the Peronist faithful. (The non-Peronists had other names for her—few of which bear repeating here.)

"La Señora" held no official position, but there was

---

[3] The money probably came from the fund for the relief of the victims of the San Juan earthquake, which was under Perón's direction before his arrest and removal from office.

not any doubt about who ran the Ministry of Labor until her death in July 1952. She was Perón's direct contact with his lower class supporters, and her attacks on the opposition were more reassuring to that strata of his backing than Perón's own more polished discourses (document 18). The top leadership of the CGT was at her beck and call. It had to be, since it could be changed at her whim. During "Evita's" reign, for example, she placed an appropriately named fellow, José Espejo (Joseph Mirror), in the CGT's highest post. Espejo's qualifications for the secretary generalship, other than having been the elevator man in the apartment house where both "Evita" and Colonel Perón lived before the October 1945 crisis, are not easy to ascertain. His removal from that high office followed hard on the death of his patroness in mid-1952.

Señora Perón also played a key role in securing the vote for Argentine women and in organizing a feminine branch of the Peronist Party. In the 1951 national elections the feminine vote contributed heavily to Perón's majority, which rose to nearly two thirds of the popular vote. (Under the 1949 Constitution, the president, vice president and national senators were chosen in direct elections.) In the Federal Capital, where a larger proportion of women voted than in the more conservative provinces, several contests for seats in the national Chamber of Deputies were decided in favor of the Peronist candidates by the feminine vote. (Each sex has separate voting urns and the results of each contest are also separated into total male and female votes.) While the Peronist Women's Party elected several of its candidates to both houses of the national Congress, the major opposition party, the Unión Cívica Radical, did not nominate a single candidate for either national senator or deputy.

While Perón was not above making violent attacks on

his opponents, he was able to leave that task largely to the other half of the Perón partnership. As a result many Argentines convinced themselves that it was "that woman" —one of the milder terms they used—who was responsible for what had happened in Argentina. Thus "La Señora" bore the brunt of the attacks on Perón. She apparently enjoyed her role as his shield in addition to serving as his "hatchet woman" in carrying out other assignments whose performance Perón found distasteful.

In the early years of his regime Perón also benefited from the benevolent attitude of the conservative members of the Argentine Roman Catholic hierarchy toward the post-June 1943 governments (document 19). In the mid-1880's Argentine liberals had secured the passage of legislation prohibiting the teaching of the Roman Catholic religion in the public schools. That prohibition remained in force, despite recurrent efforts to remove it, until December 1943, when the Ramírez government decreed its repeal. Subsequently, the Perón administration passed legislation confirming the Church's right to teach its dogma in the public schools to all children except those whose parents specifically requested that they not receive such instruction.

The pastoral letter issued by the Argentine hierarchy during the 1945–1946 election campaign was also helpful to Perón. It instructed Argentine Catholics not to vote for candidates of any party supporting separation of Church and state, divorce laws, or other anticlerical measures. Since both the Socialist and Communist parties were members of the Unión Democrática and had long urged such measures, the implication of the pastoral message was quite clear.

In the first years under Perón Catholic priests participated openly in Peronist political rallies. One parish priest, Padre Virgilio M. Filippo, ran on the Peronist Party ticket and was elected to the Chamber of Deputies.[4] In a predominantly Roman Catholic nation such partiality was a valuable political asset. There was also in the Argentine Church an anti-Perón faction led by Monseñor Miguel de Andrea, but it was much less influential and was kept in line by the arch-conservative Argentine primate, Santiago Cardinal Copello. During Perón's last years in power, however, many of the Church leaders, despite Cardinal Copello, did oppose the regime's deification of the Peróns and usurpation of the Church's traditional pre-eminence in charitable activities.

As Professor George Blanksten points out (document 19), Perón found the national school system already prepared for him to take over and use in securing and consolidating his control of the country. The military regime that came to power in June 1943 had begun the process of indoctrinating the nation's students with its own particular brand of nationalism—exalting military deeds. Those Argentine educators opposing this process, as well as the Catholic Church's resumption of a prominent role in the public education system and other changes effected by the post-1943 military governments, were dismissed in a purge that continued throughout the entire period Perón was in control.

There was resistance from university students determined not to give up the hard-won reforms of 1918, which included a substantial degree of student participation in university administration and policy-making. The resistance by the students was supported by many of their professors, but was forcibly suppressed by Perón's predecessors in

---

[4] Filippo also delivered political speeches from the pulpit of his parish church in Belgrano, a suburb of Buenos Aires, which caused some of his parishioners to leave the premises.

power and by his lackeys once he had obtained effective control behind the scenes in the Farrell government.

Perón's manipulation of the educational system as a propaganda instrument in the service of his regime caused a serious deterioration of the quality of Argentine education on all levels. However, even prior to Perón that system had not achieved the role its great proponent, Domingo F. Sarmiento, had envisaged for it—namely, to prepare the Argentine people to govern themselves wisely. Outside of the cities, and particularly in the interior provinces, educational facilities were sadly deficient before 1943. A university, and even a secondary, education was beyond the reach of the great majority of Argentines. Thus when Perón opened new primary and secondary schools where none had existed before, the parents had additional reason to be grateful to their benefactor who continually intoned that "Argentina's only privileged are its children." When university education was made tuition-free, students who could not have attended under the pre-Perón system were usually grateful and not inclined to support their fellows in attacking their benefactor. In 1951, at the apogee of his power, Perón could proudly declare that more schools had been constructed during his five years in office than in the preceding hundred years (document 19).

Furthermore, Perón's emphasis upon social justice was a decided asset in his rise to power and the retention of his mass popular following. The appeal to the long-neglected Argentine masses was obvious, and he delivered on many of his campaign promises. As the Peronist political doctrine evolved, it became known as *justicialismo*. In domestic affairs the doctrine was identified as a "Third Position" which avoided both the extreme collectivism of communism and the extreme individualism of capitalism. Since where it happened to be located between those two extremes at any particular time depended upon the attendant circumstances, justicialismo was made to order for that master opportunist, Juan Domingo Perón! His role was the balancing of the various forces in Argentine society to maintain a proper equilibrium. As Perón himself summed it up, "Our 'Third Position' is not a centrist position. It is an ideological position which is in the center, on the right, or on the left according to specific circumstances." [5]

In the field of international relations Perón's Third Position received acceptance among many who repudiated the domestic version. His determination not to follow where the United States led had won him support in his struggle to gain power, and he fell back on "plucking the eagle's tail feathers" whenever it seemed to be a useful maneuver to rally nationalist support. To emphasize his administration's independence of the United States, Perón also established diplomatic relations with the Soviet Union shortly after assuming office.[6] At that time the Soviet resistance to the Nazi war machine had won much sympathy among moderates as well as leftists, and Perón's action received little criticism except from extreme rightists. When the Cold War developed, Perón played on traditional Argentine opposition to involvement in great power struggles by declaring his Third Position would keep the country from becoming involved. Until the consequences of his disastrous economic policies forced him to seek foreign aid, and particularly from the United States,

---

[5] Quoted in George I. Blanksten, *Perón's Argentina* (Chicago: University of Chicago Press, 1953), p. 292. Professor Blanksten's discussion of *justicialismo* is highly recommended for anyone desiring more information on the subject.

[6] Argentine-Russian relations had been broken off at the time of the Bolshevik Revolution because of physical mistreatment and imprisonment of the Argentine Chargé d'Affaires in Moscow, and had stayed that way until mid-1946.

Perón exploited every possible nuance of Argentine xenophobic nationalism.

Finally, Perón's awareness of the value of an efficient propaganda machine—probably acquired during his tour of duty as a military attaché in Mussolini's Italy and during his visits to Hitler's Third Reich and Franco's Spain —was displayed in his regime's use of modern communications media. Before he came to power the bulk of the nation's press was opposed to him, particularly *La Prensa* and *La Nación,* the great metropolitan newspapers widely acknowledged as among the hemisphere's finest. Once Perón was in power the Argentine press was either brought over to Perón's side by pressure or purchase; was rendered largely neutral, as in the case of *La Nación*; or, as in the case of *La Prensa,* was silenced. Radio, and later television, broadcasts were brought into the service of the Peróns, as were wall posters, billboards and other advertising media. Posters with pictures of the Peróns and carrying the slogans "Perón cumple" and "Evita dignifica" appeared at the site of every public works project begun under Perón's aegis.[7] In every way possible the Peróns reiterated again and again that they and their Peronist followers were the only political force interested in the welfare of the masses and able to do something about improving conditions for the workers, their aged relatives and their children. It is a sad commentary on the state of the other political parties that, in general, the Peróns' claims were accurate.

In summary, then, the answer to the question "Why Perón?" lies in the Argentine past and in the failure of previous governments to satisfy the needs and aspirations

---

[7] Some of these projects were inaugurated with much fanfare and then quietly abandoned once their publicity value had been exhausted.

of the Argentine masses and of other groups dissatisfied with a *status quo* maintained by force and by fraudulent elections. Unfortunately, Perón created an even greater imbalance in the society, setting class against class and discrediting "popular democracy" by his corrupt and authoritarian methods. That he responded to the deeply felt needs of many Argentines, however, is clearly evident in the persistence with which more than one third of the Argentine electorate continues to support Peronist candidates. The expectations of Perón's opponents, that Peronism would "go away" after the dictator's overthrow, have been rudely dashed. In the period since September 1955 the persistence of Peronism has remained the nation's number one political problem and a challenging question for foreign and Argentine observers (documents 20, 21, and 22).

I

❖

THE BACKGROUND

———◆◆●▶◆———

This first section in the readings presents aspects of the historical, economic, and social background that set the stage for Perón. In many respects it is the story of the failure of representative government and democratic institutions in Argentina.

1

DOMINGO F. SARMIENTO

———◆◆●◆◆———

LIFE IN THE ARGENTINE
REPUBLIC
Civilization or Barbarism

*Argentina's famed schoolmaster-president, Domingo
F. Sarmiento (1811–1888), has been called his country's first sociologist. The fifty-two volumes of his*
Obras completas[1] *reveal again and again his passion
for educating his countrymen—and anyone else he
encountered in his travels. His* Facundo, *written in
1845 while Sarmiento was in exile in Chile, has
been praised by many literary critics as one of the
masterpieces of Latin American literature. It is also
a penetrating analysis of the Argentine society that
produced the dictator Juan Manuel de Rosas. In
the following selection (from the English translation
by Sarmiento's friend, Mrs. Horace Mann), Sarmiento describes the political forces that developed*

From Domingo F. Sarmiento, *Life in the Argentine Republic in
the Days of the Tyrants: or Civilization and Barbarism,* translated
by Mrs. Horace Mann (New York: Hurd and Houghton, 1868),
pp. 122–133.

[1] Domingo F. Sarmiento, *Obras completas* (Santiago de Chile
and Buenos Aires, 1887–1902).

during the revolutionary and early independence periods in the Argentine. To Sarmiento the forces of civilization and barbarism were personified in Bernardino Rivadavia and Rosas, respectively; and the Argentine problem was not merely how to overthrow the dictator but, even more importantly, how to correct the situation that had enabled the dictator to come to power. A century later, Argentine liberals, including many admirers of Sarmiento, would be faced with a similar problem.

In 1806, the attention of English speculators was turned to South America, and especially attracted to Buenos Ayres by its river, and its probable future. In 1810, Buenos Ayres was filled with partisans of the revolution, bitterly hostile to anything originating in Spain or any part of Europe. A germ of progress, then, was still alive west of the La Plata. The Spanish colonies cared nothing for commerce or navigation. The Rio de la Plata was of small importance to them. The Spanish disdained it and its banks. As time went on, the river proved to have deposited its sediment of wealth upon those banks, but very little of Spanish spirit or Spanish modes of government. Commercial activity had brought thither the spirit and the general ideas of Europe; the vessels which frequented the waters of the port brought books from all quarters, and news of all the political events of the world. It is to be observed that Spain had no other commercial city upon the Atlantic coast. The war with England hastened the emancipation of men's minds and awakened among them a sense of their own importance as a state. Buenos Ayres was like a child, which, having conquered a giant, fondly deems itself a hero, and is ready to undertake greater adventures. The *Social Contract* flew from hand to hand. Mably and Raynal were the oracles of the press; Robes-

pierre and the Convention the approved models. Buenos
Ayres thought itself a continuation of Europe, and if it
did not frankly confess that its spirit and tendencies were
French and North American, it denied its Spanish origin
on the ground that the Spanish Government had patron-
ized it only after it was full grown. The revolution brought
with it armies and glory, triumphs and reverses, revolts
and seditions. But Buenos Ayres, amidst all these fluctuations, displayed the revolutionary energy with which it is
endowed. Bolívar was everything; Venezuela was but the
pedestal for that colossal figure. Buenos Ayres was a
whole city of revolutionists—Belgrano, Rondeau, San Martín, Alvear; and the hundred generals in command of its
armies were its instruments; its arms, not its head nor its
trunk. It cannot be said in the Argentine Republic that
such a general was the liberator of the country; but only
that the Assembly, Directory, Congress, or government
of such or such a period, sent a given general to do this
thing or that. Communication with all the European nations was ever, even from the outset, more complete here
than in any other part of Spanish America; and now, in
ten years' time (but only, be it understood, in Buenos
Ayres), there comes to pass a radical replacement of the
Spanish by the European spirit. We have only to take a
list of the residents in and about Buenos Ayres to see how
many natives of the country bear English, French, German, or Italian surnames. The organization of society, in
accordance with the new ideas with which it was impregnated, began in 1820; and the movement continued until
Rivadavia was placed at the head of the government.
Hitherto Rodríguez and Las Heras had been laying the
usual foundations of free governments. Amnesty laws, individual security, respect for property, the responsibility
of civil authority, equilibrium of powers, public education,
everything, in fine, was in peaceful course of establish-

ment when Rivadavia came from Europe, brought Europe as it were, but Europe was yet undervalued. Buenos Ayres —and that means, of course, the Argentine Republic— was to realize what republican France could not realize, what the English aristocracy did not even wish for, what despotic Europe wanted still less. This was not an illusion of Rivadavia's; it was the general thought of the city, its spirit, and its tendency.

Parties were divided, not by ideas essentially opposed to each other, but by the greater or less extent of their aims. And how else could it have been with a people which in only fourteen years had given England a lesson, overrun half the continent, equipped ten armies, fought a hundred pitched battles, been everywhere victorious, taken part in all events, set at nought all traditions, tested all theories, ventured upon everything and succeeded in everything; which was still vigorous, growing rich, progressing in civilization? What was to ensue, when the basis of government, the political creeds received from Europe, were vitiated by errors, absurd and deceptive theories, and unsound principles? For the native politicians who were as yet without any definite knowledge of political organization, could not be expected to know more than the great men of Europe. I desire to call attention to the significance of this fact. The study of constitutions, races, and creeds, in short, history, has now diffused a certain amount of practical knowledge which warns us against the glitter of theories based upon *a priori* conceptions; but previous to 1820, nothing of that had transpired in the European world. France was roused into insurrection by the paradoxes of the Social Contract; Buenos Ayres was similarly roused; Montesquieu designated three powers, and immediately we had three; Benjamin Constant and Bentham annulled power; here they declared it originally null; Say and Smith preached free-trade; "commercial liberty," we repeated; Buenos Ayres confessed and believed all that the learned world of Europe believed and confessed. Not till after the revolution of 1830 in France, and its incomplete results, did the Social Sciences take a new direction and illusions begin to be dispelled. From that time European books began to come to us, which demonstrated that Voltaire had not much reason, and that Rousseau was a sophist, and Mably and Raynal anarchists; that there were no three powers, nor any Social Contract, etc. From that time we learned something of races, of tendencies, of national habits, of historical antecedents. Tocqueville revealed to us for the first time the secret of North America; Sismondi laid bare the emptiness of constitutions; Thierry, Michelet, and Guizot, gave us the spirit of history; the revolution of 1830, all the hollowness of the constitutionalism of Benjamin Constant; the Spanish revolution, all that is incomplete and behindhand in our own race. Of what then were Rivadavia and Buenos Ayres accused? Of not knowing more than the European savants who were their guides? On the other side, how was it possible not to embrace with ardor the general ideas of a people who had contributed so much and so well to make the revolution general? How bridle the imaginations of the inhabitants of an illimitable plain bordered by a river whose opposite bank could not be seen—a step from Europe, not knowing even its own traditions, indeed without having them in reality; a new, suddenly improvised people, which from the very cradle had heard itself called great?

Thus elevated, and hitherto flattered by fortune, Buenos Ayres set about making a constitution for itself and the Republic, just as it had undertaken to liberate itself and all South America: that is, eagerly, uncompromisingly, and without regard to obstacles. Rivadavia was the personification of this poetical, utopian spirit which prevailed. He therefore continued the work of Las Heras upon the large scale necessary for a great American State—a republic. He brought over from Europe men of learning for the press and for the professor's chair, colonies for the deserts, ships for the rivers, freedom for all creeds, credit and the national bank to encourage trade, and all the great social theories of the day for the formation of his government. In a word, he brought a second Europe, which was to be established in America, and to accomplish in ten years what elsewhere had required centuries. Nor was this project altogether chimerical; all his administrative creations still exist, except those which the barbarism of Rosas found in its way. Freedom of conscience, advocated by the chief clergy of Buenos Ayres, has not been repressed; the European population is scattered on farms throughout the country, and takes arms of its own accord to resist the only obstacle in the way of the wealth offered by the soil. The rivers only need to be freed from governmental restrictions to become navigable, and the national bank, then firmly established, has saved the people from the poverty to which the tyrant would have brought them. And, above all, however fanciful and impracticable that great system of government may have been, it was at least easy and endurable for the people; and, notwithstanding the assertions of misinformed men, Rivadavia never shed a drop of blood, nor destroyed the property of any one; but voluntarily descended from the Presidency to poverty and exile. Rosas, by whom he was so calumniated, might easily have been drowned in the blood of his own victims; and the forty millions of dollars from the national treasury, with the fifty millions from private fortunes which were consumed in ten years of the long war provoked by his brutalities, would have been employed by the "*fool*—the *dreamer*—Rivadavia," in building canals, cities, and useful public buildings. Then let this man, who died for his country, have the glory of representing the highest aspirations of European civilization, and leave to his adversaries that of displaying South American barbarism in its most odious light. For Rosas and Rivadavia are the two extremes of the Argentine Republic, connecting it with savages through the pampas, and with Europe through the River La Plata.

I am not making the eulogy, but the apotheosis of Rivadavia and his party, which has ceased to exist as a political element of the Argentine Republic, though Rosas persists in calling his present enemies *"Unitarios."* The old union party, like that of the Girondists, disbanded many years ago; but with all its impossibilities and fanciful illusions it had much that was noble and great to which the succeeding generation should do justice. Many of those men are still among us, though no longer as an organized party; they are the remains of the Argentine Republic, as noble and as venerable as those of Napoleon's empire. These Unitarios of the year 1825 form a distinct class of men, recognized by their manners, tone of voice, and opinions. A Unitario would be known among a thousand by his stately bearing, his somewhat haughty manner of speaking, and his positive gestures; on the eve of a battle he will pause to discuss a question logically, or to establish some new legal formality; for legal formulas are the outward worship which he offers to his idols—the Constitution and individual rights. His religion is the future of the Republic, whose image, sublime and colossal, is ever before him, covered with the mantle of its past glory. Never was there a generation so enterprising, so gifted with reasoning and deductive powers, and so wanting in practical common sense. A Unitario will not believe in the evident success of his enemies. He has such faith in the greatness of his cause, that neither exile, nor poverty, nor lapse of years can weaken his enthusiasm; and in calmness of mind and in energy of soul he is infinitely superior to the present generation. These men also excel us in ceremonious politeness and refinement of manner; for conventionalities are more and more disregarded among us as democracy progresses, and it is now difficult to realize the culture and refinement of society in Buenos Ayres before 1828. Europeans who went there found themselves, as it were, still in Europe, in the saloons [sic] of Paris; nothing was wanting, not even the insolence of the Parisian *élegant,* which was well imitated by the same class of young men in Buenos Ayres.

I have been particular in mentioning these little things in order to give an idea of the period when the Republic was in the process of formation, and of its different elements struggling for precedence. On one side Cordova, Spanish in education, in literature, and in religion, conservative and strongly opposed to all innovations; and on the other, Buenos Ayres, revolutionary by nature, ready for any change and progress.

These were the types of the two parties that divided every city; and I doubt if there is another such phenomenon in America; that is, two parties, conservative and revolutionary, retrograde and progressive, each represented by a city having its own peculiar form of civilization, and receiving opinions from entirely different sources: Cordova, from Spain, the Councils, the Commentators, the Digest; Buenos Ayres, from Bentham, Rousseau, Montesquieu, and French literature in general.

To these elements of antagonism must be added another not less important, namely, the want of any national bond after the provinces became independent of Spain. When government authority is removed from one center to another, time is necessary for its firm establishment.

The "Republican" recently declared that "government is no more than a compact between the governors and the governed." Evidently there are still many Unitarios among us! *Government is in reality founded upon the unpre-meditated consent which a nation gives to a permanent fact.* Where there is deliberation, there is no authority. This transition state is called a confederation. Out of each revolution and consequent change of government, different nations derive their ideas and modes of confederation.

I will explain myself. When Ferdinand VII was driven from Spain, government—*that permanent fact*—ceased to exist; and Spain was formed into provincial assemblies which denied the authority of those who governed in the name of the king. This was the *Spanish Confederation.* When the news reached America, the South American provinces revolted from Spain, and being divided into sections, formed the *South American Confederation.* From Buenos Ayres came at the end of the contest, four states, —Bolivia, Paraguay, Banda Oriental, and the Argentine Republic; these formed the *Confederation of the Vice-royalty.* Finally, the Argentine Republic was divided, not as formerly into districts, but according to its cities, and so became a *confederation of cities.*

It is not that the word confederation signifies separation, but that when separation has already taken place, it expresses the union of the different parts. The Argentine Republic was at this crisis social, and many persons of note in the cities believed that, for mere convenience, or whenever an individual or a community felt no respect for the nominal government, a new confederation might be formed. Here then was another apple of discord in the Republic, and the two parties, after having been called "Royalists" and "Patriots," "Congresistas" and "Executivistas," "Conservatives" and "Liberals," now bore the names of "Federales" and "Unitarios." [2] Perhaps, to finish

---

[2] *Federales,* those who held to a confederation of the old provinces, or a union of states. *Unitarios,* those who advocated a consolidated central government.

the list, I should give the name bestowed upon the latter party by Don Juan Manuel Rosas, that is, *"salvajes inmundos Unitarios."*

But the Argentine Republic is so situated geographically, that it is destined to a consolidation, whatever Rosas may say to the contrary. Its continuous plain, its rivers confined to one outlet, and therefore to one port, force it inevitably to be *"one and indivisible."* Rivadavia, who well understood the necessities of the country, advised the provinces to unite under a common constitution, and to make a national port of Buenos Ayres. Aguero, his supporter in Congress, said to the citizens of Buenos Ayres, "Let us voluntarily give to the provinces what, sooner or later, they will claim by force." The prophecy failed in one respect; the provinces did not claim the port of Buenos Ayres by force of arms, but by force of the barbarism which they sent upon her in Facundo and Rosas. Buenos Ayres feels all the effects of the barbarism, while the port has been of no use to the provinces.

I have been obliged to explain all these antecedents in order to continue the life of Juan Facundo Quiroga; for, though it seems ridiculous to say it, Facundo was the rival of Rivadavia. Everything disconnected with these men was of little importance, and left no impression. There were in the Republic two parties: one in Buenos Ayres, supported by the Liberals in the provinces; the other originating in the provinces and supported by the provincial commanders who had obtained possession of cities. One of these powers was civilized, constitutional, European; the other barbarous, arbitrary, South American.

These two parties had reached their full development, and only needed a word to begin the contest; one, as the revolutionary party, was already called "Unitario," the opposite party assumed the name of "Federal," without well understanding it.

But that barbarian party or power was scattered throughout the Republic, in the provinces, and in the Indian territories, and a strong arm was needed to establish it firmly in a compact form, and Quiroga offered his for the work.

Though the Argentine gaucho has some qualities common to all shepherds, he has strong local attachments. Whether he belongs in Buenos Ayres, Santa Fé, Cordova, or the Llanos, all his aspirations are confined to his own province; and he is an enemy or a stranger to all the others. These provinces are like different tribes ready to make war upon one another. López, as governor of Santa Fé, cared nothing for what was passing around him, except occasionally when obliged to drive out troublesome intruders from his territory. But as these provinces had points of contact, nothing could prevent them from finally joining in a common interest, thus bringing about that consolidation which they had so struggled against.

2

RICARDO LEVENE

THE CHIEFTAINS

Ricardo Levene (1885–1958) was one of the grandes
valores *of Argentine historiography. His numerous
works included a ten-volume history of Argentine
law and the two-volume* Lecciones de Historia Argentina, *as well as several chapters in the multi-volume*
Historia de la Nación Argentina, *which he organized
and directed. Dr. Levene served as professor, dean,
and president in the National Universities of Argentina, was Director of the Archivo Nacional de la
Provincia de Buenos Aires, and held several other
professional and honorary posts during his long and
distinguished career, including the direction of the
Academia Nacional de la Historia for many years
until his death in 1958. The following selection, from
one of the most widely read histories of a Latin
American country, describes the caudillos who dominated Argentine society and politics in the decades
following independence from Spain.*

From Ricardo Levene, *A History of Argentina,* translated and
edited by William Spence Robertson (Chapel Hill, N.C.: The
University of North Carolina Press, 1937), pp. 396–403. Reprinted
by permission of the publisher.

The political anarchy that broke out in 1820 and 1827 had its personification in the caudillos or chieftains. Behind them moved legions of people, impelled by respect for courage. Anarchy was a social condition; the chieftains were the visible expressions of this anarchy. If, after 1810, Argentine democracy broke out in a turbulent and revolutionary fashion, the elements produced by it bore traits of the original democracy. The Argentine social masses possessed an instinct for their own government and for popular sovereignty; they displayed it in numerous revolutionary movements that occurred during the colonial era and particularly in the Revolution of 1810. In the political realm, the democratic sentiment, turbulent and inorganic, had produced the crisis of the patriotic governments; and when these organizations, for reasons of stability and national order, tried to establish strong and absorbing governments or to transplant a monarchy, the popular masses moved against Buenos Aires by a single impulse. The battle of Cepeda had a double significance; it represented the democratic opposition of popular instinct to the monarchical leanings of statesmen, and also involved the principle of federation *de facto* in opposition to the unitarian tendency of Buenos Aires. The chieftains, who were faithful exponents of the instincts of the masses, raised the banner of democracy and federation. The cause was great, but the means employed by the chieftains to secure its triumph were barbarous; "because the social nucleus which executed it was barbarous; because its methods were barbarous and the roads into which it flung the people were bloody." [1]

This important phenomenon of Argentine caudillismo has been explained by Domingo Sarmiento in his famous book *Facundo,* as the result of the struggle of the country

---

[1] J. M. Estrada, *La política liberal bajo la tiranía de Rosas* (Buenos Aires, 1917), pp. 30–31.

districts against the cities, of barbarism against civilization. With more exactness, other writers take the view that the gauchos did not constitute the conscious people but that neither were they a plague of bandits. They formed the population of the country districts, dislodged and corraled by the governments of the cities. Once they triumphed, the chieftains engaged in cajoling those people but they did nothing to promote their welfare. The historic period which extends from 1820 to 1830 has been called the Argentine middle ages to signify that it was an era of chaos and retrogression.

In European history the term "middle ages" is applied to the period that extends from the fall of the Western Roman Empire (fifth century) to the fall of the Eastern Roman Empire (fifteenth century). The middle ages were characterized by one typical institution, feudalism, which involved the division of land and of political authority among numerous "feudal lords." There were feudal lords more powerful than the king himself, who for a considerable time played a role that was purely decorative. Many historians, in fact, affirm that this epoch is the "night of history," but more careful studies have demonstrated that, if the middle ages were not a brilliant period, they were a fruitful period in the sense that our modern civilization grew and evolved thereupon. In fact, during the ancient period there existed the vast Roman Empire which included almost the entire known world that had been subjected to a single authority; during the middle ages, and as a result of feudalism, the western part of this huge empire broke up into small states that were subordinated to the authority of feudal lords, and when these lords were eliminated, these states were subordinated to the authority of a king. Thus there were born from the extensive Roman Empire the modern nationalities of Europe. Accordingly, the middle ages was not a barbarous epoch.

Some analogies exist between that period and the age of the Argentine chieftains. The caudillos, like the feudal lords, were petty kings in the territories under their control; some of them were more powerful than directors or presidents. The chieftains López and Ramírez vanquished Director Rondeau. Quiroga and Bustos disobeyed President Rivadavia. The epoch which was dominated by the caudillos was one of chaos and anarchy; but just as the feudal lords furnished the bases for the European nationalities, so the Argentine caudillos assured the triumph of democracy and asserted the principle of federalism.

In addition, the chieftains were nationalists, that is, they promoted the organization of the nation, but upon the basis of provincial autonomy. All the movements of rebellion against Buenos Aires, and of rivalry among the provinces had, nevertheless, an instinct and a common tendency toward nationality. Two facts disclosed this tendency on the part of the caudillos: (1) The inter-provincial treaties which they framed. (2) The meeting of national congresses which they promoted by their initiative.

The first important inter-provincial treaty was that of Pilar, signed after the battle of Cepeda by the provinces of Buenos Aires, Santa Fe, and Entre Ríos. The first article of this convention provided that:

> The contracting parties declare that the vote of the nation, and in particular that of the provinces under their control, with regard to the system of government that should be adopted, has been cast in favor of the federation which in fact they accept. As they are convinced that all the provinces of the nation aspire to the organization of a central government, they pledge each one of the contracting parties to invite the other provinces to cooperate by sending their respective deputies in order that they may agree to whatever may suit them and promote the general welfare.

At the same time that this treaty manifests the national spirit of the caudillos, it affirms the principle of federalism.

On February 8, 1822, a treaty was signed by the governments of Buenos Aires, Santa Fe, Entre Ríos, and Corrientes which recognized the principle of Argentine nationality and pledged the contracting parties to convoke a national congress. By this treaty the differences that might arise among the provinces were "reserved to the sovereign, legitimate, general congress of all the provinces upon the occasion when the condition of American affairs should be marked by perfect tranquility and by the absolute cessation of political operations—a congress whose apt innovations would be obeyed as the emanations of national sovereignty."

In the same year, 1822, Martín Rodríguez, the governor of Buenos Aires, signed with the riparian provinces the so-called quadruple treaty by which they promised to aid each other and to promote the entry of the other states into the pact. Other treaties were later signed by the provinces, by the initiative or consent of their respective caudillos. All of these insisted upon the recognition of the autonomy of the states as integral parts of the nation. Another manifestation of the national instinct of the chieftains was their notion that national congresses should be assembled. This spirit of organization, by which they were animated, was certainly personal and egoistic. Each caudillo desired to organize the congress in his own way in order to decide its measures, but these plans were in the end proposals of organization.

The caudillo, Bustos, promoted the meeting of a general congress in the city of Córdoba. By the treaty of peace arranged between Buenos Aires and Santa Fe in the end of 1820, during the administrations of Rodríguez and of López, respectively, the province of Córdoba was the intermediary in the negotiation and its governor, Bustos, caused the insertion of a stipulation in the treaty to the effect that the provinces of Santa Fe and Buenos Aires should be obliged to send deputies to the congress which, at the end of two months should assemble at Córdoba. In fact, on October 21, 1821, there gathered in that city the deputies of ten provinces; the civil war which was raging in the north prevented the provinces of Salta, Tucumán, Santiago del Estero, and Catamarca from sending representatives to congress. The deputies who assembled at Córdoba addressed to the governments that had not sent representatives a note which contained this passage: "Appointed as deputies to the next general congress, we have met at a convenient point animated by the purest intentions, profiting by the lessons of bitter experience, guarding, so far as possible, against ulterior misfortunes, and desiring to give to the country a new era of glory and peace." But all was in vain. The deputies who had gathered at Córdoba returned to their respective provinces feeling that the attempt of Bustos to convoke a general congress had failed. Henceforth, the desires of the chieftain Bustos took another direction; for some years later he dissolved the junta of representatives and levied contributions at will.

After 1818, the caudillo López of Santa Fe, championed the autonomy of that province. In 1819, when the congress of Buenos Aires framed the unitarian constitution—an occasional cause for anarchy—López joined the chieftain Francisco Ramírez of Entre Ríos, and routed the soldiers of Director Rondeau at the battle of Cepeda. At this juncture, the Treaty of Pilar was signed, which recognized the autonomy of the contracting provinces; in the same year, 1820, López triumphed over General Miguel Estanislao Soler at the glen of Cruz; Dorrego routed him in the ravine of Pavón, but López avenged himself at Gamonal. In the personal struggle for supremacy between López and his rival, Ramírez, the caudillo of Entre Ríos, the latter was killed. Already eliminated from these struggles, the Uruguayan caudillo, Artigas, had taken refuge in Paraguay. When the congress which had assembled in Buenos Aires framed the unitarian constitution of 1826, the province of Santa Fe refused to obey the national government. But when the constituent congress had dissolved, the provincial deputies reassembled, and formed a national convention in the city of Santa Fe. Although the delegates of eleven provinces made their appearance, yet the convention did not open its sessions because of the obstacle interposed by the chieftain Bustos. In accordance with the terms of previous pacts, the members of the convention had authority to designate a general executive and to convoke a constituent congress for the purpose of framing a federal republican constitution.

Tucumán had its caudillo, a type that represented its people, Bernabé Aráoz. In 1814, Director Posadas appointed him governor-intendant of the new province of Tucumán, which by a decree of that period had been carved out of the province of Córdoba, and which had within its limits Santiago del Estero and Catamarca. In 1819, Aráoz promoted an uprising in order that he might once more gain control of the government, and on March 22, 1820, the province declared itself to be an "independent republic," with him as supreme president. In the same year, a congress assembled in the city of Tucumán with representatives from that province and from the province of Catamarca. The historian, López, justly criticizes this miniature congress and states: "It is composed of three persons: Dr. Arteaga, the curate, Pedro Miguel Aráoz, and José Antonio Olmos. The first is a miserable pickpocket, the second, a generous spirit but incapable of resisting the suggestions of his relative Bernabé, and the third is a flute that simply pipes the tune furnished by Arteaga." Nevertheless, this congress did not, as has been claimed, entertain a desire to separate from the rest of the nation. In 1824, Bernabé Aráoz was shot by order of the governor of Tucumán, Abraham González.

The caudillo Quiroga, "the tiger of the llanos," played a prominent role in the political history and the sanguinary wars of our republic. We have seen him in action, triumphing over La Madrid in the battles of El Corneta and Tala, and vanquished at La Tablada and Oncativo by the forces of General Paz. At the fortress of Tucumán, he struck another blow at La Madrid, who had taken charge of the army of General Paz when the latter was made prisoner. After an agitated and unfortunate career the chieftain, Quiroga, came to reside in Buenos Aires. To quote Saldías again:

> In his conversations with the leading men, whose society he frequented, Quiroga ingenuously confessed his errors, and admitted that he had more than once regretted having rejected the constitution of 1826; that he had acted as he did because of suggestions from men residing in Buenos Aires. The most curious fact is that he sought to associate with the unitarians who were in Buenos Aires and that they reasoned with him concerning the necessity that he should promote the organization of the nation under a federal régime, because this was the undying wish of the people. One night, in the house of Simón Lavalle, he avowed that Rosas was in accord with him in that respect; that as soon as the provinces should be at peace both of them would take steps to convoke a congress at Santa Fe [he should have said in Buenos Aires]; and that he would stake his life that the constitution framed there would be federal. Availing themselves of his offers, various leaders and émigrés of the unitarian party obtained favors of him. By his interposition, Colonel Wenceslao Paunero was al-

lowed to proceed from Bolivia to rejoin his family at
Colonia; and he offered Rivadavia his guarantee and
his services to the end that he might be allowed to remain in Buenos Aires.[2]

Was Rosas in accord with this desire of Colonel Quiroga?
In 1834, a sanguinary dispute arose between the governors
of Tucumán and Salta. Rosas asked Quiroga to proceed to
the northern provinces charged with a special mission to
prevent civil war, but as the latter insisted that as soon as
possible a congress should be assembled for the purpose of
framing a constitution, Rosas addressed a letter to him in
which he expounded the reasons that rendered the convocation of a congress inopportune. Let us quote some paragraphs of the letter:

> No one can be more fully convinced than you and I
> of the necessity of organizing a general government
> and that this procedure is the only means of insuring
> existence and respectability to our republic. . . .
> Who in order to form an orderly and compact entity
> does not previously arrange in a regular and perma-
> nent form the parts that should compose it? Who
> organizes an army out of groups of men without com-
> manders, without officials, without discipline, with-
> out subordination—men who do not for a moment
> cease to spy upon and struggle with each other, thus
> involving the others in their disorders? Who forms a
> living and robust being from limbs that are dead or
> that are torn asunder and diseased with the most cor-
> rupt gangrene, for the life and vigor of this new com-
> plex being can be no different from that which it
> receives from the very members that compose it?
> . . . Notice that a federal republic is the most chi-
> merical and disastrous which can be imagined, when-
> ever it is not composed of states well organized among

[2] Adolfo Saldías, *Historia de la Confederación Argentina,* Vol.
II (Buenos Aires, 1911), p. 223.

themselves, for, as each state preserves its sovereignty and independence, the force of the general authority with respect to the internal affairs of the republic is almost negligible.

Was this letter due to the inspiration of Rosas? Some writers affirm that it was not. Did Rosas express with sincerity the sentiments that it contains? Here the reply of most writers is again in the negative. They adduce other documents, in sharp contrast with this letter, in which Rosas seems to make a farce of the plan of federation. From this analysis it may be deduced that the caudillos, with the possible exception of Rosas, were not the disorganizers of the nation; and that the delay in framing a constitution for all the provinces was rather due to the condition of society and of the age.

We wish to repeat the words with which we began this chapter: our democracy was turbulent and inorganic, and the caudillos, its fruits and typical exponents, possessed such traits.

3

GEORGE PENDLE

GAUCHOS AND TOWNSMEN

*One of the most perceptive foreign observers of the
Argentine scene is the English writer George Pendle,
who during the last three decades or so has lived in
Argentina for lengthy periods while studying its
history and society. He is the author of admirably
written, informative, and objective histories of Argentina, Uruguay, and Paraguay, published under the
auspices of the Royal Institute of International Affairs. In the following selection from his* Argentina,
*Mr. Pendle provides an impartial view of the dicta-
tor Rosas, his downfall, and the problems his successors encountered in organizing the Argentine
nation.*

The Río de la Plata, so recently freed from colonial rule,
was not yet ready for representative institutions of the
British or North American kind, or for the social reforms
which the intellectuals of the revolution had imagined that

From George Pendle, *Argentina,* published by Oxford University
Press, under the auspices of the Royal Institute of International
Affairs (London, 1963), pp. 36–44. Reprinted by permission of the
author and the publisher.

they could carry out forthwith; and in the Plata, as else-where in Spanish America, anarchy inevitably prepared the way for despotism. It has been said that 'From one point of view . . . the dictators who so early arose were as much the expression of the Spanish American revolutions as Napoleon was an expression of the French Revolution. From another, dictatorship represented the triumph of experience over theory.' [1] In the revolutionary wars the people had grown accustomed to military leadership, and during the civil wars the provinces were dominated by caudillos. Thus by the end of the 1820's the personal rule of a military chief was generally accepted as a natural form of government. Indeed, the tradition of *caudillismo* is still not extinct today.

Rivadavia's high-handed attempt to impose a 'unitarian' pattern on the country had produced unparalleled chaos, and now was the opportunity for his opponents, the *Federales,* to endeavour to create order after their chosen fashion. However, the leader of this reaction—Juan Manuel Ortiz de Rosas—did not come from a province of the interior, but from the province of Buenos Aires itself, and, paradoxically, although he styled himself a *Federal,* throughout his long period of power he was almost constantly at war with one or more of the caudillos of the inland provinces. Furthermore, although Rosas was supported by the gauchos and the urban working class of Buenos Aires, he was in fact one of the wealthiest *estancieros*[2] in the land, the owner of a valuable *saladero*[3] and of the ships in which he exported his salted meat to Brazil and Cuba. But this offspring of aristocratic families

---

[1] R. A. Humphreys, *The Evolution of Modern Latin America* (Oxford: Oxford University Press, 1946), p. 84.

[2] In Spain the word *estancia* means a stay or sojourn. In South America it signifies a large country estate; its owner is called an *estanciero.*

[3] *Saladero:* meat-salting plant.

had spent his childhood in the 'camp', where he became a consummate horseman and won the admiration of the gauchos and Indians, whom he formed into a courageous and devoted militia. A traveller who met Rosas when he was at the height of his power wrote:

In his character of a country gentleman he gained the hearts of the peasantry: he surpassed them all in feats of activity and address, in taming wild horses, and in throwing the lasso; and his management of an estancia was excellent. Throughout his entire career, his administrative skill, and his art of ingratiating himself with his associates, obtaining their confidence and securing implicit obedience from all under his control, have been very remarkable. My first interview with General Rosas was in one of the avenues in his pleasure grounds. . . . On this occasion he wore a sailor's jacket, with blue trousers and cap, and carried a long crooked stick in his hand. His handsome ruddy countenance and portly aspect (he is of sanguineous temperament), gave him the appearance of an English country gentleman. . . . In referring to the motto, which is worn by all citizens: *'Viva la Confederación Argentina! Mueran los Salvajes Unitarios!'* ('Live the Argentine Confederation! Death to the Savage Unitarians!') he explained to me . . . that on occasions of popular excitement it had been the means of saving many lives—it was a token of brotherhood, he explained; illustrating it very forcibly by embracing me. The word death was only meant to express a wish that the Unitarians, as a political party, in opposition to the government, should be destroyed. Many Unitarians, it was true, had been executed; but only because twenty drops of blood shed at a proper moment might save the spilling of twenty thousand.[4]

---

[4] William MacCann, *Two Thousand Miles Ride through the Argentine Provinces* (1853), pp. ii, 4–5.

During the civil disturbances following Rivadavia's fall the authorities at Buenos Aires had appealed to Rosas, with his militia, to restore order, and so he had come to be recognized as the strong man of the province. In 1829 the legislature appointed him for three years Governor of the Province and Captain-General, with dictatorial powers. At the end of this term he led a campaign against the Indians in the south, thereby adding to his territorial possessions and to his reputation. In 1835 he was again summoned to assume the governorship, and his rule continued without interruption until the year 1852. Although Rosas was a *Federal,* no more 'unitarian' régime than his can be imagined. Everyone in Buenos Aires was obliged to wear as a sign of loyalty a red ribbon inscribed, as mentioned above, with a denunciation of the *'salvajes Unitarios'.* Even the ladies of the aristocracy did not dare to be seen in the street without their red ribbon or sash. Doña Encarnación, Rosas's wife and ardent assistant, wore evening dresses of scarlet satin. *Estancieros* wore scarlet *ponchos.* The dictator's spies and secret police, the *Mazorca,* intimidated and assassinated his enemies. His portrait was exhibited throughout the city, and was even displayed on the altars in the churches; intellectual activity was discouraged; schools were closed. Rosas quarrelled with France, and the French fleet—later joined by the British—blockaded Buenos Aires, bringing disaster to local commerce; he himself prohibited traffic up the river to Paraguay, in an unsuccessful attempt to subdue that country; and for nine years—unsuccessfully, also— he laid siege to Montevideo, where many of his opponents had sought refuge. Rebellions by provincial caudillos and by *estancieros* were ruthlessly crushed, the leaders being decapitated and their heads exhibited in public. Then suddenly in May 1851 one of the caudillos whom the dictator imagined that he had permanently tamed—General

Urquiza, of Entre Ríos—renounced his allegiance and began to collect together a formidable army. Rosas was decisively beaten by Urquiza's forces at the battle of Monte Caseros on 3 February 1852. He went to live in England in exile near Southampton, where he died in 1877 at the age of eighty-four.

Rosas lived in violent times, when it was not unusual for a victorious leader to execute his defeated rivals; but never before had terror been organized systematically. It can be argued, however, that the tyranny of Rosas had beneficial consequences. This *estanciero,* who governed with a gaucho's violence and lack of respect for human life, did remind the people of the city of Buenos Aires that in future they would ignore the provinces at their peril; and although the only interests that the tyrant served were his own, the provinces did at least learn during his rule that one government in Argentina at a time was enough.

The Constitution of 1853

After the battle of Monte Caseros the Argentines were ready to enter the modern period in their evolution. At this stage four fundamental characteristics may be noted: first, the population was still small, there being only about 1,200,000 inhabitants; second, the people still despised agriculture and were almost exclusively interested in horses, cattle, and sheep; third, there was an abundance of free land of excellent quality for cattle-raising and for the cultivation of grain; and fourth, as a result of the distribution of vast tracts of public land by Rivadavia (to secure collateral for a British loan) and Rosas (to reward his supporters), the large private *estancia* had become an established feature of the country. Another circumstance was to have vital consequences: there was now a growing recognition, alike among the 'unitarian' *émigrés* who returned to their homeland from Montevideo and Chile and among the victorious provincial leaders, that some form of constitutional compromise must be negotiated. Because of the traditional rivalry between Buenos Aires and the interior, this process of adjustment was delayed by suspicion and jealousy and disturbed by civil war; but the foundations of national union were quickly laid.

In May 1852 General Urquiza invited the provincial governors to meet at San Nicolás de los Arroyos, and at this conference it was agreed that a Constituent Convention should be convoked forthwith. The Convention began its deliberations at Santa Fe in November, but without the participation of the province of Buenos Aires, which rejected Urquiza's leadership, continued to refuse to be merged with the less prosperous inland provinces, and proceeded to organize itself as a separate State. The delegates at Santa Fe, however, were undeterred: they set to work to draw up a constitution which, with only minor modifications, eventually became the basic law of the whole nation and survived as such until the year 1949. As their model they took the Constitution of the United States, adapting it to local conditions in accordance with the recommendations of the Argentine publicist Juan Bautista Alberdi, who argued that, while the republic must be organized on a federal basis (because the provinces were so diverse physically and had experienced such long periods of isolation and autonomy), there must nevertheless be a strong central authority to prevent a recurrence of anarchy. The Constitution was proclaimed in May 1853. As Buenos Aires would not yet join the so-called 'Argentine Confederation', a temporary capital was established at the small town of Paraná. Elections were held in November 1853, and General Urquiza was proclaimed the first constitutional President of the Confederation.

The points at which the Constitution[5] differed from that of the United States were significant. In particular, so that he might be able to maintain national unity, the Argentine President was given considerably more power than that accorded to the President of the United States; and this arrangement followed Spanish tradition, it being contrary to Spanish ideas (and South American custom) that an executive should be subordinate to the legislature. Thus the Argentine President was authorized to frame and introduce his own bills in Congress (Art. 68); he was empowered to appoint and remove the ministers of his cabinet, and many other officials, without requiring the approval of the Senate (Art. 86, cl. 10); and in certain circumstances he might suspend constitutional guarantees by declaring a state of siege (Art. 86, cl. 19). The function and nature of the state of siege were defined in the following terms:

> In case of internal commotion or foreign attack, endangering the exercise of this Constitution and of the authorities created by it, the province or territory in which the disturbance of order exists shall be declared in a state of siege, the constitutional guarantees there being suspended. But during this suspension the President of the Republic shall not condemn by himself nor apply penalties. His power shall be limited in such a case, with respect to persons, to arresting them or conveying them from one point of the nation to another, if they should not prefer to leave the Argentine territory (Art. 23).

[5] For an English translation of the complete text of the Constitution of 1853, see R. H. Fitzgibbon, ed., *The Constitutions of the Americas* (1948); also Austin F. Macdonald, *Government of the Argentine Republic* (1942), pp. 429–52.

The state of siege is still frequently used today, enabling the President to dispense with such democratic forms as he may declare to be contrary to the national interest.

Another provision of the Constitution of 1853 gave additional power to the federal government—i.e. to the President, since the members of the cabinet were merely his nominees. For the preservation of order and unity the executive was to be permitted, whenever he should consider the step to be necessary, to 'intervene' in the provinces (Art. 6). When these occasions have arisen in practice it has been customary for the President to remove the governor, the members of the local legislature, the municipal officials, and the judges of the provincial courts, and to appoint his own federal representative—an *interventor*—with full authority to manage all provincial affairs and to supervise elections so as to make certain that the results should be favourable to the candidates enjoying federal support.[6] Thus, under the cover of one of the articles of an essentially 'federalist' Constitution, it has been possible for 'unitarian' presidents at Buenos Aires to dominate the provinces to a degree which would not have been tolerated in pre-constitutional times.

In other respects the Constitution of 1853 was remarkably liberal, and many of its clauses revealed the influence of the far-sighted intellectual, Alberdi. The opening section was a bill of rights wherein all the inhabitants of the nation were guaranteed the right to work, trade, enter, remain, or leave, 'to publish their ideas through the press without previous censorship'; and 'of freely professing their religion' (Art. 14). Further it was stated that 'the Argentine Nation does not admit prerogatives of blood or of birth; in it there are no personal privileges nor titles of nobility. All its inhabitants are equal before the law, and admissible for employment without any other requisite

---

[6] Fitzgibbon, *The Constitutions of the Americas,* p. 169.

than fitness. Equality is the basis of taxation and of the public burdens' (Art. 16), and 'no inhabitant of the Nation may be punished without previous trial, based on an earlier law than the date of the offense. . . . The prisons of the Nation shall be healthy and clean, for the safety and not for the punishment of the prisoners confined in them' (Art. 18). 'Aliens enjoy in the territory of the Nation all of the civil rights of the citizen; they may exercise their industry, commerce, and profession; own landed property, purchase it and sell it; navigate the rivers and coasts; freely practise their religion' (Art. 20). Alberdi had declared that the country required immigration and foreign capital, and that railways would unite the people better than any political measures could do. His ideas inspired, among many other clauses, the following:

Congress shall have power . . . to provide whatever is conducive to the prosperity of the country, for the progress and welfare of all of the Provinces, and for the advancement of learning, enacting programs of general university instruction, and promoting industry, immigration, the construction of railways and navigable canals, the colonization of lands of the national domain, the introduction and establishment of new industries, the importation of foreign capital, and the exploration of the interior rivers, by protective laws and by temporary concessions of privileges and the offering of rewards (Art. 67, cl. 16).

Argentina was now split into two separate states: the wealthy province of Buenos Aires and the inland Argentine Confederation. Urquiza's Government at Paraná made an honest and vigorous attempt to develop the economy of the territory under their control; but, as Buenos Aires monopolized the overseas trade of the Río de la Plata—and, thereby, the Customs duties—the Confederate provinces lacked the financial resources necessary for their projects for agricultural settlement, railway construction, education, and so forth. In 1856, hoping to attract shipping directly to their upstream port of Rosario, the Paraná Congress introduced a system of 'differential duties', imposing a higher rate of duty on all 'indirect' imports—i.e. on all European merchandise entering the Confederation via Buenos Aires. This measure naturally caused resentment and a further deterioration in the relations between the *porteños* and the Confederates. In 1859 Congress authorized Urquiza to subdue Buenos Aires by force. A *porteño* army, under General Bartolomé Mitre, was routed at the battle of Cepeda (October 1859), and a pact was then signed by the two parties, Buenos Aires agreeing to join the Confederation. The Constitution of 1853, with some very slight modifications, requested by the *porteños,* was finally adopted for the whole nation in October 1860. The old conflict was then revived, however, because the province of Buenos Aires insisted on electing its deputies to the first national Congress in accordance with its own provincial electoral laws. The national Congress therefore refused to recognize the Buenos Aires deputies. On this pretext the *porteños* renounced the pact of 1859; civil war broke out again; and, reversing the previous outcome, General Bartolomé Mitre defeated the Confederate army at Pavón (September 1861). This had been an unnecessary war, caused, in part at least, by Mitre's personal antipathy for Urquiza; but after the victory at Pavón the *porteño* leader magnanimously and wisely refused to follow up his military success: instead, he entered into negotiations with Urquiza and formally accepted, once again, the Constitution of 1853. National elections were held in 1862, as a result of which Mitre became the first constitutional President of a united Argentine republic.

4

THOMAS F. MCGANN

THE GENERATION OF EIGHTY
Politics and the New Liberalism

*Thomas F. McGann is presently Professor of Latin
American History at the University of Texas. His
fine monograph on Argentine economic, social, cultural, political and diplomatic history in the 1880–
1914 period provides valuable insight into why post-
Rosas liberalism failed to maintain and to perfect the
substance of representative democratic government,
thereby preparing the way for a latter-day Rosas to
come to power.*

Before the Argentine revolution of 1810, land was the
principal source of wealth and the sanction of social position in the otherwise resourceless Viceroyalty of the Río
de la Plata. The revolution for independence did not
significantly alter the fundamental social, political, and
economic relationships between the masses of the people,

Reprinted by permission of the publishers from Thomas F. McGann,
*Argentina, the United States, and the Inter-American System 1880–
1914* (Cambridge, Mass.: Harvard University Press, 1957), pp. 20–28,
31–34, and 42–45.

the landowners, and the soil. And although the administration of Rivadavia in the 1820's and the dictatorship of Rosas in the next two decades were poles apart in their philosophies of society and government, each bore the same fruit in the further concentration of land in the hands of a relatively few men. After the fall of Rosas and the return of the exiles in 1852, the position of the landed gentry was not changed despite the work of men like Urquiza, Mitre, and Sarmiento, who applied themselves to the task of awaking Argentina from its long sleep of reaction. These victorious leaders were liberal and pragmatic, but there was no Argentine Homestead Act during their administrations. They accepted the land system as it was and tried to build upon it by spinning out the means of communication and transportation and technical development that would make it workable and by bringing in immigrants to make it fruitful. Aside from the establishment of a few colonies, the methods of land distribution and the laws of land ownership remained essentially unchanged. Indeed, the governments that came after the Rosas regime, needful of revenue and concerned with the white elephant that was the government domain, embarked on much the same types of real estate deals as had the dictator. In one case, in 1857, the government leased 3,000,000 hectares (1 hectare = 2.47 acres) of land to 373 people; in 1867 Mitre's government sold this land on easy terms to its renters.

By 1880 the land pattern of the nation centered on personal holdings which by almost any standard ranged from big (15,000 or 20,000 acres or more) to enormous (200,000 acres and upward). The most valuable land was in the province of Buenos Aires, a sparsely settled region of great estancias, streaked by an increasing number of railroads. Here pasturage was rapidly giving way to tillage and the landowners were making the most of their new position in the expanding national economy. Sheep were replaced by wheat and the Irish herders by Italian farmers; but Irish or Italian, the men who worked the land did not own it. Some estancias covered entire departments of the province—departments in which there was "neither church nor chapel, the landowners being utterly heedless of the condition of their people." [1] The Department of Maipú, write two Anglo-Argentine observers, "has fine pastures, teeming with flocks and herds, but the poor gauchos are utterly uncared for, the whole country being owned by Alzagas, Acostas, Lastras, Pereyras, and Ramos Mexías. The last-named family has an estate of 400 square miles. The people live in mud huts." Again: "The department [Necochea] was founded in 1865 and is owned by forty large proprietors, the Alzagas, Anchorenas, Casares . . . and others, who take little heed of the condition of their people.[2]

Despite the unbalanced social situation, of which the system of property ownership and tenure was a primary cause, this was an era of marked vitality—the vitality of a frontier region, rich in its soil, chaotic with diverse races and new economic techniques, and possessed of a boundless faith in the future. The fact of surging economic expansion validated the pattern of landownership. The successful landlords—the *terratenientes*—together with other men who were less well-established but equally far-sighted, were in a mood to indulge in that orgy of land speculation which, lasting for a decade after Roca's conquest of the Indian lands in 1879–1880, ended with a few more people (and many of the same people) in possession of still more land.

---

[1] M. G. and E. T. Mulhall, *Handbook of the River Plate, Comprising the Argentine Republic, Uruguay, and Paraguay* (6th ed.; Buenos Aires, 1892), pp. 99, 346.

[2] Mulhall, *Handbook,* pp. 348–352.

Many native Argentines who were not lucky enough to be born in or to join the ranks of the terratenientes became tenants or peons, working in fields owned by other men. These *criollos* were frequently no more prosperous than the newest immigrant who wandered out into the countryside to make his fortune. Some there were of both groups, native-born and foreign, who through good fortune and wit and work acquired enough land to warrant inclusion, if not of themselves, at least of their sons and daughters in the upper ranks of society. But for every Basque or Italian or Argentine who went out into the alternately dusty and muddy *pampa central* and struck it rich, there were many who made only a marginal living year in and year out, "playing the crop lottery" on land rented from a *latifundista* whom they never saw.

The masses of foreign immigrants who settled in Argentina in these years—and their numbers diminished in proportion to the distance from Buenos Aires—made possible the nation's mounting prosperity, but they also created problems which affected the social and political fabric of the country. For one thing, the newcomers were curiously hybrid persons before Argentine law. They were under no obligation or compulsion to adopt Argentine citizenship, yet they received the same civil rights of the Argentine constitution as did native-born citizens. They could not vote (legally), but neither were they required to perform military service. An alien could become naturalized by petitioning to that effect after two years of residence, but there was complete official and popular indifference as to whether a man became naturalized or not. Naturalization, in fact, did not offer an immigrant any advantages which he did not already possess, and entailed at least one severe disadvantage—the obligation to do military service. Consequently, most of the immigrants who came to Argentina devoted themselves to the pursuit of their livelihoods and left their new homeland severely alone. The immigrant could go on with his old citizenship, his old language, his old friends, his old ideas. If Argentina gave him a job, it did not, in the vast majority of cases, offer him land to buy and the chance to play a more stable and responsible role in society and the economy. All too often when land was offered the promise was false, or the colony of which the immigrant became a part failed, or he found that clear title to his land was a mirage concocted by criollo owners who preferred to have tenants and renters rather than competitors. Under such conditions there was little assimilation into the established forms of national life of the tens of thousands of foreigners who descended on Argentina in the eighties. This was painfully clear in that activity which is one of the most objective expressions of a nation's social cohesion—politics.

The native landowning aristocracy was in a commanding political position with respect to the bulk of the population. In the immigrants they found not only laborers but semicitizens whose failure (or inability, for whatever reasons) to share in the institutionalized activities of the nation assured the criollo minority of the opportunity to continue in control of the machinery of the state. The large number of European immigrants also provided solid reinforcement for the ruling minority's basic policy, which was close collaboration with the principal nations of Europe.

An examination of Argentine politics in the eighties reveals a situation of political corruption organized around the only viable, formal party in the nation, the P.A.N. (Partido Autonomista Nacionalista). The P.A.N. was more than a party; it was for a generation the government of Argentina and a political instrument of the ruling element. Varying with the combinations of men who formed its leadership, it was the core of support for every president from Roca in 1880 to Roque Saenz Peña in 1910.

Roca's military and political authority after he defeated the porteño revolt of 1880 gave the P.A.N. its initial grip on the city and province of Buenos Aires. In a few years the use of national power by the president and his clique and their solicitude for the economic progress of the nation brought about a coalition of the conservative element of the entire country behind the shrewdest leader their class would ever have.

Oficialismo was the order of the day. This is not to say that President Roca or his successor Juárez invented the techniques of federal executive interference in elections and in the operation of the provincial governments. Before the final centralization of the national government in Buenos Aires in 1880, provincial governors had continued to rule their regions with much of the authority and many of the methods of the old-time caudillos. The federal government had rarely been free of a large measure of dependence upon these local chiefs who could marshal their voters and send the right people to the national Congress. Roca was a product of the combination of provincial leaders against Buenos Aires, but after assuming the presidency he showed no disposition to subordinate the national executive to the men who had helped him to power. New and relatively great financial and military strength, together with the normal instrument of patronage, lay in his grasp. With consummate political skill he exercised these weapons during the six years of his first administration. No parties of declared principles or broad organization confronted him; there were only *personalista* groups functioning within the practical objective of securing control of the local political machines. Through these cliques Roca threaded his way, aided by loyal and efficient agents such as Bernardo de Irigoyen, Juárez, Pellegrini, and Wilde. Elections meant that the P.A.N. was pitted against *ad hoc* groups organized by men of the same fundamental social and political views as their opponents, the chief distinction between the former and the latter being that one was "in" and the other "out." Opposition tickets were fluid in the extreme, to the point of merging with the government forces or disappearing entirely just before an election. The struggle for spoils was characterized by fierce partisanship in press and speech and the engendering of personal antagonisms that are perpetuated to this day among some prominent Argentine families.

A mainstay of the P.A.N. and therefore of the president of the nation, who was the head of the party, was electoral corruption. Every device of political fraud seems to have been known and tried in Argentina in these years. The purchase and falsification of votes was a major occupation of the national and provincial governments. One unnamed contemporary sourly but succinctly described the situation when he wrote: "In the deserted electoral registration offices one could hear nothing but the scratching pens of the government clerks writing imaginary names." The problems of controlling the electorate were simplified for the dominant interests by a limited suffrage, indirect election of the president, and the system of the *lista completa,* by which the entire ticket was elected if its leading candidate won a plurality of votes. As the power of the president grew at the expense of the provincial governors, control of the provinces and their elections became fairly routine. Carlos D'Amico was a living testimony to that fact. D'Amico was a man of distinguished family and personal ability who as governor of the province of Buenos Aires during part of Roca's first term fought against the president's encroachment upon the affairs of the great province. The upshot of this political struggle was unusual in a period when many leaders acquiesced to presidential pressure with more or less profitable results

to themselves: D'Amico was forced not only out of
political life, but out of the country. In the book which
he wrote in his Mexican exile, the former governor defined the composition of a typical provincial government
as he knew it to be under Roca and Juárez: "A delegate
from the national government, a bookkeeper, a cashier,
and the Chief of Police are all the staff required." [3] When
force and corruption at the provincial level failed to produce the desired results, the national Congress could annul
the provincial election, expel undesired colleagues and hold
another election, with closer attention to a more productive
outcome. As D'Amico wrote: "The only elector in Argentina is the President of the Republic, who elects the
provincial governors, the legislatures, the national Congress, and his own successor." [4]

As early as the day after Roca's inauguration the great
newspaper of Buenos Aires, *La Prensa* (Oct. 13, 1880),
foresaw the continuation of political *caudillismo* in the nation. Of the revolution just ended, which many people
interpreted as the signal for the opening of a long awaited
era of purity in Argentine politics, the newspaper gloom-
ily asked: "Who has triumphed in the end? No one. Political justice remains unachieved; the people will continue
to suffer their hard lot . . . Their struggle has not ended;
their cause is only latent, and the danger persists of a
series of uninterrupted outbreaks . . ." *La Nación,* also
great, commented on Roca's slogan "peace and administration." "The country needs peace," said Mitre's paper,
"but peace with justice and liberty."

The outbreaks came, during the next three decades, in
the form of scores of minor blood-lettings in local po-

---

[3] Carlos Martínez [Carlos Alfredo D'Amico], *Buenos Aires: su
naturaleza, sus costumbres, sus hombres. Observaciones de un
viajero desocupado* (México, 1890), pp. 131–132.

[4] Martínez, *Buenos Aires,* pp. 53–58, 123–137.

litical struggles, and in three major revolutionary attempts (1890, 1893, 1905) to pry loose the grip of the ruling class on the government. But the ten years from 1880 to 1890 were comparatively halcyon. Roca's superb political talent and the lavish corruption of the Juárez government, combined with the diversion of popular interest into economic activities, served temporarily to dampen the fires of civil strife. At the same time the dominant interests in the nation, through their chief representative, the president, extended the area of their authority and influence, in part as a response to Argentina's crying need for greater political centralization and in part as satisfaction of their private aims.[5]

Roca led the nation along these new paths. He was a master of the possible in politics. His own correspondence is the best witness to his abilities as a conscious realist in the affairs of men. He knew his Machiavelli, writing to Juárez, his protégé and successor, that "Political force lies in knowing how to play the lion and the fox at the same instant." Again, in a letter to Juárez dated almost two years before the election of 1880, in which he discussed his plans for surmounting the considerable obstacles which lay in his road to the presidency, Roca wrote: "It is necessary, as you see, to avoid these reefs, and so I shall begin to maneuver with the skill and prudence of which you know me capable." [6]

---

[5] José Nicolás Matienzo, *La revolución de 1890 en la historia constitucional argentina* (Buenos Aires, 1926), pp. 6–7, where this leading Argentine authority on the political history of his country and class writes: "In the decade from 1880 to 1890, not only did the personal power of the president grow immeasurably, but a deep political and administrative corruption spread throughout the nation, converting the government into an instrument for the satisfaction of private interests."

[6] Agustín Rivero Astengo, *Juárez Celman, 1844–1909; Estudio histórico y documental de una época argentina* (Buenos Aires, 1944), Roca to Juárez, October 26, 1879, p. 144; Roca to Juárez, July 24, 1878, p. 105.

This skill was demonstrated in 1886 when Roca imposed his successor upon the country. In the years of his first administration, Roca's political power was centered in the interior province of Córdoba where Juárez was his principal agent. It was from there that the president brought his wife's brother-in-law, via a seat in the national Congress, to be his heir in the Casa Rosada, for Roca was bound by the Argentine Constitution of 1853 which prescribed that no Argentine president could succeed himself in office.

Roca was neither the first nor the last Argentine ruler to select his successor and arrange for his accession. There is much to be said for Roca's administration, despite the rough edges it may present to those who have the advantage of hindsight. Roca no doubt hoped to perpetuate through Juárez the regime of relative "peace and administration" which he himself had given the country from 1880 to 1886, during which force had been generally supplanted by more subtle political methods. The men of the Generation of '80 were the sons of murdered or exiled fathers. They had cut their first teeth amidst civil war, turmoil, and hate. In their maturity, particularly after the last war in 1880, they desired surcease from revolution, and peace and prosperity for themselves and their land. Behind the still harsh and vindictive struggle for power in the eighties, there became apparent a spreading acquiescence to the need for mastering the forms, if not the content, of democratic government, in order that the weak but growing national unity might be preserved and the business of building the nation's wealth carried forward.

With the astute grasp of Argentina's destiny which his remarkable career displays, Roca struggled to secure the elements of peace, unity, and progress which the country needed. He was no mere fox, sniffing silently from prey to prey, as his enemies would have him appear. An answer to such charges may also be found, not in his acts alone, but in his correspondence. There is, for example, the letter that he wrote in 1880 when he was under heavy pressure to withdraw his presidential candidacy in the face of the civil war it would almost surely precipitate. "This," wrote Roca, with a depth of understanding which few of his contemporaries possessed, "is no mere election contest, but a question of whether or not we are an organized, united nation, not just one of those 'South American' places upon which the world sneers." It was on this basis—the establishment of a modern Argentina—that Roca fought a revolution and devoted his life to the development of his country's resources and its relations with other nations.

.   .   .

. . . Argentina in the eighties had that peace which Roca advocated in his first message to Congress—the internal imposed peace of a dominant minority, yet a not unworthy advance over former conditions. Roca returned to this theme in his exultant final message to that body in 1886: "I successfully conclude my government without having had to inform you during its whole course of civil wars, of bloody interventions, of the rebellions of caudillos, of loans wasted in repressing disorders and suffocating rebellions, of Indian depredations. . . . Peace . . . has never before reigned in this land for six consecutive years."

The land was indeed relatively tranquil, but there were some who took a different view of this presidential dispensation of peace. For *La Prensa* (Oct. 12, 1886), it was peaceful simply because, "The parliament is silent, and the ministers speak only to receive at once the votes of great majorities, attained without effort and without agitation." And to Belín Sarmiento, who inherited some of the vitriolic vigor of his illustrious relative, Argentina was the tragic original of his book—*Una república muerta.* He accused the rulers of the nation of concealing the realities of their regime under myths of a heroic past and dreams of a fantastic future, substituting the promises of their inflated oratory for a healthy internal policy.[7] The republic was dead; silence had settled over the field of political liberties which had formerly seen bitter but fruitful contests for freedom. The Argentina army acted as a praetorian guard to support the *status quo*. Even the firemen of Buenos Aires carried rifles. Political passivity was preached by the upper class as a soft name for choking oppression.

Yet Belín's solution to Argentina's distress was typical of the pointless theorizing so common in Argentine political writing. He proposed a revised and strictly enforced suffrage law and the creation of an active elite imbued with honesty and true patriotism, capable of leading the nation to higher and purer levels. He did not indicate how these ends could be accomplished. Roca, not so troubled by these ideals as Belín, wanted peace for a purpose. Peace meant tranquillity, a word much used in Argentina in the next thirty years. Political and social tranquillity were synonyms for the *status quo*—for the chance to develop the nation's pastoral and agricultural potential, obtain foreign loans, build waterworks and railroads. Without this internal peace Argentina would continue to be an outcast in European eyes, merely another South American country, as Roca had put it. In short, a bad risk.

If the slogan "peace and administration" provided respite from generations of conflict, it also was the frame on which were woven patterns of economic exploitation and political reaction. To that formula the word *oligarquía* is inextricably tied.

"The oligarchy" is a term used in the 1880's and after in Argentina by *La Prensa* and by people opposed to the rule of the land by an increasingly tight-knit group. By this

---

[7] A. Belín Sarmiento, *Una república muerta,* introducción por Lucio V. López (Buenos Aires, 1892), p. 1.

opprobrious word was meant the political organization composed of the president and his associates, the provincial governors and their supporters, the national representatives who obeyed the behests of the executive, whether national or local, and the economic interests, mainly landowners, which allied themselves with these men.

The Argentine oligarchy was described many years ago by José Nicolás Matienzo, a distinguished member and student of the class which he analyzed, in these words:

> The governing elements [of the nation] are recruited from a class of citizens which, if it does not properly constitute a caste, nonetheless forms a directing class. . . . This class corresponds approximately to the highest social stratum, formed by the members of the traditional families, by the rich, and by the educated (*hombres ilustrados*). The members of this class maintain among themselves more or less tight social and economic relations and, as is natural, share common sentiments and opinions. . . . Without this common code there would not exist that interchange of services and favors which they reciprocally lend without distinction of party politics. It is this moral code of the directing class which the citizens designated for the different government positions carry into the public administration, whence they manage the interests of the country.[8]

The ruling class reinforced this conception of the government as its special preserve with an absolutist and centralist doctrine of the executive power. Congress, the banks, the local governors, the party organization, and the formulation of foreign and domestic policies increasingly came under the authority of a small group of leaders, of which the president was the head. These leaders were the active

---

[8] José Nicolás Matienzo, *El gobierno representativo federal en la República Argentina* (Buenos Aires, 1910), p. 322.

representatives of the aristocratic class and the faithful executors of the common code to which Matienzo refers.

Such a development was inherent, although not necessarily inevitable, in Argentine history. The declaratory act of May 1810, in which the leaders of the Argentine revolution made their first attack on the royal government, contained a phrase to the effect that the governing class of the country should consist of "la principal y más sana parte del vecindario"—"the chief and most stable part of the citizenry"—literally, of the list of neighbors or residents, those who had property and position in the community. The conservative traditions of Spain, transmitted to her colonies, were retained and reinforced by the structure of landownership which persisted after the political revolution of the first decades of the nineteenth century. The Argentine landed aristocracy lived within its traditions, not as with a sere verbal heritage but as a legacy of success—the success of their victorious struggle for independence, of their endurance and in many cases increased power under the tyranny of Rosas, and, finally, of their successful reorganization of the nation between 1852 and 1880. After 1880, when immigrants and foreign capital descended on the immense properties of this class, the efforts of the past were redeemed. New problems also appeared, but they were for the future; today was for work and wealth.

The men of the Generation of '80 embodied the hopes of their fathers and the teachings of Sarmiento, Alberdi, and other early Argentine liberals. They had been taught from childhood that the salvation for their glorious but backward land lay in adopting European and North American modes of production and in imitating the cultural pattern of progressive foreign nations, including their methods of education, customs of work and standards of values, all these to be erected upon the basis of an invigorating

European immigration. In these formulations of liberalism is the source of the positivistic and materialistic society of Argentina after 1880. Roca, Pellegrini, Juárez, and their peers were the heirs and executors of the preceding generations. They were men "individualistic, pacific and cosmopolitan." To them fell the task of Europeanizing Argentina. They fulfilled the dream—and transformed the nation.

.   .   .

Whatever we call it—liberalism, positivism, or a Spanish equivalent, _cientificismo_—the doctrines which came into full practice in Argentina in the eighties were stamped with a European trademark, adopted by Argentine leaders, and sanctified by success. The history of Argentine liberalism extends from the radical leaders of the 1810 Revolution through Rivadavia and his University of Buenos Aires with its preaching of utilitarianism to Urquiza, Mitre, and Sarmiento, who took the refounded nation in hand after 1852. The victory of liberalism was complete by 1880. The nation for the first time could gather in abundance the slowly matured harvest of the past. But the years had worked profound if little understood alterations in the old doctrine. In conformity with the rapid economic and social changes which were twisting the nation into a new shape, liberalism took on restricted and special meanings.

Roca, Juárez, and the governing class which they represented knew with Victorian certitude what this new liberalism meant. It meant peace—Roca's peace—"the resolute elimination of any fair struggle for power, a struggle that could be dangerous for the country, which was in a process of transformation, and even more dangerous for their own class [the oligarchy]." And liberalism meant administration—Roca's administration—"the fulfillment of the . . . ideals of progress and enrichment." In achieving these objectives the oligarchy was far from being a consciously selfish minority intent upon choking back the rights of other groups. There can be little doubt that the Argentine rulers believed in the rectitude of their program. The bloody sacrifices which had been made before 1881 in the name of internal peace and liberty, together with the tangible benefits accruing to the nation during the years following the federalization of Buenos Aires, were sufficient warrant for the continued application of the liberal creed. History had placed the Argentine landowner—and the city of Buenos Aires—in a position midway between the rich pampas and Europe. It was fitting that the men of property should derive the principal benefits from that coincidence. But the double impact of European capital and immigration on the liberal Argentine ruling class transformed a hitherto somewhat paternal creole aristocracy into an elite increasingly isolated from the mass of the people. The new liberalism was no longer a radical doctrine but a shield for the privileges of an aristocracy.

A restricted and inflexible form of liberalism, a "sectarian liberalism," came to the fore in Argentina after 1880. Although historians have demonstrated that the zenith of liberalism in England had been passed by the 1880's, it would be a rewarding study in social dynamics to show that the lag between Argentina and Europe was such that the Argentines did not yet perceive that they too had lost the old liberal *élan* and had begun to retrench on the practice, if not on the theory, of liberalism. Certainly for Argentina, just emerging on the world scene, liberalism seemed to be an inexhaustible guide to the perfect society, as it had been the touchstone of success for the most powerful nation on earth. The Argentine aristocracy found economic collaboration with England an admirable complement to ideologic imitation.

However, beneath the surface uniformities of sectarian

liberalism (under the liberal spell men even trimmed their moustaches in the "liberal" style) there were grave problems such as that involving freedom of the press. Why did an oligarchic government which maintained itself through rigged elections and federal interventions permit the existence of a bitterly hostile and usually free press? One of the answers to this question seems to be that the oligarchy believed that it could counter the opposition press with its own newspapers. Another is that in the view of the ruling class a free press could accomplish little so long as the instruments of political control remained in the proper hands. There is further consideration: the free press—and this comes down to *La Prensa* and *La Nación*—was, after all, part of the heritage of the ruling class, and the owners and editors of these papers were members of that class. Freedom of the press was a necessary condition of the intense personal struggle for power among the members of the oligarchy; it was part of their liberal doctrine and it was an escape valve for pressures within the elite, as well as a means of battling the enemies of the moment. Furthermore, the independent press made up for the disservices it did to the men in power by its services as the medium of ideas, as the purveyor of the economic doctrines of the oligarchy, and as the chief link with European thought and economic activity. Finally, the opposition press could be, and sometimes was, silenced by the government. Argentine liberalism was autocratic; it provided freedom for the press to print anything that might contribute to the material growth of the community, but not the freedom to report the simple fact that the administration-controlled congress had met in secret session.

Such peculiarities of sectarian liberalism reflected the concepts of liberty, order, and progress held by the ruling elements. In practice these good words seem to have meant liberty for the governing class, order ("tranquillity") for the rest of the people, and progress for the individual who could make the most of the economic free-for-all. Political ideas, however, were not the only European concepts which the oligarchy imported for its own use. Social Darwinism also made its appearance, providing support for the dominant group and a ready reference for reasons as to why the economic and political bounds of the people should be restricted. Principal spokesmen of the aristocracy such as Pellegrini insisted that the untutored masses were unfit to assume the burdens of liberty. The time for all that would come, of course, but for the present anarchy would be the only result of an extension of popular freedom. The people should be content with the guidance of the enlightened elements in the nation. A definition that fits the Argentine aristocrat of this era may be found in the observation that "only the nineteenth-century liberal could combine contempt for the common man with faith in democracy." [9] In economic matters, despite preachments of equality of opportunity, the common man had to run fast to keep up with those on the inside. The national government was Janus-like in its economic policies. On one side the president and Congress employed their wide authority to facilitate and subsidize "public works," a series of projects which served public interest and private profit. On the other, when it served its interests the policy of the government was a most chaste laissez-faire—no tariffs that might interfere with the flow of trade, no labor unions to interfere with the "natural movement" of business, and no taxes to reduce the possession of wealth.

[9] Crane Brinton, "The New History Twenty-Five Years After," *Journal of Social Philosophy*, I (January 1936), 145.

5

JAMES R. SCOBIE

CONSOLIDATION OF A NATION

*Professor James R. Scobie, who teaches Latin Amer-
ican history at Indiana University, has devoted particular attention to Argentina in his research and
publications. In this selection from one of his latest
works Scobie describes the growth of nationalism
and underscores the disillusionment of the urban
middle classes with "democratic" processes in the
last years of the nineteenth century. He shows how
the newly formed Unión Cívica Radical (Radical
Civic Union) rose to power, indicates its achieve-
ments, and tells how its failures, in Yrigoyen's second term, set the stage for the military coup d'état of
September 6, 1930.*

Along with the superficial aspects of a national culture
came definite pressures to enforce "Argentinism"—exerted
strongly on and by the new citizens born to immigrant

From James R. Scobie, *Argentina: A City and a Nation* (New
York: Oxford University Press, 1964), pp. 194–208. Copyright ©
1964 by Oxford University Press, Inc. Reprinted by permission of
the author and the publisher.

parents. The educational system provided the most effective means to instill conformity and patriotism. The children naturally treated as superior the values of the society in which they lived and looked down upon parents who spoke Spanish badly or were not adept in Argentine surroundings. Poverty, illiteracy, and lack of instruction made it virtually impossible for the great majority of immigrants to counteract such rejection. Only in the middle class families of English and German managers and technicians were children raised somewhat outside the Argentine environment and sent to private schools that emphasized the language and culture of their parents.

The anticlerical legislation of 1884, which removed the Church from a teaching role in the public schools, led to greater government control over education. During the first years of the twentieth century the minister of education took further steps to insure the indoctrination of the rising tide of school children. All instruction had to be given in Spanish, and a uniform curriculum was taught in all public and private schools—although less stringently adhered to in the latter institutions. New textbooks were commissioned for the school system. School children actively joined in the parades and ceremonies for May 25 and July 9, and teachers preached a cult of such national heroes as San Martín and Belgrano. Boundary difficulties with Chile in the late 1890's and the centennial celebrations of 1910 provided additional opportunities to reinforce the children's patriotic ardor.

The Argentine government made its authority felt in other areas as well. At the turn of the century all young men were required to register for compulsory military service and were subject to call at the age of twenty. The disciplined and regimented Argentine Army, strongly influenced by German military missions after 1910, did not teach democracy, but a year in the barracks provided illiterates with the rudiments of reading and writing and gave conscripts elementary concepts of public health and some notion of the existence of a national authority. Official policy sought to mix conscripts from all areas and classes, and the Indian from the *puna* or the Chaco frequently found himself drilling alongside a clerk from a porteño bank or a son of an Italian peasant. This might lead to understanding, but at least it made the extremes aware of each other's existence. In 1912 a significant measure extended the privileges and obligations of citizens in electoral matters. After two decades of struggle by the Radical Party, all men (and women after 1947) over eighteen years of age received the right to vote by secret ballot but with the added prescription that suffrage was mandatory and failure to vote was punishable by fine. The enrollment booklet the men received upon registration for military service served as the voter's identification, as his record of having voted, and as a document for all civic and legal matters. The expansion of government bureaucracy made the individual increasingly aware of the state's authority and, consequently, of nationalism. In the late nineteenth century civil registers replaced the files of parish churches; licenses were required for marriages; education, health, and welfare institutions, fire brigades, waterworks, postal and police departments—in short, the whole gamut of public services—expanded prodigiously under municipal, provincial, and federal authorities.

The significant political developments of the 1890's, however, did not come from immigrants or nationalist pressures but rather from another new element of modern Argentina, the middle classes. This group, which played such a vital role in the expansion of coastal cities and reaped so many benefits from the agricultural revolution, aspired to join the oligarchy in directing the political destinies of the nation.

Elections were mere pantomimes, although not all were as lopsided as the plebiscite in 1835 that gave Rosas absolute powers over the province of Buenos Aires by a vote of more than nine thousand ayes to four nays. The voice of authority inevitably determined the outcome, and the sympathies and loyalties of local caudillos decided how and for whom votes were cast. Even when the caudillo descended from his horse after mid-century and addressed himself to the urban populace as a politician, the ballot box continued to cause violence. Now bricks, swords, and revolvers controlled the results at electoral tables, where the voter had to present himself and openly attempt to deposit the distinctively colored ballot of his party. By the 1880's some of the cruder methods of influencing the outcome were modified by stuffing the ballot box and purchasing votes. But these measures merely confirmed the control over elections exercised by incumbents. The upset of a favored candidate in one of the provinces inevitably brought rapid intervention and a new election to remedy the error.

The boom of the 1880's, with its balm of prosperity, gathered all elite groups—anticlerical liberals and pro-Church conservatives, soft-money *estancieros* and hard-money bankers, francophile porteños and creole provincials, autonomists and centralists—into one national party and blotted out earlier political conflicts. Even the wounds of the porteños' revolution against federalization of their city were quickly healed. Gradually control of both party and government was centralized in the hands of the president.

But the unprecedented wealth and the undivided power of the elite class in the eighties were not wisely handled, and self-interest led to economic and political crisis in 1890. The absence of a national currency long obstructed sound fiscal planning. Paper notes, of which the most

widely used and acceptable were the porteño issues originally supported by the Buenos Aires customhouse, fluc-
tuated wildly in gold value with every revolution, war,
depression, or boom. Early in his administration, Roca
established a national currency freely convertible to gold
—a reform which he ranked alongside the Conquest of the
Desert in importance to Argentine development. Yet by
1885, inflation and a lack of gold reserves forced authorities to declare the inconvertibility of the paper peso and to
revert to the daily market quotation for the country's
principal economic interests, especially the estanciero,
agriculturist, and exporter who paid their local costs in
depreciating paper and received pounds sterling or the
equivalent for their products. From this, however, followed an inflationary cycle of paper emissions to meet
government expenditures and to stimulate further economic expansion. Faced with disaster, the Juárez Celman
administration in 1890 even resorted to clandestine printing of banknotes. But as the peso fell from 100 to the gold
ounce in 1884 to 350 in the early 1890's, the benefits even
for agricultural interests began to dwindle. Much of the
boom had been financed with land mortgage bonds. These
bonds, widely accepted in Europe during the late 1880's,
were repayable in paper currency, the depreciation of
which seriously curtailed Argentine credit abroad.

But it was the emerging middle classes of the coastal
cities which were most affected by the spiraling currency.
Inflation cut deeply into salaries, pensions, and profit margins and magnified the gap in economic interests between
the landed class on one side and the storekeeper, small
merchant, clerk, army officer, schoolteacher, officer man-
ager, and engineer on the other. At the same time these
middle class groups were thoroughly disillusioned in regard to the processes of so-called democracy. Total apathy
greeted elections. No doubts existed as to which party

would win, for, barring military revolution or intervention by the national government, the incumbent invariably chose and elected his successor. In the city of Buenos Aires, where more than half the names on the election registers were fictitious or invalid, those in charge of electoral tables possessed a convenient margin to assure victory. Yet, even with the stuffing of ballot boxes, the vote in this city of half a million inhabitants rarely exceeded ten thousand during the 1880's for the average bourgeois saw little point in endangering job, life, and limb for a lost cause. In other cities, especially those of the interior, citizens had little role in determining the outcome of elections, while in the countryside the *jefe político* (an appointed political administrator of a rural district) or military commandant delivered the votes of gauchos and peons in accord with higher orders.

The widespread corruption and peculation of the late eighties reflected still further discredit on the oligarchy and fueled middle class discontent. Congressmen, ministers, and judges now had the opportunity to decide upon authorizations to build railroads, acceptability of public works, or permissions to colonize lands—each project involving enormous sums of money. A rapidly expanding bureaucracy with a characteristic fondness for paperwork and the long-established legalism of the Spanish mind added administrative procedures or *trámites,* until only experts armed with ample funds and know-how could finally emerge with desperately sought authorizations. In this situation speculation and the craze for making money swept away a public morality established by earlier and poorer administrations. To the profits from railroad ventures, wine and sugar industries, public works programs, and agricultural exploitation of the pampas were added fortunes and bribes wrung from public office. Corruption infected all levels of the Juárez Celman administration, from the customs inspector who looked the other way for a ten-peso bill to the judge who gave a favorable decision to whichever party offered the most in terms of his personal gain. The public came to believe that any government official, from the president down, could be bought.

Disillusioned by corrupt government and hurt by unbridled inflation, the middle classes began to demand a voice in political matters. A protest movement, largely composed of university students and professional men, took shape in the city of Buenos Aires. Most of its members were of creole origin, for, in the beginning, it attracted few immigrants. The principal objective was enunciated at a mass meeting in late 1889: "The guarantee of public liberties, especially effective suffrage, without fraud or government intervention in elections." Around this banner rallied the most heterogeneous elements: formerly elite families who, with the rise of the oligarchy, had fallen back into the middle classes; Catholic groups angered by the anticlerical bias of the oligarchy; fragments from all the traditional political tendencies whose only common goal was the overthrow of the present regime; and reformers who sought government by will of the majority. Despite the potential divisions, the protest momentarily captured porteño imaginations. The movement, which initially incorporated the words "Civic" and "Youth" in its title, emerged in early 1890 as the Unión Cívica and was hailed by 15,000 followers in the largest political rally Buenos Aires had ever known.

At this moment Argentina received the full impact of the financial crash. With the exception of the railroads, the credit that Europe extended to Argentina during the 1880's went largely into loans to national, provincial, and municipal governments and into land mortgage bonds. Once the reliability of Argentine schemes became suspect, many of the ambitious projects dissolved overnight. Governments found themselves without funds. Public works were halted. Banks closed their doors and in mid-1890 declared a moratorium. The influx of European immigrants ended, and emigration increased. The collapse of the stock exchange ruined many who had speculated wildly, and the peso's value declined at an ever sharper rate. The urban middle classes suffered acutely, for the crash wiped out prospects and savings. Hatred welled up against the oligarchy, and by May 1890 some of the leaders of the Unión Cívica felt they had sufficient support to organize a rebellion against the Juárez Celman regime. Military elements joined with the civilians, but divided counsels and lack of co-ordination postponed plans. When disclosure of vital secrets threatened the conspiracy in late July, the revolutionaries launched their attack, and street fighting broke out in the city of Buenos Aires.

The suppression of this revolt after three days of bitter conflict revealed both the disunity of the protest movement and the flexibility of the oligarchy. The revolutionaries held an initial advantage in the city of Buenos Aires, but they failed to capture the president of the vital control centers of government. Outside of Buenos Aires and perhaps Rosario they stirred little sympathy. Uncertain division of command between civilians and military gave the national authorities the chance to bring supplies and loyal forces from garrisons in Rosario and Córdoba. At the same time the oligarchy proved more than willing to sacrifice Juárez Celman as a symbol of all the mistakes and grievances of the eighties. "The revolution has been crushed, but the government is dead," was the epitaph voiced on the floor of the Senate, and few were willing to listen to the defense: "Whatever the President's errors, every one of us has been his collaborator." Abandoned by his colleagues, Juárez Celman turned over executive powers to his more astute and acceptable vice president.

The sacrifice was sufficient. The oligarchy maintained political supremacy and extended its control for another quarter century. Some of the elite learned from the crisis. Prosperity became tempered with stability. If the depression momentarily slowed economic development, it was followed by the even greater economic boom of 1904 to 1912. Roca, the symbol of expansion and confidence, returned to the presidency for a second term in 1898. The following year he took advantage of the peso's recovery to re-establish its convertibility to gold—but at 227 instead of 100 pesos to the gold ounce. Production and exports based on an accomplished agricultural revolution now kept pace with speculation. With meat and cereals Argentina turned its former deficits with England into favorable trade balances. The oligarchy accepted new elements and new ideas within its ranks. As long as rising opportunities for urban middle classes lessened the effectiveness of the appeal for suffrage, the elite class could continue to control the ballot box and the public till.

The reformers emerged from the 1890 revolution as divided as they had entered it. A sizable portion of the Unión Cívica followed Mitre, that venerable elder statesman of the porteño nationalism, into an electoral accord with Roca and the oligarchy. The hard core of the Unión Cívica reconstituted itself in mid-1891 as the Unión Cívica Radical, or Radical Party,[1] pledged to a nationwide campaign to secure the universal secret ballot for male citizens by all available means, including revolution. Appeals to civic ardor in 1893 and 1895 temporarily captured

[1] The party officially accepted the designation "Radical," already sanctioned by popular use, at the end of 1892. The translation is not a happy one, for the original sense was one of vindication of basic civil rights and adherence to the true purpose of the Unión Cívica rather than the advocacy of extreme change connoted by the English word. Once this middle class party achieved the presidency, its basically conservative nature was clear, for its economic and social policies were anything but "radical."

large parts of the provinces of Buenos Aires and Santa Fe by revolution, but the Radicals proved unable to resist the oligarchy's skillful manipulation of armed force, intervention, amnesty, and conciliation. In each case the revolts flickered out after a few weeks of demonstrations and some sporadic fighting. In 1896 two principal leaders of the Radical Party died, and the following year yet another important segment of Radical opinion surrendered to Roca's blandishments.

By 1900, however, a new principle and a new caudillo had taken control of the Radical movement. "Intransigence" became the guiding force of Radicalism—the refusal to vote or to participate in public life until free elections were guaranteed. Beneath this philosophy lay the personality of Hipólito Yrigoyen. University and business associations linked him to leaders of the oligarchy, but he became the champion of political justice, and at his funeral in 1933 he was honored by sorrowing multitudes as the first Argentine president to defend the common man. He possessed few of the characteristics of Argentina's nineteenth-century leaders. Taciturn, introverted, a poor orator, he nevertheless galvanized the middle and lower classes by a certain mystical leadership. A meticulous organizer who created a disciplined and loyal party structure through countless individual interviews and small informal gatherings, he built an electoral machine which paralleled and often excelled that of the oligarchy. To Yrigoyen, revolution or the secret ballot afforded the only means by which the Radicals could capture power. But in his expert handling of both weapons he neglected all others: the Radical Party, even after gaining power, was never able to carry out effective economic and social reforms or to make more than symbolic appeals to the lower classes. The political issue of democracy was suffrage, and with that all problems presumably could be solved.

The Radicals' pretensions that they represented the disfranchised mass of citizens were challenged from both the
left and the right. The Socialist Party, which emerged in
the 1890's, attempted to capture leadership of the urban
working classes with specific proposals for shorter working
hours and better labor conditions. Yet the Socialists were
divided between international, anarchist, utopian, and
nationalist philosophies and torn between theoretical discussion of their principles and the practical need to organize strikes and labor unions. After 1900 an increasing
influx of anarchists from Spain and Italy secured impressive support from discontented industrial workers, although
the movement suffered from a similar division into intellectual and syndicalist groups. The violent aspects of an-
archism eventually created fear and hatred among the
middle classes as well as the oligarchy. Anarchists and
some Socialists were singled out for arbitrary arrest,
deportation, and police torture—repression not usually
meted out to Radicals, who played politics under the established rules of revolution and amnesty. Finally, within the
oligarchy itself there developed a significant movement to
extend suffrage and even to guarantee the secret ballot as
the best means to win public support and retain the elite's
control of Argentine politics.

Despite the formidable odds of apathy and opposition,
Yrigoyen spun his party network across Argentina, in provincial capitals and coastal towns, in army garrisons, and
even in government offices. With tenacity and patience he
repaired the holes torn in his web by police surveillance,
arrests, dismissals, and transfers and steadfastly refused to
compromise with regimes that did not guarantee free elections. Early in 1905 another Radical revolution broke out
simultaneously in the provinces of Buenos Aires, Santa Fe,
Córdoba, and Mendoza, only to face the usual process of
rapid suppression and amnesty. Almost immediately Yri-

goyen returned to tireless reconstruction and extension of the party. The times favored Yrigoyen's and the Radical Party's immediate objective, for a substantial number of the oligarchy recognized the growing appeal of political reform. Presidents now repeatedly consulted with Yrigoyen, not only in the hope of overcoming his intransigence but also with a view toward instituting acceptable electoral reform. Behind such proposed changes lay no romantic concept of surrender to Jacksonian democracy but rather the realistic expectation that the oligarchy might steal the mantle of reform and deprive the Radicals of their only popular appeal or unifying purpose.

In 1910 the oligarchy chose Roque Saenz Peña, the spokesman of this liberal or reform wing, as president, with the clear realization that he would seek electoral reform. Two years later, after a bitter congressional struggle, Saenz Peña secured the law of universal and secret male suffrage that thereafter carried his name. As youths of eighteen registered for military service, their names were entered on election registers, and they incurred the obligation to cast their ballot in national elections. No longer did voters have to vote orally or deposit the distinctively colored ballot of their party before the watching eyes of their fellow citizens. The law afforded the voter the secrecy of a closed booth, where he selected a list of candidates, and the security of a sealed urn, into which he deposited his vote. As a final assurance to the minority, the party that ran second in any province received one third of the seats at stake in the national Chamber of Deputies while the majority party was limited to two thirds of the representatives.

Free elections, however, depended on enforcement of the law, and that the oligarchy was not willing to guarantee. Yrigoyen struggled to maintain the principle of intransigency until such guarantees were forthcoming, but he struggled vainly against the enthusiasm of his own party. In the city of Buenos Aires and in the province of Santa Fe, the Radicals won their first seats in Congress, albeit with slim margins and amid scenes of violence and fraud. The law's principal guarantor, Saenz Peña, died in 1914, and Yrigoyen redoubled his insistence that the Radicals return to intransigency. But, despite Yrigoyen's reluctance to run for office, the 1916 election carried him to the presidency by a margin of one electoral vote.[2]

The Radicals won the presidency in 1916 with an electoral machine built during twenty-five years of revolution and preparation. In the coastal cities the Radical cause was strengthened by the entrance into political affairs of urban middle and lower classes, especially the native-born sons of immigrants who had settled in Argentina during the 1880's. The rejuvenated and liberalized elite still suffered from the label of "oligarchy," and the intellectual Socialists and hunted anarchists showed little promise of achieving political control. In contrast, Yrigoyen surrounded himself with a mystique of democracy and political rights that turned him into the caudillo of these new voters.

The ascendancy of the Radicals from 1916 to 1930 altered Argentine politics in several aspects, but it failed to strengthen or perpetuate democratic institutions and stability. The Radicals, disclaimers notwithstanding, consecrated party organization and revolution as the principal means to gain power. The opposition, therefore, necessarily resorted to the same proven tactics. Political machines served to harden divisions into what Argentines have characterized as "political hatreds." The oligarchy, for all its

---

[2] The election hung in the balance until the electoral college met, because, although Yrigoyen won a majority of the popular vote, he did not secure a majority of the electors. A group of dissident Radicals from Santa Fe controlled the deciding votes. Finally, despite Conservative blandishments and their own personal opposition to Yrigoyen, they gave support to a Radical victory.

exclusiveness, not only had drawn on a wide range of opinions and trained abilities within the elite but also had received constant renewal of talent from below. Party organization, on the other hand, thrived on service, seniority, and patronage which reduced flexibility in recruiting talent. Professional politicians who had risen through the ranks increasingly dominated ministries, congresses, and the country. The figures whom Yrigoyen appointed in 1916 provided a refreshing change from the families who had dominated porteño, and consequently the nation's, social and political life under the oligarchy. Yet government by unknowns brought not so much an introduction of new ability as the discarding and alienation of all those who had not served in the Radical cause.

The other avenue to power—revolution—was no Radical innovation, but its glorification as a viable political weapon brought unfortunate consequences. Now even the most pacific civilian leadership had to respect the military and rely on it for support and protection. The Argentine Army had fought its last foreign war in the 1860's and faced its last border tension at the turn of the century. Rather than losing importance in the twentieth century, however, the Army increased its role in national life and politics. Universal military training merely provided a mass of raw recruits to fill the ranks. But the cadre and regular army developed a sense of autonomy. German training missions, modern weapons and techniques, and *esprit de corps,* all contributed to the disdain felt by middle class officers for politicians and political parties. Although one sector stood for constitutionalism, the Army as a whole tended to intervene more and more in politics, not only to secure larger appropriations and broader privileges but also to influence economic and foreign policy.

These potential dangers to democracy in Argentina were further accentuated by the Radicals' inability to carry out a program that would meet middle and lower class aspirations. Certainly a large part of the failure can be attributed to obstruction by Conservatives. Yrigoyen embarked on the presidency in 1916 with a minority in the Chamber of Deputies, only one representative in the Senate, and provincial control limited to Santa Fe, Córdoba, and Entre Ríos. Despite wide use of presidential powers of intervention, the Radical advance beyond the coastal cities was extremely slow. Political change had little chance in those interior provinces where society remained untouched by prosperity, immigration, urbanism, or a middle class, and where stability contributed to Conservative control of government. At the national level, the Senate, elected by provincial legislatures, remained a bulwark of Conservatism until 1930. The overthrow of Yrigoyen by a military coup in that year was apparently influenced by the threatened loss of such a vital Conservative veto. But Yrigoyen himself shared responsibility for the difficulties encountered by the programs of the Radicals. The caudillo's overwhelming personal domination of party and government accentuated conflicts within Radicalism. His successor in the presidency represented the conservative wing of Radicalism, which soon began to resist the caudillo's supremacy—a split that widened still further when a nearly senile Yrigoyen was re-elected president by popular acclamation in 1928.

Of the many proposals for reform advanced by the Radicals, few survived the combination of Conservative obstruction and internal party divisions. The general balance sheet, therefore, remained one of failure. In the distribution of land, in the establishment of controls over transportation and public utilities, and in government exploitation of natural resources, especially of oil, Radical projects were repeatedly defeated or postponed. While neighboring Uruguay developed one of the most advanced programs of social legislation in the world, the Radicals disillusioned the working classes by violently repressing industrial strikes. During the postwar depression Radical authorities were faced with severe outbreaks of labor violence in the city of Buenos Aires, aggravated by Conservative intrigues. The strife reached a climax in the Tragic Week of January 1919 when streetcars were burned, machinery destroyed, and citizens shot. Finally, military intervention was required to restore order. Less dramatic but nonetheless damaging to Radical prestige in the cities were defeats imposed on social security and minimum wage laws. In economic policy the Radicals proved equally unsuccessful in implementing programs for industrial development or tariff protection. In a word, the Radicals, having achieved power on the platform of political reform, could not maintain leadership in other areas and consequently abandoned the urban populace to political drifting.

The major Radical accomplishment occurred not in the political arena but in the field of education. At the University of Córdoba in 1918 there developed a movement known as the "University Reform" that soon spread throughout Latin America. Fundamental to Latin America's present-day university structure, the "Reform" program secured autonomous university government shared equally by students, alumni, and professors. Finances and ultimate authority remained in the hands of the national government, but middle class groups were now able to break the Conservative monopoly of university administration and teaching. Student and alumni participation in governing councils and in the selection of university officials and faculty stimulated improvements in curriculums and teaching. In the long run, however, abuses of the reform spirit brought higher education increasingly into the realm of politics and led frequently to a breakdown of standards in the universities.

The political drift experienced during the relatively prosperous twenties turned into disaster for the Radicals with the advent of the world depression. By 1930 Yrigoyen and the Radicals were thoroughly discredited on all fronts. The government took no measures to meet the impact of the depression on the cities. Graft and intervention flourished. The Conservatives conspired openly with elements of the army. Congress, newspapers, and even the people who had re-elected Yrigoyen now repudiated the aged caudillo. Chaos threatened to overwhelm the country. On September 6, when a column of troops left the military college located just outside the city of Buenos Aires, the doors to the capital and to the Casa Rosada lay open to them. The commanding general of the revolution quietly assumed control of the country with the open support of Conservatives, Communists, and many Radicals and the acquiescence of the great majority of the population.

Thus ended Argentina's first attempt at government by the middle classes. In less than two years the military turned over powers to a constitutionally elected president. The ensuing Conservative regimes that ruled the country from 1932 to 1943 renewed some of the benefits as well as many of the faults of the former oligarchy. As we have noted, the rising tide of economic nationalism and industrialization forced the government to walk a tightrope between world markets for meat and grains, secured by the Roca-Runciman pact, and the demands for protection and support from its own industry—a dilemma temporarily resolved by the outbreak of World War II. In the political field the Conservatives regained control of the ballot box, the Saenz Peña Law notwithstanding, and sought to capture leadership of the middle sectors by the selection of anti-Yrigoyen Radicals as presidents and ministers.

Political drift, however, only worsened under the Conservatives. The sons of Argentina's second wave of immigration reached voting age in the 1930's, yet in political terms these citizens hardly existed. Politics became increasingly divorced from economic and social reality. A disillusioned citizenry found few contacts or responses on the political scene. The Conservatives provided traditionalist rule by an elite class that remained closely allied to British interests. The Radical and Socialist parties offered only the unappealing alternatives of old men and old ideas, unchanged since the once dynamic era of the 1910's. Even the Communists suffered from dissension. The Church, more concerned with prestige and pageantry than with fundamental social problems, contented itself with perfunctory support of the regime. The labor union movement, torn by various socialist and syndicalist tendencies and unable to strengthen itself during Radical administrations, found organization even more difficult under the frankly hostile Conservatives. Finally, those sectors of the Army which supported Conservative ambitions in 1930 now added admiration for Fascist techniques to their previous disdain for politicians. In moments of crisis these officers were only too willing to assert autonomy and independence of any civilian government.

Renewed prosperity built on Europe's gathering war clouds momentarily obscured this real poverty in Argentine politics, and world opinion in the late 1930's accepted Argentina as one of the most stable and progressive democracies in Latin America. It was true that half a century of political consolidation had gradually built a central authority and a national spirit, but little integration of the parts resulted. Military groups, political parties, and economic classes, rather than promising unity, represented sources of division and conflict. A military coup against the Conservatives in 1943 merely ripped off the façade of democracy, revealing many of the present-day political problems in their stark reality.

6

GINO GERMANI

━━━━◆◄●►◆━━━━

TRANSFORMATION OF THE
SOCIAL AND
POLITICAL STRUCTURE

*The transformation of Argentine society from rural
to urban as a result of immigration and internal
migration had important consequences for Argentine
politics. For an analysis of this phenomenon we turn
to Professor Gino Germani, an Italian-born, Argen-
tine-trained sociologist, who has also studied and
taught in the United States, most recently at Colum-
bia and Harvard Universities. He is the author of
numerous monographs and articles on Argentine
society, including his pioneering* Estructura social
de la Argentina.[1]

The generation that assumed the task of developing Argentina into a modern national state was very aware of the

From Gino Germani, *Política y sociedad en una época de transición*
(Buenos Aires: Editorial Paidos, 1962), pp. 220–231. Translated
and printed by permission of the author.

[1] Gino Germani, *Estructura social de la Argentina* (Buenos Aires,
1955).

contradictions between the simple rationalism of the independence-minded elite and the true nature of colonial society, which persisted during the first half of the nineteenth century as a result of the autocratic rule of the *caudillos*. Its members understood that no political reform would be possible until radical changes were effected in the social structure.

This generation was made up of "social realists" who used the philosophical and sociological thought of their time to understand the national reality, and they arrived at a distinct plan to effect substantial changes in the Argentine society. The essential measures for achieving this end were: education, foreign immigration, and economic development. These points summarize the plan of the so-called "Generation of 1837," of Sarmiento, Alberdi, Echeverría and others who formulated it and in part carried it out from the moment they secured power. But the ruling groups' action in fulfilling this program was no less contradictory than had been that of the revolutionary elite of May: it should be remembered that in the end they constituted what came to be called "the oligarchy," a landholding bourgeoisie, despite its liberal motivation and sincere concern with transforming Argentina into a modern state. Undoubtedly, it was this position in the social structure that was the principal source of contradiction in its reformist efforts.

Let us see what happened with immigration. Its purpose was twofold: to "populate the desert" and to transform the population by giving it those features deemed necessary for developing a modern nation. In effect the ruling group tried to replace the "traditional" social pattern with one more appropriate for a modern industrial structure. At that time this transformation was regarded as a "racial" change and not the result of moving from one social structure to another. In the language of the times, it was a question of "bringing Europe to America," of Europeanizing the population of the interior, considered the major source of political instability and of backward economic practices.

With this in mind, the elite emphasized "colonizing" to make sure that the European immigrants would be rooted to the land. Although a surge of urban activities, industry, services, etc., also was desired, there can be no doubt that the immigration was definitely directed "toward the desert." What transpired only partially fulfilled these aims. Certainly the population was radically changed, and one of the features essential to understanding present-day Argentina is its large element of immigrant origin.

A radical change in the economic structure also took place with the emergence of Argentina as one of the world's leading producers of cereals and meats. But the social structure of the countryside was not changed as desired. No large and strong agrarian middle class, based on land ownership, emerged. Instead of "colonization" there resulted what some called a colossal land speculation that increased and reinforced the predominance of the great landholdings. By the early stages of massive immigration, the greater part of the most accessible and arable land was already in the hands of a few landholders. In 1914, after a half century of immigration, with foreigners representing no less than half the total active population, immigrants still made up only 10 per cent of the landowners. The traditional families had succeeded in maintaining and increasing substantially the latifundist pattern and in 1947 three fourths of the land was still concentrated in little more than 20,000 farming enterprises, less than 6 per cent of the total.

The legal pattern of land use was and continues to be land rental—or less favorable forms—and the place of a rural middle class was occupied in large measure by renters and small landowners, continuously exposed to all the favorable or unfavorable fluctuations of climate and the world market. Although some managed to prosper, the unfavorable economic conditions of the majority obliged them to be constantly moving in search of better working conditions and subjected them to all kinds of restrictions. In even worse conditions than these small landowners and renters were the landless peasants—salaried workers exposed to seasonal crop rotations, low levels of employment and low standards of living. One of the major and undesired results of this situation was the concentration of foreigners in the cities and the extraordinary urban growth.

TABLE 1 / *The Process of Urbanization in Argentina 1869–1957*

% Urban Population (Defined as those living in areas with 2,000 or more inhabitants)	Years
27%	1869
37	1895
53	1914
62	1947
65	1957

Undoubtedly, massive immigration and other innovations attempted by the elite directing the "national organization" from the second half of the past century onward meant a profound change in the country. But the social structure that thus emerged contained certain deviations from the ideal of achieving a stable base for a democracy. One of the most important impediments to democracy was the unfavorable rural structure and the resulting population distribution.

The elite wanted to populate the desert, and, in a certain sense, they did. But the population was largely concentrated in the cities; and instead of lessening the disequilibrium between the underdevelopment of the interior and the development of the Littoral, this further accentuated it. The consequences were made clear by the middle of the century.

The process of urbanization in Argentina developed in two great phases: the first, between 1869 and 1914, involved massive immigration from Europe; the second, corresponding to the period 1930/1935 to 1950/1955, was fed by internal migration on a massive scale.

The role of foreigners in the formation of the Argentine urban structure is clearly evident. Not only in cosmopolitan Buenos Aires, where 50 per cent of the population was made up of foreigners between 1869 and 1914, but also in the other cities where the proportion was also exceptionally high. Significantly, the larger the city, the greater the proportion of foreigners. Thus in cities of 100,000 and more inhabitants, more than one third—between 1895 and 1914—had been born outside the country. It should also be noted that in addition to this urban concentration there was another regional pattern. All the large cities were located in the Littoral zone, and foreigners generally settled there. As a result metropolitan Buenos Aires and the provinces of the Littoral always retained approximately 90 per cent of the immigrants.

This geographical concentration had a series of far-reaching effects on the social structure, involving the typical differentiation between "central" and "peripheral" areas with all its consequences for the political life of the country. Urban growth, combined with the expansion and transformation of the economy, inspired substantial changes in society: already, in the beginning of the present century, what we could call the traditional "boss" had been destroyed and replaced by figures more like the modern model. Also, as a result of other measures to spur economic development—attraction of capital, construction of railroads, legal reforms—the country became a great export center for cereals and meats. The new requirements of foreign trade, the impulse to internal activities given by great urban concentrations, and the accrued wealth of the country, stimulated the first industrial development.

Since the last quarter of a century modern industrial activity has emerged and expanded throughout the country, replacing the traditional handicraft methods; and although still centered on agricultural production, it had already reached a respectable volume by the first decade of the present century. At the same time the lower strata of the old society, largely rural, saw themselves replaced by an urban proletariat and a rapidly expanding middle class. Thus the "bipartite" traditional society (an upper class of large landholders versus a low stratum composed of the bulk of the population, with an intermediate stratum of little significance and usually identified with the upper class) was replaced in the central areas by the tripartite system (upper, middle, and lower classes). It could also be called multi-partite, since the differentiation between levels, especially in the cities, becomes indistinguishable, and the structure assumes the image of a continuing series of overlapping positions in which the transition from one to another becomes difficult to perceive.

An Argentine middle class of a size and social and economic significance sufficient to be politically influential first appeared between 1869 and 1895. By the last decade of the nineteenth century it had become a group of great importance. It is necessary to remember that in the main it is an urban middle class, concentrated in the Littoral. Therefore, its weight is greater in the areas which play a central role in national life. Also, one must take into account the qualitative changes produced by the transition of the traditional boss to more modern types. The middle class, from its beginnings until the early part of the century, was composed mainly of men who had begun new activities: medium and small enterprises that comprised the commercial activity and nascent industry. Meanwhile the upper class—the traditional families—retained its broad control over the agricultural sector.

A smaller rural middle class was also formed from among the country people (*campesinos*) who achieved some prosperity and economic solidity. But this involved a minority group in comparison to the foreign immigrant masses and to the native rural population. Later, particularly after 1910, the middle class probably owed its growth largely to expansion of its "dependent" sectors— "white collar" workers, employees and public officials, professionals and technicians of the private and public bureaucracies. This change in the composition of the middle class also had political significance. In the lower, populous strata, the rural peons, the unskilled workers, the jobless, the old artisans, the domestic servants were increasingly becoming urban workers in industry, commerce, transportation, and services—that is, in activities carried out by modern enterprises and concentrated in the cities. This resulted in the movement of people from the "central" areas of the country to the cities, creating conditions favorable for the upsurge of proletarian movements which, in the pattern of the early stages of industrialization and urbanization, appear as social protest movements.

End of Limited Democracy and Political Participation of the Middle Classes

The political significance of these changes is obvious: they brought about the entrance into national life of groups which had been separated from the old traditional strata. This implied the possibility (and necessity) that a functioning democracy—particularly in its most immediate manifestation, universal suffrage—would also include the recently formed classes. In other words, it involved political integration of the recently mobilized sectors of society.

Faced with this process, which would provide a base for the forming of a democratic state, the ruling elite did not seem disposed to share power, much less to cede it to the new groups being incorporated into the national life. The elite continued to aspire to a liberal democracy, in which participation was limited to the upper strata of society. Although in many other aspects the ruling elite's activities were progressive and open to greater participation of the popular strata in national life—for example, in education— there were certain limits which were very difficult or impossible to overcome in economic and political matters. In the first place, not only were the elite groups unable to renounce their monopoly of land, but they themselves profited from the economic transformation. Often the measures for development they chose were oriented more toward their own class interests than toward those of the nation. In the political field a prolonged struggle was necessary before the most progressive elements of that same "oligarchy" finally made universal suffrage possible and consented peacefully to participation in power by the new social groups. The first elections in which all the citizenry participated were held in 1916 and gave the government to men of the middle class, organized politically around the Radical Party formed three decades earlier.

This date, 1916, can be taken to mark the end of limited democracy in Argentina, and the beginning of representative democracy with full participation of the population, though it is difficult to fix rigid demarcations within such complex social processes. Moreover, this date was only the beginning of a long process which is still developing.

The transition from one type of democracy to another

was characterized in Argentina by various features that
helped make it particularly traumatic. In the first place, the
country found itself in a somewhat paradoxical situation
as a result of massive immigration. One essential but
seldom remembered fact is that for thirty or forty years
foreign-born people were much more numerous than natives. If one considers the effects of a double concentration
—geographic and by age—the percentage of foreigners in
categories most significant politically (male adults) and in
the "central" zones (the capital and the provinces of the
Littoral) one discovers the extraordinary fact that this
figure reached some 50 to 70 per cent.

In terms of elections this meant that where participation
in voting could have greatest importance, some 50 to 70
per cent of the inhabitants were not able to participate. In
absolute figures, in 1895, of the 216,000 male inhabitants
of the city of Buenos Aires, only 42,000 were native
Argentines (and those naturalized amounted to less than
2 per cent). At this same date, in the provinces of the
Littoral (Buenos Aires, Santa Fe, Mendoza, Córdoba, La
Pampa, Entre Ríos), of over 600,000 adult males, 287,000
could exercise the right to vote as natives. If one considers the further drastic reduction in political participation derived from other social conditions, one can realize
the full significance of the term "democracy with limited
participation."

This problem of the lack of political participation by the
majority of the population concerned the ruling groups of
the era, but it is well known that in this respect the elite
maintained its characteristic ambivalence. The stability of
"limited" democracy was actually due in large part to this
fact. It is very likely that the political effects of the appearance of the middle strata were considerably retarded
by their predominantly foreign composition. The failure of
the lower classes to form a party capable of representing

them politically, was probably due to similar reasons. . . .

Landed property continued almost entirely in the hands of Argentines. Compare this with the situation in commercial and industrial development, where the managers of commerce and industry, and the industrial workers, were largely foreigners, and constituted a higher proportion of the middle class in the entire active population. Furthermore, in the lower, populous strata engaged in industrial activities (old handicrafts, domestic service) the native majority predominated. And of course among the rural population, especially in the interior provinces, natives also predominated. While the elite retained firm control over landed property, the middle class and the proletariat were formed in the cities on the basis of massive immigration.

As the children of immigrants became active and as the extraordinary proportion of foreigners began to lessen, these newly formed classes began to have a chance to exercise a *direct* influence on political activity. Here the word "direct" has particular importance. Obviously these majority masses, although marginal from the viewpoint of their electoral rights and of their political interest, exercised an indirect pull of great importance, although there are no studies or data that permit precise evaluation. In relation to the lower, populous class, the new classes nourished—as leader and as mass support—the great protest movements of the first decades of the century, and the middle strata provided the human element most propitious for the emergence of the movement that should have represented this sector politically in national life.

Thus in Argentina, the passage from elite government, with limited participation in democracy, to middle class government meant the incorporation of the foreign immigrant masses, or of their sons, into political life. But it is probable that the peculiar make-up of the population, and particularly the predominance of foreigners in the protest movements in the first decades of the century, meant a considerable delay in the formation of political organisms suitable for the urban proletariat. That element supported Radicalism, the expression of the middle classes, instead of forming a sufficiently strong party of their own (the Socialist Party had only local importance in the country's capital).

The Radical Party which governed the country for fourteen years until 1930 should have represented during that period all the new, emerging strata, but it did not fulfill that function. In fact, in no way did the Radical Party use power to bring about those changes in the social structure that might have assured a sounder base for the functioning of democratic institutions and tended to prepare the integration of all social strata as they emerged. It did nothing, or very little, to solve one of the basic problems of the country, the agrarian problem. Although until the end of this period conditions in the countryside were generally rather better than later on—and the stability of the rural population was much better, so that in those years there was less urban growth—the socio-economic structure of the countryside remained practically unchanged, since the means adopted were completely insufficient, when one considers the magnitude of the problem. With respect to the urban proletariat, the attitude of the Radical Party was no less ambivalent. Although numerous measures of social protection for the worker were adopted, the legislation was not only rather moderate, but it also often had no practical application. On the other hand, in spite of the climate of liberty enjoyed during the period, the workers' organizations did not see their functions facilitated. Legislation did not explicitly recognize the legal status of trade unions, although of course their functioning was permitted by the general dispositions of the Constitution. This lack of recognition, in an atmosphere where the higher strata openly opposed such organizations, made their work difficult and provided a very serious obstacle to the unions' role as a vehicle for progressive incorporation of the populous strata into the nation's political life. It is symptomatic that the Radical parliaments maintained the repressive legislation created by the oligarchy at the beginning of the century, opposing the first expansion of the workers' movements. In 1919 the Radical government did not hesitate to solve the social problems and commotion created by the post-war situation with a bloody repression.

The high percentage of foreigners during the era of emergence and development of labor movements probably served to impede the formation of a party that might have integrated them within the democratic structure of the country. On the one hand, in spite of their numerical and social importance in the population, they had to remain in a marginal position within the electorate. On the other hand, their foreign composition, combined with the internationalist ideology that so intensely characterized movements on the left during this era, probably contributed to placing such movements in an unfavorable light. This occurred precisely at the time when the incorporation of sons of immigrants was at its height, necessitating their firm identification with the new fatherland. One example is the undoubtedly nationalist character (in a democratic sense) of the UCR [Unión Cívica Radical] and its refined "isolation," particularly during World War I. . . .

Thus if the Radical Party, in spite of popular sympathy and support, was not capable of representing the proletariat politically, neither were the Socialist Party or the other organizations of the left. Moreover, as the Socialist Party "aged," it was gradually becoming more and more composed of middle class groups (owing to the intense ascendant mobility of the immigrants) and ended up representing only an alternate radicalism for the independent electorate.

Finally, the existence of "peripheral" areas, those large zones of the country in a state of underdevelopment, and the fact that the progressive incorporation of the inhabitants into national life was realized only in the central areas, in the Littoral and in zones of high urbanization—while the interior and the rural sections of the coast remained completely marginal—constituted another disturbing factor of fundamental importance for later development. In effect, it would have been essential for the political balance of the country (that is with regard to assuring the functioning of a representative democracy) that the strengthening of a democratic leftist party, endowed with the support and cohesion of the masses, be produced in the proper ideological climate; that is, within the tradition of leftist democratic thought such as occurred in the European countries that led the way in industrialization.

The Great Internal Migrations and Integration of the Popular Strata

Such was the situation in 1930, when as a repercussion of . . . the particular social structure of the country . . . and the world depression that rudely struck the Argentine economy, there was a change in the Argentine government. For the first time in many decades a constitutional government was overthrown by military intervention. This movement, which also reflected the new international political climate created by the emergence of Fascism in Europe, fundamentally signified the return of the "oligarchy" ousted from power by the Radical majority. But this "return" could not mean a return to the past and a kind of limited democracy in which political participation would be restricted to certain classes. It was to have meaning and consequences very different from the apparently analogous situation of a half century earlier. It was no longer a matter of the exclusion of the less developed sectors of the population as a result of the political "absence" or "passivity" of the less developed sectors of the population. Rather, the strata already fully "mobilized" would use compulsive means to ensure "exclusion." The principal means employed by those groups lacking the electoral support needed to secure power was systematic fraud, without the formal denial of the exercise of civil rights. Freedom of the press and of association were more or less respected, as were other rights sanctioned by the Constitution. But union activities encountered increasingly greater difficulties, and this, together with the frustration produced by the systematic manipulation of the popular will in elections, created a feeling of deep skepticism among the majority of people. This was a skepticism which continued to be influenced by the general crisis of democratic ideologies during the 1930's. Moreover, the parties of the opposition were not at the height of their effectiveness at this moment when the country was experiencing a new stage in its socio-economic development.

In effect, as a repercussion of new conditions created by the world crisis of 1929, two convergent processes were produced in Argentina: a new and decisive phase of industrialization was begun; and urbanization gained an unusual impetus with the massive migration to the cities from the country's interior. The intensity of these internal migrations was very great, and during the period of 1936–1947 the proportion of Argentines born in the provinces who moved to metropolitan Buenos Aires was equivalent to almost 40 per cent of the natural population increase of these same provinces. It was a mass exodus by which vast layers of people from the underdeveloped zones—masses until then completely on the fringes of the political life of the country—established themselves in the large cities and particularly in Buenos Aires.

TABLE 2 / *Population of the Buenos Aires Metropolitan Area**
Internal and External Source of Its Composition (1869–1957)

Year	Total Population	% Born Abroad	% Born in the Interior	Average Annual Number of Migrants from the Interior
1869	250,000	47%	3%	
1895	783,000	50	8	8,000
1914	2,035,000	49	11	
1936	3,430,000	36	12	83,000
1947	4,720,000	26	29	
1957	6,370,000	22	36	96,000

* These figures for the metropolitan area, the city of Buenos Aires, plus the surrounding populated area of the province of Buenos Aires, are similar to those cited for the Federal Capital on p. 20 of the Introduction. The city of Buenos Aires and the Federal Capital are coterminous. [Ed.]

It was a process in a way comparable to what had happened in the massive foreign immigration half a century before but with three great differences: (1) the rhythm was then much slower, since the growth of the urban population took place over at least three decades; (2) the masses that exerted political pressure and led the movement for effective universal suffrage were not the immigrants themselves (who, because they were foreigners, did not participate except indirectly in political processes), but their sons; and (3) it was a matter of the recently formed middle class emerging, leaving a nascent proletariat in a subordinate situation. These great masses, transplanted rapidly to the cities and changed suddenly from rural peons, craftsmen, or laboring personnel into industrial workers, acquired a political significance without at the same time finding the institutional channels necessary for their integration into the normal functioning of the democracy. The repressive policy of the governments from the end of the past century until the beginning of the present, the ambivalence and relative failure of the governments of the middle class between 1916 and 1930, the severe limitations on the functioning of democracy after 1930, and the general disbelief and skepticism created by all this experience, coupled with the absence of political parties capable of expressing their sentiments and needs, left these masses "available" (*en disponibilidad*), making them a displaced element to be taken advantage of through whatever happenstance offered them some form of participation.

Meanwhile, other events also pressured Argentina; the expansion of Nazism in Europe and its first triumphs during the first three years of the war precipitated those events. A new military intervention in 1943, this time with open totalitarian designs, interrupted the conservative experiment with "democracy limited by means of fraud." But the social structure of Argentina, particularly at this stage of its evolution to an urban society and the type of masses "available" for use as a human base for a totalitarian movement, was very far from lending itself to a Fascist experiment of classic type, a simple reproduction of the Italian or German experiments. It was necessary to effect great changes in that scheme, and *Peronism,* which emerged starting with the military revolution, was the fitting expression of the particular conditions created in Argentina by an accumulation of old and new factors which we have tried to summarize.

There resulted, thus, another of the paradoxes in which the country's history abounds. A movement of the Fascist type set off a regime that was undoubtedly totalitarian in character, even though endowed with features very different from its European model: it was a type of authoritarianism based on the consent and support of the majority, which for the first time in sixteen years could express its wish in regular elections. This fact is of singular significance, since free elections were beginning to be transformed into the principal, if not the only, symbol of democracy, and had constituted one of the most insistent rallying cries of the parties of democratic opposition, particularly the Radicals, during the conservative regime.

7

JOHN J. JOHNSON

THE ARGENTINE MIDDLE SECTORS ON THE POLITICAL DEFENSIVE

John J. Johnson, Professor of Latin American History at Stanford University, has made important contributions to the literature on Latin American middle sectors and military forces in a number of articles and monographs. His analysis of the Argentine middle sector's failure to provide the substance as well as the form of representative democracy reveals the divisive forces at work among the country's middle groups.

In so far as the political role of the Argentine middle sectors is concerned, the historical past falls into three rather clearly defined periods. The first period preceded

Reprinted from *Political Change in Latin America: The Emergence of the Middle Sectors* by John J. Johnson (Stanford, California: Stanford University Press, 1958), pp. 94–104, *passim*. Reprinted with the permission of the publishers, Stanford University Press. © 1958 by the Board of Trustees of the Leland Stanford Junior University.

the election, in 1916, of Hipólito Irigoyen, whose eleva-
tion to the presidency marked the beginning of fourteen
years of middle sector leadership on the national level. The
second period corresponded to that fourteen-year era,
which terminated with Irigoyen's overthrow, in 1930, by
the military in alliance with the conservative oligarchy.
The third period extends from 1930 to the present; an
era characterized by efforts on the part of the middle
sectors to evolve a program that would permit them again
to dominate the Argentine government. It is within the
framework of these three periods that the political role of
the Argentine middle sectors is discussed.

During the half-century prior to the election of Irigoyen
the histories of the Argentine nation and the Argentine
middle groups were, broadly speaking, not unlike those of
Uruguay and Chile. In every major area of human relations the predominant philosophy in each of the republics
was essentially the same—democratic and representative
government, laissez-faire economics, Catholic religion, and
cultural dependence upon Europe. In all three countries
the members of the privileged groups were highly individualistic. To the extent that developments were conditioned by local circumstances the differences seemed, in
general, to favor the Argentine middle elements.

At the turn of the century, the status of the Catholic
Church in Argentina was similar to its position in Chile,
and to its position in Uruguay prior to the advent of José
Batlle y Ordóñez. The Argentine Constitution of 1853,
which was still in force, had set the pattern. That document provided for the support of the Catholic Church by
the Argentine government but it also recognized freedom
of worship. In the 1880's the anticlerical elements had
forced the passage of legislation that prohibited religious
instruction in public schools. The Church had not been
particularly active in politics, and there had never been

a clerical party such as was found, for example, in Mexico or even in Chile where the Conservative Party was said to be more Catholic than the Church.

The record of the Argentine armed forces in staying out of civilian matters was better than that of Uruguay's prior to 1910 and compared favorably with Chile's. They had not engaged in politics on their own account since 1852, when they were instrumental in the overthrow of the tyrant, Juan Manuel de Rosas. Thereafter they remained aligned with the ruling oligarchy, and in 1890 and again in 1905 they efficiently suppressed uprisings of the "untried new groups" against the established authority. But when Irigoyen was elected, the armed forces accepted the shift of power from the elites to the new groups without serious incident. At that time there was good reason to believe that the military had become professional and would henceforth devote itself to those functions assigned it by the Constitution.

Relative to its neighbors, Argentina had enjoyed an abundance of the benefits resulting from the influx from abroad of investment capital, technological know-how, and skilled labor. The nation had by far the most highly developed land and water transportation system to be found anywhere in Latin America, which had given its people considerable mobility and numerous contacts with Europe, from which new ideas were flowing to all parts of the world. It had also contributed to the development of a truly national economy. With the aid of foreign capital, the firm foundations of a commercial and industrial economy had been laid. The republic, with 50 per cent of its people already living in cities, was the most urbanized in Latin America. It had received more than its share of immigrants, who had played a major role in making the pampas one of the richest agricultural areas in the world. The impact of the immigrant upon fast-growing

Buenos Aires, whose population in 1890 was 50 per cent foreign born, was equally apparent.

Argentina had also usurped Chile's leadership in education. The republic's claim to cultural superiority in Latin America could not be challenged. The Generation of the 1890's (*La Noventa*), which included such names as Alejandro Korn, Carlos Bunge, Lucas Ayarragaray, and José Ingenieros, comprised the greatest single collection of scholarship and ability ever assembled in Latin America up to that time. The graphic arts were more highly developed than anywhere else in Latin America.

The celebration of the centenary of the winning of independence, observed in 1910, had given encouragement to the growth of an ardent patriotism without producing an ardent nationalism. Argentine patriotism was predicated primarily upon future potential rather than upon past achievement. Although there were isolated outbursts against the foreigner, the majority opinion was that the foreigner would and should continue to play a significant role in building the new Argentina. There was little wonder that such was the case. If Argentina had a distinct national characteristic in 1916 it was that it contained a higher proportion of new blood than any country in the Western World, including the United States. The honor rolls of public figures and scholars and artists were peppered with Italian, French, German, Irish, and English family names. In the economic area there was little of the antiforeignism that in Uruguay had led to a national policy designed to eliminate the foreigner from direct participation in the economic life of the republic.

Xenophobia, however, had already entered into the nation's thinking on foreign policy, and the United States was the bête noire. Argentina foresaw itself as the leader of a South American bloc, and a strong United States, dominating a Western Hemisphere union of nations, stood between

Argentina and that goal. By 1916 the narrow area of agreement in foreign policy between the two republics foreshadowed the strained relations that have become normal in this century. The United States recognition of British claims to the hotly disputed Falkland Islands added to the leadership's sensitiveness.

The preparation of the Argentine middle sectors for political leadership compared favorably with that of their counterparts in Uruguay and Chile. In the 1860's and 1870's the Argentine middle elements had exercised a pronounced influence upon the administrations headed by Bartolomé Mitre, Domingo Faustino Sarmiento, and Nicolás Avellaneda. Each of those regimes encouraged education and cultural development; probably the two foremost newspapers of Latin America, *La Prensa* (1869) and *La Nación* (1870), were founded during the presidency of Sarmiento. The three executives also promoted immigration and technological development, both strong planks in the middle sectors' political ideology. Finally, each of the presidents lent his support to the growth of representative government. Thus, the Argentine middle sectors gained valuable experience in policy-making at about the same time as the Chilean middle groups, and earlier than the Uruguayan elements.

The Conservatives, controlled by landed oligarchs, returned to power in 1880 through resorting to extensive electoral coercion. But the groups led by the urban middle sectors were literally growing by the day in numbers and prestige, and within a decade they rose in armed revolt against the fiscal bankruptcy and official malfeasance of the Conservatives as represented by President Juárez Celmán (1886–1890). The "Revolt of 1890" was short-lived, as the military remained loyal to the legal government. The uprising, nonetheless, signaled a new era in the republic's political life.

During the new era the urban middle sector-led groups so strengthened their claims to a greater share in the government that the Conservatives were finally compelled to give those claims legal recognition. The Civic Union, which had provided the intellectual ferment for the Revolt of 1890, was established as a political party in 1892. The new party was known officially as the Unión Cívica Radical, but traditionally it has been referred to as the Radical Party or simply as the Radicals. Although it drew support from wide segments of society and had a broad geographic base, it was from the start the party of the middle sectors, particularly those in Buenos Aires. Soon after the founding of the Radical Party, the highly regarded Argentine Socialist Party was established (1894) under the extremely able Juan Justo. It appealed both to the intellectuals, especially the university students, and to the rising industrial workers, who were beginning to organize in unions.

In 1905, largely to call attention to the pressures that were building up in the boiling political cauldron, the Radicals again arose in a revolt that was promptly quashed by the military. But throughout the 1890–1916 period, probably the Radicals' most effective tactics were the political education of the electorate through the press and party organizations and abstention from the polls. Abstention, used widely at times in Latin America to avoid a show of strength, repeatedly called public attention to the frauds that the Conservatives were perpetrating against society. The very fact that the middle sectors were free to make their objections known is highly significant. It suggests above all that the Republic had passed out of the stage of brute force and into one of greater political refinement and finesse. This development was made manifest when the mounting agitation of the Radicals, and to a lesser extent the Socialists, forced the passage of the Reform Bill of 1912. Popularly known as the "Sáenz Peña Law," it was introduced and passed by a Conservative government. The law, for the first time in Argentina, established the secret ballot and provided for broader suffrage and minority representation. It was under the terms of this bill that the middle sector-dominated Radical Party was victorious in the national elections of 1916.

The 1916 elections placed Argentina under the leadership of the middle groups. But control was not firmly in their hands. The Radical Party won narrowly and only with substantial and absolutely essential assistance from the rural elements who supported it because they disliked it less than they disliked the Conservatives.

Middle sector leadership was destined to last fourteen years. No middle sector leadership in Latin America ever came to power under more auspicious circumstances or, once in control, had more with which to work. There was not, for example, an armed revolt such as had confronted Batlle in Uruguay. Also, Irigoyen soon built up the presidential power to the point where it far exceeded that exercised by Alessandri in Chile, who was hamstrung by a malfunctioning parliamentary system. Nor were the Radicals faced with an aroused working element, as were the Mexican and Brazilian middle sectors when they took over control of their governments.

No middle sector element in Latin America ever inherited a more financially sound government. Argentina had already largely recovered from the first shock of economic dislocation following the outbreak of World War I. By the time Irigoyen took office, the nation's products were being urgently sought by the Allies. After the war, Argentina's prospects for future development along modern, progressive lines remained highly favorable in relation to the other four republics. The war had proved an incentive to industrial development more or less to the same degree that it had in the other countries, but in other respects the advantages lay with Argentina. It possessed the most highly integrated railroad system in Latin America and one of the seven best in the world. Its working elements were the healthiest, the best fed, and the most literate in the area. There were, of course, in some of the more backward farming regions hundreds of thousands of workers who were neither healthy and well fed nor literate. Land values rose precipitously after the economic readjustments of the early 1920's. Foreign investment capital and credit were available in plentiful supply. Throughout the decade following the end of the war, there were signs that Argentina was in balance and at peace with itself.

But then the depression struck and the nation was shocked out of its complacency. Overseas markets dried up, and easy credits from abroad disappeared. With them went the supreme confidence in the republic's future that a rising crest of prosperity had produced. For the first time in a decade and a half there was widespread discontent. For the first time the record made by the middle sectors since 1916 was closely scrutinized. The findings revealed that the Radicals had been largely unaffected by what was going on around them. The 1916 platform that had brought victory still provided the guiding spirit of the Party. The Radicals had been successful in carrying out some of the highly commendable goals of that platform, but they had failed to cope successfully with certain other developments that had not been foreseen in 1916.

The 1916 program had called for political democracy, and the Radicals had assiduously promoted representative government and freedom of expression. They had broadened the electoral base. They had maintained an atmosphere of freedom. They had permitted the waging of campaigns and the holding of elections. In most instances they had seen to it that ballots were fairly counted and that the victors were sworn into office. The picture, however, was not entirely favorable. Irigoyen's record of intervening in the political life of the provinces had been surpassed only once, by Justo José de Urquiza (1852–1860). Irigoyen's centralization of authority in the national government had been recognized as posing a threat to democratic government. Patronage had been used to buy political support. Official corruption had not been cured; if anything, it had become more widespread. But these adverse developments should not be permitted to discredit the very solid contributions that the Radicals made to the growth of representative government between 1916 and 1930. For in the latter year no other country in Latin America gave the impression of being as politically mature as Argentina.

.   .   .

In so far as the Radicals' political future was concerned, their contribution may be considered largely to have ended with what they did by way of promoting the development of democratic-representative government and education. That was, of course, no small contribution; nonetheless, it must be recognized that it represented primarily the fulfillment of the principles they had held in the nineteenth century rather than a response to the changing conditions of the postwar world.

One of the significant failures of the Party was its inability to galvanize major segments of the middle sectors into a political unit. In fact, the leadership's conduct had had the opposite effect, and by 1930 the middle groups had become increasingly fragmented. There were good social and economic reasons why this was true, and they are discussed below; but politically, the responsibility for diffusing the middle sector political strength would seem to lie primarily with Irigoyen. He had been a member of the Party since its founding and its leader since 1896. Almost from the start he had viewed the Party as a personal vehicle and, as he strengthened his position, he became a personalist in the extreme. Before 1916 his capriciousness had driven the "Santa Fé Agrarians," under Lisandro de la Torre, out of the Party, and they returned only long enough to provide Irigoyen with the votes he needed to unseat the Conservatives in 1916. By 1922 his tyranny as president of the nation and as head of the Party had forced the antipersonalists, made up of the more conservative elements of the Party, into secession. Thenceforth, *Irigoyenistas* and the antipersonalists, who continued to consider themselves Radicals, were at loggerheads. When the antipersonalists won the presidency in 1922, Irigoyen used his influence in Congress to void a large part of the antipersonalist legislative program. When Irigoyen lost his popular support and faced an armed revolt during his second term in the presidency, the antipersonalists refused him their backing.

.   .   .

The Radicals' record in support of the "neglected" elements of society was checkered. During their fourteen years in office they produced nothing to compare with the progressive and enlightened constitution that Chile had promulgated in 1925. Unlike in Uruguay and Chile, where the State had assumed a "social responsibility," in Argentina the Radicals had been content to leave the welfare of the less fortunate elements in the hands of Catholic charities. The Party could not point to anything concrete that it had contributed by way of permanent gains for organized labor. Following the week-long strike of 1919, which Irigoyen finally broke with the help of the police and the national army, and at a heavy cost in lives, the Radicals at no time demonstrated an abiding faith in the political capabilities of the workingman, although they continued to rely upon the votes of the urban workers to stay in office. They did place in the law books a considerable body of piecemeal legislation in favor of industrial labor. But their labor philosophy was heavily impregnated with paternalism and reflected a profound conviction that the benefits of the nation's prosperity would eventually filter down to the working groups whether there was legislation or not.

Any possibility of labor's profiting from the laws passed by the Radicals was largely nullified by the government's failure to provide for the enforcement of labor legislation, by the government's liberal use of court injunctions to prevent strikes, by the government's use of armed police as strike breakers, and by the government's imprisonment of labor leaders who refused to show their gratitude for favors received. The over-all view of labor's status under the Radicals revealed that the leadership's thinking had not been affected by the Mexican Revolution or the world trade union movement.

The Radicals' failure to respond favorably to the plight of the urban labor forces drove many socially conscious members of the middle sectors into the Socialist Party. By 1930 the Socialists had won over an important part of the laboring element of the city of Buenos Aires. Although Irigoyen retained to the end a large following among the working groups of the city, the inroads made by the Socialists forced him increasingly to rely upon that portion of his political organization centered in the province of Buenos Aires. In the national legislature the Socialists comprised the third middle sector-led element—the anti-personalists and the Santa Fé agrarians being the other two—that opposed the Irigoyenistas and in so doing they dissipated the energies of the middle groups.

8

ARTHUR P. WHITAKER

FLOURISH OF TRUMPETS
Enter the Military
1930–1943

The September 6, 1930, military overthrow of President Irigoyen was an important bench mark in Argentine history. During a period of more than a half century the country's military leaders had largely abstained from direct intervention in national politics. For an analysis of the consequences of their abrupt re-entry into Argentine politics we now turn to one of the most perceptive scholars in the Latin American field, Arthur P. Whitaker. During the last years of his nearly three decades as Professor of Latin American History at the University of Pennsylvania, he conducted an advanced graduate seminar in Argentine nationalism. Among his numerous articles and monographs on Latin American subjects, several have been devoted to Argentina. In addition to Argentina,

From Arthur P. Whitaker, *Argentina*, © 1964, pp. 83–103, *passim*.
Reprinted by permission of Prentice-Hall, Inc., Englewood Cliffs,
New Jersey.

these include The United States and Argentina
(*1954*), Argentine Upheaval: Perón's Fall and the
New Regime (*1956*), *and a substantial chapter in*
Nationalism in Latin America, Past and Present
(*1962*), *on which Professor Whitaker and David
Jordan collaborated.*

The revolution of 1930 marks the assumption by the Argentine armed forces of the new role of decision maker
in public affairs, which they were to play in various ways
for the next third of a century. But that revolution also
revealed a persistent flaw that has made it difficult or impossible for the military to perform their self-appointed
role successfully, namely, their incessant internecine discord. Due in part to personal and interservice rivalries,
their schisms also reflect the fragmentation of the Argentine civilian society from which both officers and men are
drawn and with which even the professionalized officer
corps continues to maintain contact.

The armed forces' inability to agree among themselves
on how to use their decisive power has been a major
source of the instability that has characterized Argentine
public life most of the time since 1930. This protracted
instability, too, was something new in Argentine history;
for combined duration and intensity, there had been nothing to match it in the century elapsed between the advent
of the tyrant Rosas and that of dictator Uriburu. . . . The
inability of the armed forces to agree among themselves
facilitated the emergence in the 1940's of still another new
power group, organized labor.

The first phase of the military's new role . . . is de-
limited by two military revolts, each successful in a single
day: General Uriburu's on September 6, 1930, and one
on June 4, 1943, which was directed not by an individual

but by a *junta*. In between, Argentina was ruled first, for seventeen months, by a military dictator, Uriburu, who sought but failed to establish a kind of fascist system. Then, for a little more than ten years, it was governed by a revised version of the pre-1914 oligarchy, under constitutional forms but on military sufferance until the second coup turned it out in 1943 and set up another military dictatorship.

The Role of the Military and the New Nationalism

The Argentine armed forces' new political role involved a sharp break with long-established principle and almost as sharp a departure from precedent. . . . Argentina's Liberator, General José de San Martín, had established that principle, summing it up in the oft-quoted apothegm, "The army is a lion that must be kept in a cage and not let out until the day of battle." Later, this principle was incorporated in the Constitution of 1853 in a clause, still unaltered, which makes the president commander in chief of the nation's armed forces; and the president, elected in substantially the same manner as the president of the United States, is of course the head of the civil government.

First among the circumstances that led to a reversal of these roles was the modernization and professionalization of Argentina's armed forces, and their consequent growth in proficiency and self-esteem. Ironically, this long process was given its first major impulse by leaders such as Mitre and Sarmiento, whose purpose was to strengthen the civil government against the militarism of that day as represented by the caudillos and their gaucho hordes. Thus, it was the "schoolteacher president" Sarmiento who founded the Colegio Militar (1870) and the Escuela Naval (1872), the Argentine equivalents of West Point and Annapolis. In the next few decades, Roca, Pellegrini, and Roca's protégé, General Pablo R. Riccheri, carried on in the same spirit. In 1884 the General Staff was reorganized; beginning in 1899 German military missions and equipment were imported; in 1900 the Escuela Superior de Guerra (a national war college for higher officers) was founded; in 1901 compulsory military service was established; and in the next few years the character of the officer corps was profoundly altered by the forced retirement of many older officers and the adoption of seniority and technical proficiency as the criteria for promotion.

As a result of this last change, the middle class supplanted the oligarchy as the main source of the officer corps. The fact that the middle class consisted to a large extent of "new Argentines," the sons of immigrants, weakened the hold of Argentine traditions, including San Martín's principle, on the nation's professionalized, self-confident armed forces. The alienation was most pronounced in the German-trained army.

In the 1920's and '30's several other circumstances reinforced the trend. Partly by contagion from abroad, two related ideas gained wide acceptance in Argentina. One was that the political parties were corrupt and incompetent and representative democracy a failure; the other, that it was the armed forces' mission to redeem the country. Both ideas fell on fertile soil in Argentina, where they had an exceptionally long and vigorous life. That they did so was partly the fault of the civilians themselves, and the Radicals were as much to blame as their right-wing opponents. When the latter used the armed forces to overthrow Irigoyen's government in 1930, they were only giving him some of his own medicine, for he had done all he could to gain military support for the revolts of 1890, 1893, and 1905; and when in office he constantly played politics with the armed forces. His successors in the Radical leadership also tried to stir up military revolts for several years after 1930, though with no better success.

Finally, nationalism conditioned the behavior and thought of most Argentines, including the military, during this period. There were, however, different kinds of nationalism and these corresponded to, if they did not cause, divisions within the military as well as the civilians. Both of the two main types of nationalism, liberal and integral, described by general students of the subject flourished in Argentina at this time. Liberal nationalism was the older type there; except during the Rosas period, it was dominant at all times before 1930. Unfortunately for its continued preponderance, liberal nationalism became identified with the oligarchy and so with exploitation of the masses and with a foreign economic and cultural penetration that was said to be stunting the country's growth, undermining its traditional culture, and making a farce of its vaunted independence. On such grounds deep dissatisfaction with Argentina's liberal or "canonical" nationalism was voiced as early as 1910 even by genuine liberals such as Ricardo Rojas.

Spurred by the deep economic depression of the early 1930's and its sequel in Argentina, integral nationalism expressed in part a revulsion against the fruits of the liberal variety. In foreign relations it was characterized by xenophobia, aggressiveness, and chauvinism; anti-imperialism and anticolonialism were among its favorite themes. In domestic affairs its proponents held that, in order to achieve the goals of "true" independence and greatness, the Argentine nation must be integrated at whatever cost to established provincial, individual, or other freedoms. They also made an effort, however misguided, to cope with new problems of great urgency, such as the rise of a rootless proletariat, social fragmentation, and economic lag in a deteriorating international situation, at a time when the political parties were apparently unable to meet the challenge under the existing rules of the game.

The foregoing descriptions of both varieties of nationalism are comprehensive models, and there were probably not many Argentines who subscribed to either type in every detail; there was certainly a wide variety of views and behavior among those associated with each. The liberal nationalists, for example, included not only the essentially democratic and civilian Sarmiento but also General Agustín Justo. Among the integral nationalists there was an even more glaring contrast between the elitist authoritarianism of General Uriburu and the popular, majoritarian tyranny promoted by Colonel (later General) Juan Perón after 1945. In short, while nearly all Argentine groups draped themselves in the national flag, there was not the remotest approach to a general consensus on the meaning of Argentine nationalism.

Uriburu: The Failure of Elitist Nationalism

After the quick success of his coup amid general applause, General Uriburu set up a dictatorship and tried to convert Argentina into a corporative state under elite control. For one reason or another, his plan, first publicly revealed on October 1, 1930, met with overwhelming opposition among his military associates as well as the civilian population. Some disliked it most because they regarded it as an alien importation, smacking of Italian Fascism; others because it would mean scrapping Argentina's traditional democratic system, to which conservatives as well as liberals had professed allegiance for generations past; and still others for more personal reasons. The last-named group included political leaders whose careers would be blighted if Uriburu succeeded in destroying the political party system; it also included General Justo's large following in the armed forces, which was a rival of the Uriburu faction. As for mass support, Uriburu made no effort to build it up until too late, and in any case it was in all probability ruled out by the elitist character of the plan; this was a sobering lesson that was not lost on one of Uriburu's junior associates, Captain Juan Perón.

. . . Uriburu failed to win the solid support of the military for the simple reason that he dispensed rewards and punishments on the basis of political loyalty to himself. As a result, the rival Justo faction was only stiffened in its determination to oust him. In fact, Justo planned a revolt in 1931, but this became unnecessary when Uriburu, baffled and mortally ill, permitted Justo's election to the presidency in November of that year.

.   .   .

The rock on which Uriburu foundered was political. As the only means of getting indispensable military and civilian support for his revolution, he had promised publicly to respect the Constitution. This won his regime a provisional but valuable endorsement by the nation's Supreme Court, which recognized it as a *de facto* government. The court's action then enabled him to issue a constitutionally valid declaration of a state of siege suspending all guarantees of individual rights. He issued the declaration at once, and maintained and enforced it throughout his brief administration. Moreover, it was soon apparent to all that he was determined to do everything in his power to scrap the Constitution in favor of his corporative system of government.

Uriburu's power was not equal to the task. The stronger Justo military faction of liberal nationalists held him to his promise to change the Constitution only by constitutional means, not by decree. This threw the question back into the civilian political arena, where our bluff soldier proved himself a complete tyro. Overconfident because of the public acclaim that had greeted his September coup, and disregarding the advice of wiser heads among his associates that time must be taken to organize and build up a popular following, he permitted a free election to be held in Buenos Aires in April 1931, only seven months after the coup. The result was a disastrous defeat for the Uriburu ticket; the worst blow to him was that the great bulk of the opposition vote went to the supposedly discredited Radicals. He canceled the election and set to work organizing paramilitary as well as political groups, but it was too late, for his military and civilian foes only redoubled the pressure on him to restore normal constitutional government.

Too ill to hold out longer, Uriburu permitted a nationwide election to be held in November 1931. It was won by a coalition of conservatives (now called National Democrats), Antipersonalist Radicals, and Independent Socialists, headed by General Agustín Justo. . . .

Decline of the Parties

. . . Extreme nationalists of both the left and the right attacked the regime with increasing vigor throughout Justo's administration.[1] The storm did not break until after his retirement and the beginning of World War II in 1939, but it was already gathering. In the atmosphere of growing national and international tension, many Argentines regarded his liberal brand of nationalism as at best outdated. In addition, the decay of the opposition parties became so obvious, and the regime's electoral frauds closed the door

---

[1] As Professor Whitaker explains in the portions of his book not included here, the nationalists' ire was provoked by a trade agreement with the United Kingdom (Roca-Runciman agreement of May 1933), which they considered detrimental to Argentine interests, and, in 1935, was further exacerbated by the "benevolent treatment" accorded British tramway interests in Buenos Aires. [Ed.]

to peaceful change so firmly, that public confidence in the country's democratic system was shaken. Clearly, the situation was shaping up for another military coup, despite Justo's efforts to keep his companions in arms out of politics.

As the presidential election of 1937 approached, the rising Radical tide made Justo himself uneasy over the chances of passing control to the right people. Accordingly, he and his followers simply stole the election by fraud and force (the force of the local police, not of the Army, which was kept in its barracks). The Concordancia ticket, headed by his hand-picked presidential candidate and fellow Antipersonalist, Roberto M. Ortiz, won by a comfortable margin.

Yet, except in the narrowest partisan sense the Concordancia's victory was pyrrhic. It damaged Justo's own reputation beyond repair by making a mockery of his vaunted restoration of normal constitutional government. In this respect, at least, he did reproduce the practices of the old oligarchical regime. For the political health of the nation, the effect was disastrous. Coming on top of all that had gone before, it seemed to confirm what nonconformists had been saying for years past: that in Argentina democracy was only a snare to facilitate the domination and exploitation of the nation at large by a privileged few.

Disintegration of the Regime

When the new president, Roberto M. Ortiz, took office in 1938, there was widespread hope that the promise to restore honestly administered constitutional government would at last be carried out. Although elected as the Concordancia's candidate, Ortiz belonged to its relatively liberal Antipersonalist Radical wing and was reputed to be a man of complete personal integrity and also to have a talent for leadership demonstrated both in public affairs and his private practice as a lawyer. The very fact that his election had been notoriously fraudulent gave ground for hoping that such a man would try to make amends by purifying the political process even at the expense of his own class, as Saenz Peña had done by his electoral reform law of 1912.

That is just what Ortiz did, but the war in Europe soon distracted him, then diabetes crippled him, and his well-intentioned but limited efforts at reform did less to improve the political tone than to weaken the regime by sowing dissension in the government party, especially in its National Democratic wing. As that was the wing to which Vice President Ramón S. Castillo belonged, there was a virtual change of administration when illness forced Ortiz to turn over his powers to Castillo in July 1940.[2]

In the next eighteen months the United States moved away from neutrality, through "all aid short of war" to Britain and the other enemies of the Axis (including, after June 1941, the Soviet Union), to entry into the war after the attack on Pearl Harbor. On the other hand, Argentina, with Castillo at the helm most of the time, moved in the opposite direction, first hardening its neutrality and then giving signs of benevolence toward the Axis. Its course is understandable, if not praiseworthy. The Axis was at the height of its power; Generalissimo Franco had won the Spanish Civil War with its aid; and the Argentines had heard reports, since confirmed, that the United States did not plan to defend South America south of the northern "bulge" of Brazil, so that Argentina would be left alone

---

[2] Ortiz never fully recovered his health, dying in July 1942. In June 1942 he resigned and Castillo, who had been exercising power as acting president, formally assumed office as president. [Ed.]

to face an attack or reprisals from Hitler. And the Argentine military, whose voice was now loud again in public affairs, fully expected him to win.

Accordingly, when Castillo responded to the Pearl Harbor attack by declaring a state of siege, the measure had no anti-Axis connotation whatever and was merely designed to cripple the domestic opposition. His last major foreign policy decision reached the public a month later, January 1942, at a meeting of American foreign ministers in Rio de Janeiro. There the Argentine delegation successfully resisted heavy pressure from the United States and its Latin American friends for a resolution requiring all the American states to break relations with the Axis. Instead, the resolution only recommended a break, and that was the end of the matter so far as Castillo's government was concerned: it simply ignored the recommendation.

Castillo acted as he did because, beset by his domestic foes, he was fighting for his political life and, however misguidedly, for that of the regime. He needed all the help he could get from the state of siege and from every other available source. Ominous rumors were circulating of new military conspiracies and of communist infiltration of the now divided labor movement. The opposition parties could hardly help Castillo, even if they would; the only two of any consequence, Radical and Socialist, were suffering from a kind of bureaucratic dry rot and had lost the confidence of the people. His own party was crippled by dissension both between its National Democratic and Antipersonalist wings, and also within each wing.

In an effort to kill two birds—one political, the other military—with one stone, he gave the now key cabinet post of Minister of War to one of the Antipersonalist Justo's military associates. In order to placate the extreme nationalists among the military, who were enraged at seeing Brazil's armed force move ahead of Argentina with

Lend-Lease aid from the United States, Castillo even tried secretly to obtain arms from the Axis. He failed, however, and in November 1942 his military critics forced him to replace the recently appointed Minister of War with one of their own group, General Pedro Ramírez. That was the beginning of the end for Castillo. He might perhaps have been saved by General Justo, but Justo died in January 1943.

Since Argentina's democratic tradition is as old as the nation itself and still had strong supporters in various political and social sectors at this time, it may be wondered why they did not join forces to meet this crisis. Such an effort, at first promising, was indeed made. It had its origin in a group organized in June 1940, under the name Argentine Action, to support the cause of Britain and its allies. The group was therefore pro-democratic as well as anti-Axis. Its initial focus was on foreign, not domestic affairs, but as the domestic crisis deepened, some of its leaders tried to convert it into an inter-party coalition for the defense of democracy in Argentina.

Despite the known imminence of the threat of subversion, this effort at democratic defense failed. The chief reason seems to have been that most of the leaders of the largest party, the Personalist Radicals, refused to join the coalition because they were determined to keep a free hand in the hope of winning the election in November 1943 with a ticket headed by an army general. Their candidate was to be no less a person than Castillo's new Minister of War, Pedro Ramírez, with whom they held secret conclaves in the spring of that year.

Before the Argentine Action group dissolved, it adopted a program that linked two increasingly important themes in Argentine public life: nationalism and the need for economic and social reform. When the coup took place, one of the first measures of the new military junta was to proscribe Argentine Action as pro-communist. Yet Juan Perón, who emerged from that military junta as the master of Argentina, developed a widely popular program remarkably like that of the proscribed group: a program of social justice, land reform, development of mineral resources, industrialization, and economic independence. Even his most familiar slogan, the "Third Position," was anticipated by Argentine Action's call for an "intermediate" position between free enterprise and a regimented economy. This democratic group was in step with the times, but it could not arouse like-minded civilians to concerted action and it had the military leaders against it.

The coup took place on June 4, 1943. It was exclusively the work of the military and was directed by a secret junta of generals and colonels called the GOU.[3] With little fighting and amidst a mixture of public applause and indifference, the GOU gained control of the government immediately. Promising to respect the Constitution, the new government was promptly accorded *de facto* recognition by the Supreme Court. Except that there was less civilian enthusiasm for the coup, it seemed to be 1930 all over again. But there was an important difference: this time there was no General Uriburu, no single commander, but a sprawling junta composed of top and middle brass, and all scrambling for power. Out of this struggle emerged a regime which, it is safe to say, was quite different from anything planned by the military conspirators.

---

[3] The letters are generally said to stand for "Grupo de Oficiales Unidos," though there are variants, including "Grupo Obra de Unificación" and "Gobierno, Orden, Unión."

9

CARLOS SÁNCHEZ VIAMONTE

CAESARISM IN CONSTITUTIONAL THEORY AND IN PRACTICE

Carlos Sánchez Viamonte has studied the theory and practice of the Argentine constitutional system from the viewpoint of the practicing politician as well as that of the scholar. In the years before Perón he held professorships in the social sciences and public law at the National Universities of Buenos Aires and La Plata, positions to which he returned after Perón's overthrow. Some of the results of his research and political experience can be seen in the lengthy list of monographs and articles he has published, including Derecho político, Historia institucional argentina, El constitucionalismo: sus problemas, *and* El pensamiento liberal argentino en el siglo XIX. *His political career has encompassed serving the Argentine Socialist Party as member of a provincial con-*

From Carlos Sánchez Viamonte, "Introducción a los poderes del gobierno," *Argentina, 1930–1960* (Buenos Aires: Editorial Sur, 1961), pp. 101–107. Translated and printed by permission of the publisher.

stitutional convention (1934) and as provincial deputy (Buenos Aires), national congressman (the Federal Capital), and vice-presidential candidate (1958). In the following selection Sánchez Viamonte examines the constitutional provisions used by "strong" Argentine presidents before Perón and those added during the Perón regime.

Our Constitution possesses a more accentuated Caesarist structure than one finds in the Constitution of the United States. In our Constitution the Executive Power is personified in a single functionary with the title of *President of the Argentine Nation* and the character of the *Supreme Chief of the Nation*. But the Caesarist theory does not terminate there, even though under the Constitution neither the President of the Republic nor the Executive Power has more assigned powers or functions than those expressly assigned. (Moreover, this follows two doctrinal Argentine principles: one designating those attributes and faculties that cannot be delegated to either the Executive Power or to the President of the Nation, in accordance with Article 29, which curbs such delegations of power as treason to the Fatherland; and the other, derived from Article 95, which forbids the President to exercise judicial functions, etc.) Caesarism in the Argentine Constitution is comprised, in the main, of what has been called both "strong executive" and "strong government," because of the erroneous tendency to call the Executive Power "the government," despite being cognizant that the government is made up of three constituted powers or knowing that three functional branches exercise power interdependently.

The preponderant role of the President vis-à-vis the legislative powers makes it clear that the principal sources of power are in his hands. Their use, even without abuse, is sufficient to constitute a form of Caesarism whenever the individual exercising such powers does not have a deep attachment to republicanism and a sincere respect for the moral value of democracy. In sum, the President's power to name or remove all functionaries and employees of the administration and—with the consent of the Senate—to name the judicial magistrates, including the members of the Supreme Court of Justice, added to his veto power over legislation and established a decisive predominance in his favor over the entire administration, including the judiciary. It is interesting to note that all administration functionaries are named without the consent of the Senate and can be removed by a simple executive resolution.

In respect to the President's relation to Legislative Power, he is able to exercise important legislative functions during the congressional recess, which normally lasts for seven months each year; sometimes by express constitutional authorization and at others by authorization said to be implicit. . . . The most dangerous of these is the power to declare a state of siege on the grounds of internal disturbances; the most potent, from the political point of view, is the power to decree interventions in the provinces. To these constitutional or quasi-constitutional powers must be added those the Executive Power employs as a result of its Caesarist tendency, and also through both the accommodating complacency of the other branches of government and the lack of major objections on the part of the public or its communications media. For example, the Constitution (Article 86, Clauses 11–12) is interpreted to mean that Congress does not convene unless the Executive Power convokes it. One ought to point out, regarding this last interpretation, however, that such executive action is not inferred from the constitutional text. Its usurpation

. . . is enough to demonstrate the contrary. (See the author's work, *Manual de derecho constitucional,* pp. 263–264.)

As for the *Federal Government's* intervention in the provinces, we believe it appropriate to make it clear that the voice of the "federal government" ought to be interpreted as meaning that of the national Congress and not that of the Executive Power. Furthermore, such an interpretation is supported as the only correct one by Article 67, Clause 28, of the Constitution, which is the source of such powers whether they are implicit, residual, incidental, or whatever they are called. Congress and not the Executive Power has those powers.

The Argentine Constitution uses an eclectic or mixed system in establishing the Executive Power—which is not unipersonal but pluripersonal or at least bipersonal. This is evident in the provisions giving a constitutional character to the cabinet ministers and anticipating the existence of the Cabinet, in Article 88, where two classes of ministerial responsibility are established, (1) one which holds each minister *personally* responsible for the actions he authorizes; and (2) another under which the ministers have *collective* responsibility for whatever they *authorize jointly* (political responsibility before the Congress). This supposes the Cabinet's concurrence and the Cabinet's existing in a form closely identical to that consecrated by France in its constitutional law of 1875.

In a country so favored by nature and so extensive as the Republic of Argentina, economic power shows itself in financial power and by means of bureaucracy the country becomes a *timocracy,* as it was called in Greece, or a *plutocracy,* as it is now called. It is the government of the wealthy—exercised not by a social class but by the citizen who occupies the Presidency of the Nation—usable as a corruptive influence on its functionaries and public em-

ployees, both those with and those without tenure, and
above all on those others aspiring to a bureaucratic position.

Thus, the Argentine Executive Power is able to impose
its will on the entire country without abusing its constitutional powers. Obviously that imposition of power is made
more onerous and prejudicial as a result of its abuse,
almost without exception, by Argentine presidents, each
one more ostensibly. The irregular governments—improp-
erly designated *de facto*—produced by coups d'état of
military character, have accentuated that Caesarist tendency
even more, accustoming the people to suffer it with resignation.

Caesarism in Practice

We have sometimes said that the President of the Argentine Nation exercises the powers which the Constitution
grants him, plus those arbitrarily attributed to him, plus
those the servility of the other public officials—including
those in the Congress and judiciary—assign to him with
complaisance. We now reiterate this assertion, which we
could demonstrate in an entire book devoted to this
end. . . .

The federal government has always been vicious in its
practice of intervention in the provinces. The number of
interventions decreed by the Executive Power, while Congress was in session, is 102 under the National Constitution of 1853 (excluding those decreed by the provisional
governments after 1930 and including 37 from 1910 to
the present [1961]). Under the presidency of Hipólito
Yrigoyen, and within a period of apparent institutional
normality, 12 of the 14 provinces experienced intervention.

It should be pointed out that Article 6 of the National
Constitution authorizes intervention in the territory of the

provinces but not in their government. It states "The Federal Government intervenes in the territory of the provinces. . . ." "Intervenes in the territory" does not mean intervening in the government or destroying provincial autonomy. Unfortunately, this observation has not been made by the Argentine authors of political treatises, and it has not been established in parliamentary debates. Instead, invariably the practice has been to intervene in the government and to annul the provincial autonomy; on many occasions the intervention has been extended to all three provincial branches of government and to the municipalities, as has just happened in the case of the province of Córdoba (June 1960), although this intervention was decreed by the Congress.

As regards the state of siege, the abuses of it are innumerable. It has been declared many times, because of an internal disturbance, while the Congress was in session; and the Executive Power, or more accurately the President of the Nation, has so exploited the use of Article 23 for his own purposes that it would be impossible to enumerate here the infractions committed. In fact, the President passes judgment on and applies penalties for unlawful acts that have nothing to do with the internal disturbance claimed to exist (Articles 23 and 95). Furthermore, the malicious procedure of referring to the constitutional provisions favorable to liberty as "guarantees" was adopted, as though they were only . . . declarations—theoretical protection rather than fundamental parts of the constitution.

Since Article 23 of the Argentine Constitution establishes a condition under which individuals can be arrested and transported during a state of siege—that is, "if they do not choose to leave the country"—a capricious terminology was invented that assigns to the exercise of this right, when not affected by the state of siege, the character of an "option" that the interested party must make before the executive, yet confers on the latter the power of whether or not to grant it.

      .   .

For a long time the Executive Power used to order the detention, and in some cases, the transfer [of individuals], by verbal order. Their counselors, in [employing] their writs of *habeas corpus,* demanded a written order, and finally this was achieved. The judicial doctrine in this field is confused and complacent, tending to favor the Executive Power in nearly all the cases we know. On the national level, Dr. Virgilio Tedín's freeing of Senator Alem and Deputy Molina in 1892 is cited as an exception, but one should point out that far from establishing the juridical rights of the detained persons, his argument was based on the division of powers since those detained were legislators.

During the so-called "Justicialista" dictatorship, the President of the Republic invented an extra-constitutional system. He called it a "state of internal war" and, since it was not provided for in either the Constitution or the law, he used it without restraint to persecute his political adversaries. But the truth is that the Argentine presidents have always made an unqualified abuse of the faculties that Article 23 of the Constitution provides them.

      .   .

Among the institutional vices that are conducive to Caesarism we can point to the interpretation of Article 55, which unequivocally assigns to the legislative chambers the obligation of meeting from May 1 until September 30, juxtaposing it against Article 86, Clause 11, which makes it obligatory for the Executive Power to authorize the annual opening of the sessions. This has been interpreted as an attribute of the executive branch to the detriment of the legislative branch and has reached the point of the Chambers not meeting until the month of August, because the Executive Power has not convoked them. This occurred in 1930, under the presidency of Yrigoyen. Furthermore, the interpretation of Article 55, which states that the Chambers "also can be convoked in extraordinary session by the President of the Nation or their sessions prorogued," has been a vicious and false one. That "also" proves that this power was accorded to the President without prejudice to that power of the legislative chambers themselves; the latter, according to the Constitution, "will convene" without anyone convening or convoking them.

In 1910 President Figueroa Alcorta abused the power allegedly accorded him by Article 55. He not only employed the provisions in the act calling for a special session; but also, when Congress attempted to defend its parliamentary rights, he closed it with police help, thereby committing a serious institutional transgression.

.   .   .

There are many cases of executive invasion into the area of congressional powers. The executive branch does it frequently on the pretext of regulating laws which do not need to be regulated. This tendency was converted into a system during recent times, with almost no objections from the legislators. (We cite, as an example, smuggling, for which the regulatory decree establishes penalties which are thus imposed on the law [regarding smuggling].) . . .

One of the formal defects of our institutional life, which favors the executive preponderance, consists in giving legal form to interference by the executive branch into areas not in its province, such as constitutional reform and the state of siege. These areas properly are the concern of Congress (Articles 30 and 86), but legal regulation opens the door for executive interference, whether by proclamation or veto.

To the foregoing it is necessary to add the cases in which the executive branch openly usurps the powers of Congress, as has occurred with the concessions relative to sources of energy (petroleum and electricity). The country's economy is under the leadership of the Congress; Article 67, Clauses 1 to 12, in addition to Clause 16, are clear and unequivocal on that point.

Finally, we consider it our duty to point out some serious cases of constitutional infringements on the part of the executive, because it is already a chronic infection that affects us, this suppressing the legislative and judicial powers as part of the government (*propiamente dicho*) and concentrating all authority in the hands of a so-called strong executive, who is in reality, dictatorial and an exponent of Caesarism.

The Constitution has created the invocation of the state of siege as the only remedy for those serious contingencies that could endanger the institutions already established, including territorial sovereignty. The dictatorship introduced, in the constitutional reform of 1949, the "state of prevention and alarm" to accentuate the arbitrary powers of the President of the Republic. As this did not seem to him sufficient, he took advantage of events to frame, without either a constitutional or a legal base, the "state of internal warfare," the true significance and limits of which were never clarified, but which an obsequious judiciary converted into "extraordinary powers," submitting to a superman from whom originated all inspiration of justice and whose word was law even over the Constitution.

In the year 1948 Law 13,234, called the "National Defense Act in the Event of War and Applicable in Peace Time," was dictated. This law annuls the 110 articles of the Argentine Constitution; replaces the Executive Power with a military cabinet presided over by the President of the Republic in his capacity as Chief of the Armed Forces; authorizes the application of martial law and of military edicts throughout the country, dictated by the military government both in the whole nation and in specific regions where the military commanders exercise *total authority*.

According to this law, the military government created by it could dispose of persons over eleven years of age, moving them to any part of the Republic whatever and obliging them to render whatever services are demanded of them; as well as disposing of the property of particular entities or of persons or its use or possession, as it would seem convenient.

The dictator authorized the application of this law with the name of "Plan Conintes" (interior disturbance of the State). The present government [the administration of Arturo Frondizi, 1958–1962] not only abstained from abolishing the law, it also kept it in force and actually applied it, by abolishing civilian jurisdiction in judicial matters, etc.

On the question of pardon and commutation of punishments, President Yrigoyen introduced, as a dangerous innovation, the exercise of this Executive Power without awaiting the termination of the trial—that is, without a firm sentence and without a punishment set by the judiciary. At the present time [1960], under the presidency of Frondizi, the same thing is occurring. In both cases the judicial community has been complacent most of the time.

.   .   .

Although one could cite an infinite number of examples, to conclude this brief introduction it is enough to point out again that Caesarism, expressed in the letter of the Constitution or deduced by extension of it, is one of the gravest ills that has afflicted the Republic and still afflicts it.

10

ALEJANDRO RUIZ-GUIÑAZÚ

---◄━►━►---

THE NECESSARY
REVOLUTION

*By the time of World War II the optimistic out-
look of many Argentines—summed up in the popular saying that "God must be an Argentine"—had
been replaced by a deep dissatisfaction with Argentina's failure to attain the position its people and national resources deserved. Alejandro Ruiz-Guiñazú,
son of a distinguished diplomat and historian, expressed this frustration of the nationalist right. Some
of the measures he urged would be adopted in the
following decade, and the following excerpt from
his work illustrates many of the dissatisfactions of
rightist nationalists with the* status quo ante Perón.

We have asserted the need for a national revolution . . .
[and] justified it, demonstrating the total bankruptcy of
democratic liberalism in the contemporary world and in

From Alejandro Ruiz-Guiñazú, "How to Effect the Revolution We
Need," *La Argentina ante sí misma* (Buenos Aires: Guillermo Kraft,
Ltda., 1942), pp. 173–185 *passim*. Translated and printed by per-
mission of Guillermo Kraft, Ltda.

our own country. Finally, the idea of the Constructive State, in its fundamental aspects, has been explained.

We declare here . . . that every responsible man who speaks, writes or works in some way in favor of revolution is obliged to respond to three major points:

1) what policy commends that revolution;
2) what form of government will be most apt to apply that policy;
3) how does that revolution expect to achieve power.

Here is my response.

I

The revolution that we need can have as its object no policy other than that of national greatness—this to be seen no longer as a commonplace abstract ideal, good for adorning sonorous paragraphs, but rather as a government program precisely defined, rigorously concrete, and susceptible to being put into practice by a state that, at last, has free hands and sharp vision.

(a) The historical destiny of a people depends above all on the character of its race. Race is not exclusively a biological fact based on a community of blood. A community of blood is highly desirable, but race can exist without it. The authentic idea of race is very much more than the natural selection practiced by a herd of swine. Race is a spiritual fact; a psychological unity rather than a physical one. Race is not the manufacture of a determined head shape. Unity of race and purity of race mean community of ideals, community of interest—a mentality, a style, a way of living, a way of suffering, a way of thinking and of feeling common to a people. The greatness of a race, its ability to resist conquest and to maintain its individuality, these are not forged in a laboratory. History creates them in time and space, and the state with full conscience of its mission will dedicate itself to nurturing them on behalf of its own whole development.

(b) But before nurturing racial virtues, it is necessary to defend the race. Every young people, sparsely inhabiting its territory, needs the contribution of foreign immigrants to attain cultural and economic expansion. However, recourse to the foreigner is always a danger to the health of races, even for those which have reached maturity. Immigration constitutes, then, the number one problem of our national defense. . . . No foreigner, however robust and intelligent, should step on Argentine soil if he does not satisfy one essential condition, that of being assimilable. . . . We are incubating in our entrails a disease that some day we shall have to cure painfully and with danger to life. This disease is that of imperialists of diverse origin and with diverse aims—banking, economics, or political influence—whose agents live and work among us at grave risk to our national integrity, not so much now as for the future. Today's intolerably liberal regulations allow them absurd ease in becoming nationals. At present no documentation of citizenship ought to be authorized before ten years' residence in the nation or before a thorough examination of his activities over that period. The state already has excellent defenses, beginning with the Residency Law.[1] But a law's worth varies according to the spirit with which it is applied.

The formation of race demands not only external defense but also internal protection and stimulation. In a new country, of a cattle-farm type whose population is 60 per cent urban and 40 per cent rural, hardly any problem requires re-examination with the urgency and over-all importance as that of urban congestion, so as to help re-

---

[1] A law enacted in 1902 that authorized the summary deportation of foreign agitators, including resident aliens. [Ed.]

establish balance and root the Argentine in the land that is his sustenance and whole life. A people is incapable of defending its independence, or of sustaining a long war, if it does not have a peasant class strongly rooted in its native soil. The man from the countryside has been and will always be a better soldier than the city man, not because he is braver but because he has better physical and moral health. . . . Today Argentina suffers from an unnatural anomaly; it carries within itself a terrible threat. To ward it off great sacrifices and a profound revolution in the national economy will be necessary. A colonization law means a step forward. But it is not enough for the Congress to sanction it and for the executive power to promulgate it. It must be applied in a rational and permanent way, correcting it as practical experience dictates. And it will not produce positive results until it forms an integral part of an over-all national policy which rigorously weaves together all levels of activity.

The vitality of a people is measured by the surplus of births that it registers annually. We, a people still in formation, already possess the most abject vice that characterizes every decadent civilization: the voluntary sterility of the female. . . . Our present regime is completely indifferent to the problem because its aims are individualistic and electoral, and because it lacks social sensibility. But the future Argentine state will regard demographic policy as one of its primary activities. Toward that end it will pursue its purpose at parallel and overlapping levels: moral, social, and economic. It will have to revoke the liberal principle that says "for equal work, equal salary" and to replace this with a family salary and family subsidy. The head of a family will enjoy privileges and rights proportionate to the number of his children. The bachelor will see his privileges reduced to a minimum. . . . These and many other measures will be integrated in inexorable legislation, destined to conserve the life of the Argentine people. The state will have to perfect a solid moral and social education that makes the citizenry understand that greatness is not in egoism but in the spirit that gives a heroic and exalted sense to life, as sublime courage is to sacrifice self for the good of all. . . .

To bring about the advent of a strong rural class and the application of an intense demographic policy; to realize our national potential at its highest in all areas, the new state must impose social justice. Class struggle is nothing other than the consequence of imbalance between capital and labor. There must be harmony between them. Work is not a punishment but a right and a duty. Work is the most sublime form of prayer. Capital is a means of production—not a privilege or a culture for the breeding of parasites. Consequently it will be necessary to associate the worker with capital by his sharing in the benefits. By the same token, the state will have the right to watch carefully the use of profits, not to curtail freedom but to avoid the dangers to which today's capitalists subject us. The worker has no right to strike, as the boss has no right to arbitrarily dismiss him or suspend his wages. On the other hand, both have the right of assembly and of making heard, with absolute freedom, their needs and their rights to property. The owner has the right to reap the benefit of his property, within the limits of a clear social ethic; the worker has that of being assisted in times of misfortune and in old age. At present there exists in more than one zone of the Argentine republic exploitation of the worker, salary abuses, unemployment, poverty, and vagrancy. And these ills are being aggravated rapidly at the same time that the first consequences of the ensuing world catastrophe [World War II] are developing. The only remedy against convulsion and explosion is justice expressed not in words but in the integral application of equitable law. In a new country, immensely big and rich, poverty has no cause to exist. The state that tolerates it loudly confesses its congenital ineptitude.

The realities of life have corrupted our federalism. For a long time, federal intervention provided provincial autonomy. But day by day the attraction of Buenos Aires is more irresistible, and we progress uninterruptedly toward centralization in *all* affairs. The fact is that authentic federalism is the crowning point of an historical evolution —the expression of a matured civic culture. But to organize the country, it was necessary to adopt a system, and we chose forms of government more appropriate to peoples who have reached their apex. . . . Let us not stubbornly cling to political federalism that is in no way indispensable to our greatness. Let us work, rather, toward a decentralization of economic activity. Because the really indispensable condition of greatness, . . . is the balanced distribution of population, of commerce, and of industry—the diversity of wealth in different regions, each of which should be autonomous in respect to its own patrimony, but should nevertheless dovetail to increase and consolidate the general patrimony of the country. We should strive for rigorous political unity and ample economic decentralization. Or, simplifying the terms: decentralization in unity. This standard contains all the others. It is the major directive in the policy of national greatness. On it depends, in fact, action on race. on attachment to the land, on demographic increase, on improvement in the workers' conditions, and on necessary military power. Therefore, the state, to be constructive and essentially dynamic and effective, should put political unity into the service of regionalism, protecting most particularly the private initiative inland, inspiring those thousand new industries that today lie inert, ending once and for all the prohibitive freights that exceed the cost of transoceanic transport, extending without interruption the road network even to the ultimate limits of the country, financially supporting the poor provinces and lifting indigent territories up from their prostration. But none of the aspects of this work will be realized without the formation of a new patriotic and economic mentality; without the assistance of an education that inculcates in Argentines confidence in their country, teaching them to invest their capital in authentic and legitimate national independence. Thus, from the university to the barracks, from the labor pool to the specialized profession, the citizen, freely and individually, will have enriched his native land.

II

Every revolution has as its object the establishment of a new order of things; to replace one state, one regime, with another. The problem of the form of government, then, constitutes the fundamental question in the constructive application of the revolutionary spirit. Therefore, since the failure of our present political regime begs for a national revolution, we must explain what form of government is needed for the future Argentine state.

If in answer to this obligation we should begin to detail here the structure of such a state we would incur exactly those vices of rationalist theorizers; we would contradict the essence of thought in these pages; we would demonstrate a lack of all realistic sense by pretending to order beforehand what belongs exclusively to the future, what ought and will surge from natural historic evolution or by accident of inevitable events.

The regime destined to take deep root in the national reality will not emerge in twenty-four hours. It is the outgrowth of the problems, needs, tendencies, and ambitions of a people. Its formation should be corrected and continuously improved by experience. Therefore, to decree years in advance a complete system drawn to the millimeter would imply a lack of intellectual honesty or would be equivalent to manufacturing recipes.

What is important, what is decisive and indispensable, is an extremely clear and firm notion of the fundamental concepts that should guide the life of the state: authority, liberty, order, responsibility, dynamism. Thus, for example, if we affirm that the state should be constructive by nature and at the same time neither liberal nor totalitarian, we understand that its executive arm will be constituted by a very strong power strictly respectful of all legitimate liberty. What practical value could it have to launch now an erudite and compact exposition of what is needed when there still does not exist among us a movement that embodies a national reformist spirit? I insist: what is decisive is to know what one wants, where one is going. The new constitution comes in steps; it is the legal expression of the new spirit.

Now then, we must establish that orientation, general lines, directives, tendencies are not synonymous with vagueness or with abstract finality. If one asks me what is the authentically Argentine form of government, I answer: democracy. The fact is that our fundamental problem does not consist in suppressing popular representation but, on the contrary, in reinforcing it to the maximum, giving it a form infinitely more true, legitimate, and rational.

The fatal end of electoral democracy is demagoguery. And universal suffrage—whose absurdity we have also proved—is the direct cause of electoralism. Therefore, no remedy, no solution, will be effective if the cause is not rooted out. Palliatives, graft, good will, negotiation, or violence—none will be effective while the root of the evil exists. Let us imagine the most favorable of circumstances: a president who, working with the necessary

means and spirit, manages to impose purity on suffrage.
Let us suppose that on departing from office, he leaves
the country in an unassailable condition for another president leaning in the same direction. It can be declared that
as long as universal suffrage lasts—along with its inevitable institution, the committee,[2] and its inevitable agents
and mentality—all progress would be illusory and provisional. Sooner or later someone would again be imposed
who knew how to appeal to the masses with demagogic
flattery. At least here in our country, the professional
politician has practiced and will always practice the
smear as the most effective method of destroying the influence of positive values introduced by a superior ad-
versary. Hence Argentine politics go on being irremediably
dragged on toward the vile and the dishonest by unscrupu-
lous candidates.

To replace universal suffrage there is no other road
than that of popular representation through syndicalist
and corporative organization. But before continuing, it is
necessary to clarify two points. First, there are many
who persist in considering corporatism synonymous with
totalitarianism—two concepts that are essentially independent of each other. Those who deny it ignore past and
present history, as well as the elements of the principal
social doctrines. It is preferable, therefore, to overlook
their ignorance and leave them to their luck. Second, there
is no lack of those who assert that a regime based on
corporate representation is not capable of expressing the
whole of the nation's life forces. . . . But, its realization
being a problem of a technical order, the solution depends
solely on the capability of those in charge of it. When we
speak of corporative and syndicalist representation we do

---

[2] Presumably the congressional committees of the World War II
period that were busy investigating the activities of suspected axis
agents and violations of civil liberties. [Ed.]

not limit ourselves to the professional and economic level; we are thinking also about the moral, social, political, and intellectual levels.

Every system of a corporative type emerges from a dilemma. If the profession so organized enjoys complete autonomy, it soon withdraws into itself. Allowing excessive liberty to the different production sectors would probably give them the faculty of price-fixing, for instance. And those prices will respond to the self-seeking criterion of their own interest, without account for the higher interest of the nation as a whole. The same selfishness would lead the corporations, in a misdirected feeling of self-defense, to prohibit creation of new industries or of new production methods to avoid other competition. In this way there would evolve a sterile rigidity such as characterized the system in the last stages of the Ancien Régime.

Inversely, if the corporation is not autonomous and is subject to state control, its functions are reduced to those of a simple machine. In effect, from the moment the state intervenes in the regulation of production and other aspects of the economy, the corporation only takes the place of a transmitter, charged with disseminating state directives.

The solution lies, therefore, in legally limiting the executive power without impairing his authority for constructive and propelling work. Indispensable to that end is the existence of a totally independent judicial power, charged with declaring the constitutionality or unconstitutionality of the executive's actions on all levels of state activity, including the economic. Special tribunals with simplified and rapid procedures will operate efficiently in their various jurisdictions. In other words, it is a matter of revising the balance of the three powers, of seating it on better bases and of making it serve a new spirit.

The presidential institution responds exactly to our national reality. Without doubt, its maintenance represents a vital need. In the election of the chief executive, only the system of voting needs to be changed to give it the benefit of a more authentic and more complete popular representation. . . .

III

How will the revolution that we need come to be consummated? Certainly not by means of a revolt supported by a local minority. A coup of this kind would remedy absolutely nothing and would instead create a climate of civil war. At the very least, the enormous confusion of ideas now existing in the country would culminate in chaos.

Here we speak of a national revolution and not of a movement organized by a group of citizens in the Federal Capital. The country has entered a decisive stage in its short political history. Therefore to be a patriot today is much more difficult than it was fifteen years ago. To be a patriot ought to mean now to resist the temptation to choose the easiest road, which is the path of violence, surprise, physical combat. Our politics have fallen so low that, at present, whatever the event, whatever the attitude, it can have irreparable consequences, which spur the descent and end by making us drown in an embarrassing mediocrity of republicanism. The responsibility is clear.

Now then, the revolution is not necessarily something catastrophic. *In the case of Argentina, for example, there could be the providential advent of a president who, intimately infused with the reformist spirit demanded by the century and by our internal reality, would execute by legal means a complete constitutional change. But this hypothesis is most improbable. Legality requires not only*

*a well-meaning will but an absolute majority in the legis-
lature.*[3]

Discarding these too-beautiful possibilities, we believe
in the necessity of a long, hard, difficult road that instead
of idle action requires silent, tenacious work, guided by
an unbreakable faith in the country's destiny and subject
to the directives of an iron will. Greatness will not be
won for the country by destructive criticism or demagogic
violence.

Among people of independent opinion, in groups of
nationalist tendency and among the militants of different
political parties, there number today thousands who feel
sincerely and deeply disillusioned with the general failure
of liberal democratic institutions. Some have already declared themselves against them, adopting different pos-
tures. Others, many others, live in disorientation and
destitution, desiring, perhaps without being able to articu-
late it, a vigorous, total, redemptive renewal. The whole
of those forces, of those values, already represents a
nucleus capable of working decisively toward national
destiny. But that potential revolution waits for the leader
who will unite it and carry it to power. And the leader
will not be fabricated by propaganda because this would
only be a false leader. He will emerge naturally, providen-
tially, to confront the internal danger. They will face each
other.

A change of regime, of system, means a change of life,
a change of spirit. It is not, then, a thing to be improvised
nor to be attained in a few months. We must understand
in its full sense that the conquest of every higher goal
demands struggle; and that the greater and higher the

---

[3] Italics by the editor. Although he quickly rejects it, the author
is here expressing the wish for the coming of a provident *Lider,*
who will solve the nation's problems. He also voices another attitude
frequently encountered in Argentina—disillusionment with the legislative branch of government. [Ed.]

goal, the greater will be its price, the greater the sacrifice. National greatness may demand of us, perhaps, life itself. Therefore it is not today a question of playing with words. It is necessary to cherish them and to give to each one a content of action.

To make us wake up, remake ourselves, be worthy of our own selves, we need a shock proportionate to our fall. The equilibrium, the apparent normality cannot prevail against the forces that are being generated, visibly or invisibly, on all levels of the country's life. Perhaps it will be necessary to endure the return of the worst of the radicals. Perhaps there will come deep convulsions brought on by the next world economic catastrophe and the lack of social justice that we bear. Or perhaps it will be the economic and political servitude that the definitive conqueror of the present world war will try to impose on us.[4] Future decades do not smile; but difficulty is a condition of greatness. I believe in the virtue of the whip.

---

[4] World War II. [Ed.]

II

THE WINNING
AND CONSOLIDATION
OF POWER

*In this section the readings reveal how Perón won
and consolidated power. The authors include two
members of Perón's Cabinet and a labor leader,
each of whom indicates the persuasiveness of
Perón's appeal and the failures of his opponents.*

11

FRANKLÍN LUCERO

LOYALTY WITHOUT RESERVATIONS

Military support was essential to Perón's rise to power. One of his stalwart supporters in the military was a career officer, General Franklín Lucero, who was Secretary of the Army when Perón was overthrown in 1955. The following excerpt reveals how Perón secured Lucero's support for plans to establish a "new Argentina."

In mid-1944 my superiors terminated my mission in Chile with the express order that I should present myself immediately to the Minister of War, Colonel Perón. In compliance with this directive, I requested an audience with the Minister of War as soon as I arrived in the country; he invited me to his private residence in Calle Posadas, where the interview was held. I found my long-time friend, accompanied by his already vigorous, fighting ally, af-

Translated from Franklín Lucero, *El precio de la lealtad* (Buenos Aires: Editorial Propulsión, 1959), pp. 22–23.

fectionately called "Evita"[1] by the public, plethoric with patriotism and enthusiasm. On offering me the post of Chief of the Secretariat of the Ministry,[2] Perón invoked the similar appointments we had occupied in our long years of past service (Infantry School, Junior Officers School, and Mountain-Training Center).

.   .   .

That conversation went on for several hours, and Miss Evita took part in it. It was owing to that fortunate circumstance that I came to understand the range of the ideals of Perón and Evita Perón. . . . I recall with deep emotion that he said to me:

> Our Fatherland needs radical changes that cannot be introduced suddenly, given the enormous interests created in all the social classes of the country, especially among the politicians and the military, dominated as you know by a powerful oligarchical, liberal, mercantilist minority. If we attempt to modify the actual state of things abruptly, we do not doubt that this minority would swallow us up at once, the same as would the military groups, like those at Campo de Mayo or those who belong to the "GOU."[3] Consequently, we will change the political, economic, and social physiognomy of the country by means of new procedures and methods that will progressively break down the old and bureaucratic organizations. We will create a new doctrine, which will assure us a just, free, and sovereign Fatherland, and fortify enormously the national spirit. I am pledged to this course and I need you, in the position of Chief

---

[1] María Eva Duarte, later Señora Perón. [Ed.]

[2] The post was one that Perón himself had held and had used to build up his military following. [Ed.]

[3] Campo de Mayo is the main army base near Buenos Aires. The "GOU" (*Grupo de Oficiales Unidos*) was the secret military lodge of nationalist officers. By mid-1944 Perón was one of the principal GOU leaders, but others were contesting his influence. [Ed.]

of the Secretariat, to replace me in as many of my functions as you can, so that I can dedicate my time to these fundamental reforms.

From that instant I committed myself to a higher ideal and to loyalty without reservation to this soldier and visionary friend, loyalty which I profess and will continue to profess, observing it at the cost of the greatest sacrifices.

In that visit I became acquainted, for the first time, with the philanthropic views of Mrs. Eva Perón in behalf of children, the aged, labor, and poor students.

Thirteen years have passed since I heard those words that seemed the utopia of a patriotic revolutionary. That period, during which I have been a modest collaborator, gives me the right to declare to the *cipayos* [Sepoys— local agents of a foreign power] that Perón continues intensely alive in the hearts of the Argentine people. The legions of workers (men and women) whom he inspired will conquer those little enemies who deny or do not understand his doctrine and his work.

12

ROBERT J. ALEXANDER

ARGENTINE LABOR BEFORE PERÓN AND UNDER PERÓN

After September 6, 1930, military presidents in the Casa Rosada were no novelty in Argentina. The June 4, 1943, military coup threw open the competition again, and Juan Domingo Perón was astute enough to recognize the value of adding popular support to his military following. Robert J. Alexander, Professor of Economics at Rutgers University, long-time student of Argentine affairs and author of numerous monographs on Latin America, including The Perón Era, The Bolivian National Revolution, *and* Communism in Latin America, *describes the state of Argentine labor before Perón entered the scene and how he used labor to gain and to hold power.*

During the 1930's and early 1940's, several significant changes occurred among the workers and in the trade union movement, particularly the CGT [Confederación General de Trabajo]. In 1930 immigration practically came to a halt. The urban working class, therefore, came to consist of second-generation Argentines and migrants from the countryside.

The second-generation workers were receptive to a native Argentine radicalism. The migrants from the countryside were politically illiterate. For them democracy had been a farce and so they were not impressed when someone who seemed to be helping them was accused of being a "Fascist." They, too, were good tinder for the fire which Perón was soon going to light.

At the same time, there was a growing tendency toward the bureaucratization of the labor movement. Trade union leadership had become a career in many of the larger unions. The labor organizations had begun to accumulate considerable property, not only headquarters buildings, but hospitals, summer camps, and other institutions built to provide social security and social service for their members.

Because unions had grown strong in such key industries as the railroads, it had become necessary for them to maintain at least an armed truce with the government. The romantic—and irresponsible—ideas of the old Anarchists, who used the unions as a weapon against the state, were not applicable to the new bread-and-butter unions which grew up in the decades before 1943.

Furthermore, there is considerable evidence that there was a growing gap between the leadership and membership of many of the unions. Attendance at union meetings fell off steadily during the 1930's, as did voting in union elections. Trade union membership became a duty rather than a privilege.

This gap was first exploited by the Communists whose influence grew in the late 1930's and early 1940's. The Communist-controlled Construction Workers' Union was the second largest organization in the CGT by 1943, and Communist influence was growing in a number of other organizations.

Finally, a large part of the working class remained outside the unions entirely. The packing-house workers, most of the metal workers, the workers on the "factory farms" of the sugar industry, and many other groups were unorganized. The trade union movement was heavily concentrated in Buenos Aires and its vicinity. Although there were some unions in the interior cities, nowhere was there the relative strength of the labor movement in the capital and its environs.

During the decades before the 1943 Revolution the important Argentine unions had established a pattern for labor-management relations that was adapted for his own purpose by Perón. Its two basic elements were collective bargaining and trade-union social insurance.

Collective contracts varied considerably in their geographical scope. In the railroad, textile, and shoemaking industries, there were nationwide collective agreements; in the printing trade, the hotel and restaurant industry, retail trade contracts were on a regional basis.

By 1943 some of the collective agreements had become fairly complicated. They dealt not only with wages, but also in many cases with the classification of workers, hours, vacations, and other fringe benefits. In some instances the contracts established social welfare funds financed by employer contributions and administered by the unions.

Negotiation of these contracts was conducted directly between the workers' and employers' organizations. The government played little or no part in the process and the

Departmento Nacional del Trabajo was little more than a statistics-gathering agency. Settlement of disputes rising within the collective agreements was also handled directly through union-management grievance procedure. The unions were organized to present those problems which needed solution in the day-to-day relations of workers with employers.

The other emphasis of the union before the Perón period was the establishment of social security and social welfare projects. The most notable examples of these activities were the health and hospital programs of the two railroad workers' unions. These were administered by representatives of the unions, though they were financed by the employers with some help from the government. They provided complete medical care for most of the country's railroaders and their families.

The railroad unions also aided their members in housing. Other unions had different social welfare programs. The Municipal Workers' Union of Buenos Aires, for instance, had a summer colony open to all members of the organization and their families.

The organizational structure of the pre-Perón unions varied a great deal. The railroad unions set a pattern of centralization. The local organizations of La Fraternidad and Unión Ferroviaria were merely sections of the national organization, with relatively little autonomy. The national unions had the right to remove officers of local units, and financial control was centralized in the Buenos Aires headquarters of the two organizations.

On the other hand, there were a number of important unions organized on a federal basis. These included commercial employees, hotel and restaurant workers, and printing trades workers. The center of power in political and financial affairs was in the local units of these unions. Collective bargaining was also done on a local or regional basis, and collective agreements were signed between local affiliates of these unions and their corresponding local employers' organizations.

In all the important unions, day-to-day business was carried on by full-time, paid union officials. Only in the Anarchist unions of the FORA [Federación Obrera Regional Argentina] did the old-fashioned prejudice against professional trade-union leaders exist.

At the time of the Revolution of 1943 there were four central labor organizations functioning. The old FORA still had a few scattered unions affiliated with it in Buenos Aires and a few provincial cities. The Unión Sindical Argentina was somewhat larger and was still nominally Syndicalist in its orientation. Its most important affiliates were the Telephone Workers' Federation and the Maritime Workers' Union.

The CGT had split into two rival factions. This division arose from a struggle over the secretary generalship of the organization in its national congress in December 1942. One faction, based mainly on the two railroad unions, sought the re-election of outgoing Secretary General José Domenech. Most of the leaders of this group were Socialists.

The other faction sought the election of Francisco Pérez Leirós, also a Socialist and head of the Municipal Workers' Union. It was also led by Angel Borlenghi, Secretary General of the Commercial Employees' Confederation and a member of the Socialist Party. However, this group received its main backing from Communist-led unions such as those of the construction workers, metallurgical workers, and textile workers.

When the two factions disagreed over who had won a very close election, they split into two different organizations, each of which called itself the Confederación General del Trabajo. They were generally referred to as CGT 1 (that of Domenech), and CGT 2 (that of Pérez Leirós).

. . .

Like the trade unions of pre-Perón Argentina, the employers' organizations suffered little or no interference from the government. Their attitudes toward collective bargaining differed considerably from one organization to another. However, many of the employers' groups had long experience with the process of collective negotiation with the trade unions or their workers.

The agriculturalists of the pampas region, which included the principal wheat- and meat-producing sections of the country, were organized in *sociedades rurales* (rural societies). In other regions, such as the sugar-growing province of Tucumán in the north, there were still other employers' groups. The small farmers and tenants were grouped in the Federación Agraria, which was very active in cooperative affairs until the advent of Perón. Few of the agricultural employers' groups had any experience with collective bargaining since there were few agricultural workers' unions before Perón.

Thus, there had developed in Argentina before the coming of Perón a pattern of collective bargaining. Both the employers and the workers adhering to this pattern had had considerable experience in making it work. Its weakness was that it covered only a small percentage of the country's urban working force, and virtually none of the workers of the countryside. The organized workers constituted a species of "aristocracy of labor" before 1943, and when the organizing fever swept over the hitherto unorganized workers after 1943, the old organizations were vastly altered.

One can draw a parallel between labor-management relations in Argentina in 1943 and labor-management relations in the United States a decade before. In both cases the situation changed suddenly. In the United States, the catalyst bringing about this change was Franklin D. Roosevelt; in Argentina, it was Colonel Juan Domingo Perón.

Government Direction of Labor Protest under Perón

The Revolution of 1943 brought about fundamental changes in labor-management relations in Argentina. Colonel Juan Domingo Perón, who emerged as the leading figure in this revolution, sought to bring under his control the whole process of negotiation between workers and employers. Ultimately, he largely substituted the government's fiat for collective bargaining.

In order to achieve this complete government direction of the grievances of the Argentine workers and of the establishment of the "web of rule" in Argentine labor-management relations, Perón had to destroy first the independence of both the workers' organizations and those of the employers. By persuasion and force he brought the labor movement almost completely under his control. He was somewhat less successful in converting the employers and in quelling their opposition to him. Nonetheless, by the end of his regime, nearly all official organizations representing the employing class were under the domination of the Perón government.

Perón

Colonel Perón used the labor organization existing in 1943 as a level to boost him into power. At the same time he tied those organizations to his own destiny, and completely subordinated them. It is interesting to note the difference between Perón's attitude toward the labor movement and that of Vargas in Brazil. Vargas destroyed most existing labor organizations and established new state-controlled groups in their place. Perón, on the contrary, bent the existing trade unions to his will. Perhaps this was why he was never as successful as his Brazilian contemporary in completely destroying the independence of the labor movement.

Although Perón was successful in gaining control of the top leadership of the labor movement, he could never completely destroy the opposition in the rank and file, and there were numerous instances during his tenure in office when the lower-echelon leadership of the unions defied the President. The result of the Perón experience was the acceptance of the fact that the labor movement had become one of the great centers of power in the country's social, economic, and political structure.

The revolution that gave Perón his chance was motivated more by the army's fear of a pro-Allied government coming to power in the middle of World War II, than by any concern with social or economic affairs. The Army, which had been trained by German instructors, had for long been strongly pro-German, and in World War II was "neutral" in favor of the Axis. The prospect that the election scheduled for the end of 1943 might bring to power the pro-British landowner Patrón Costas undoubtedly was at the root of the June 4, 1943, rebellion.

The military government which took office under the leadership of the new President, General Pedro Ramírez, dissolved Congress, which under the control of the Radical and Socialist parties had been the center of democratic and pro-Allied agitation for a number of years, and suspended freedom of the press.

Most important of all, as things turned out, the military regime suppressed CGT 2 on the grounds that it was "Communist-dominated," and ousted the leaders of some of the country's principal labor organizations, namely La Fraternidad, Unión Ferroviaria, and the Unión de Obreros Municipales, placing military officers in charge.

By September 1943 there were widespread demonstrations. This discontent was shared by an impressive number of retired generals and admirals who issued a statement calling for a restoration of constitutional government. Some of the younger members of the dominant military group saw that the regime was either going to become a violent dictatorship, in which case its tenure would probably be short, or it was going to have to seek support from civilian elements.

The first move was an attempt to win over the industrial middle class. This group had been discontented with the landowner-dominated governments and might have been expected to be friendly to a regime that had overthrown the last of these governments.

However, the industrialists had traditionally supported the Unión Cívica Radical, and they felt that ultimately this party would come to power when constitutional government was restored. They saw no point in mortgaging the future Radical government's position by making what they considered an unnecessary alliance.

The next move was to turn to the industrial working class. This group had also been unfriendly toward the landed oligarchy and had not received sympathetic treatment from any government since the first administration of President Hipólito Irigoyen (1916 through 1922).

Furthermore, a number of the military men already had contact with the labor movement. Colonel Juan Domingo Perón, the leader of this group, had been named Director of the Department of Labor soon after the June 4 revolution and had set about expanding its power and activities. Other officers closely associated with him had been placed in control of the unions taken over by the government. This group of military men conferred at length with leading trade union officials, in an effort to find out what it was the latter wanted and whether or not an alliance could be formed between military and trade union officialdom. These inquiries met with limited success.

The result of this change in direction of the June 4 revolutionary regime was the move in November 1943 to convert the old Department of Labor into a new Secretariat of Labor and Social Welfare, with cabinet status for its chief. The first Secretary of Labor was Colonel Perón.

PERÓN AS SECRETARY OF LABOR · During the next two years, Perón rose rapidly, becoming Minister of War and Vice President, as well as Secretary of Labor early in 1944. He also set about to win over the workers. In doing so, he sought to convince them that only through his office could they get vindication for their grievances.

In his assault upon the labor movement, Perón used both the carrot and the stick. For those trade union leaders who resisted his blandishments he reserved prisons, concentration camps, and exile, and made it increasingly difficult for their unions to function. Meanwhile, many labor leaders who might have wished to resist Perón found that more and more of the rank and file were being won over by his promises and performance.

During the 1943–1945 period, Perón threw his efforts into helping the labor movement expand. There had been perhaps 300,000 to 350,000 organized workers in Argentina when he took office. Within a couple of years this number was increased several fold. Perón forced employers to recognize their workers' unions and to negotiate with them. He personally led campaigns among packinghouse workers, sugar plantation peons, and various other labor groups in the interior of the republic. Where dual unions existed, he encouraged rival groups to forget their differences and to launch intensive organizing campaigns with the government's support.

On the other hand, Secretary of Labor Perón intruded his department into the field of collective bargaining negotiations. He first encouraged and then insisted that collective conflicts be brought to the secretariat for conciliation and decision. Many times, after collective negotiations conducted at the secretariat had been concluded, he presided over the formal signing of the new contracts. The workers soon came to the conclusion—which was frequently correct—that Colonel Perón had been more responsible for their wage increases and other benefits than had their own union leaders.

Finally, the Secretariat of Labor began an extensive job of enacting labor and social security legislation. In this field Argentina was considerably behind most of its neighbors in 1943.

This legislative work—by decree—extended into various fields. A more effective system of factory inspection was instigated. Social security legislation was enacted which brought under its scope the great majority of the country's wage- and salary-earning population. During the 1945 election campaign, Perón's successor as Secretary of Labor decreed that all employers must pay an extra month's pay to their workers at Christmas time. A number of legal, paid holidays were established.

HIS CONTROL OF THE LABOR MOVEMENT • The result was that by the middle of 1945 Perón had converted the trade union movement into a powerful personal political machine. He had conquered the Confederación General del Trabajo in the middle of 1944 when he had won its support for a government-sponsored Independence Day (May 25) celebration, the real purpose of which was to indicate political support for the regime then in power. Although certain unions remained hostile to Perón, their number was comparatively small by the end of 1945. The Unión Sindical Argentina was almost liquidated when most of its more important unions joined the Perón-backed CGT.

The degree of support which Colonel Perón enjoyed among the workers was demonstrated in the events of October 1945. On the ninth of that month a military coup by hostile elements of the army resulted in his forced resignation and temporary imprisonment. However, the new military group was unable to rally the support of the civilian politicians and for over a week the country got along without any cabinet.

In the meantime, Perón's labor supporters began to mobilize. A major role in this action was played by Cipriano Reyes, the leader of the packing-house workers in the areas near Buenos Aires. These and other workers began to descend on the capital by train, truck, auto, and even by foot. Civilian opponents of Perón were forced to go into hiding, while the military group in charge of the government did not dare order their troops to halt the mobs.

As a result, on October 16, Colonel Perón was brought back from prison and the next day appeared on the balcony of the Casa Rosada, arm in arm with President Farrell, to address the cheering crowd of supporters. Although Perón did not return to any of his offices, he was from that time on in full control of the government.

A few days after Perón's restoration to power, a campaign to choose a constitutional President of the Republic was launched. Perón announced his candidacy, although he had no political party supporting him. To fill this gap, he organized three new political groups. The largest of these —which won a majority in both houses of Congress on February 24, 1946—was the Partido Laborista, organized by most of the principal trade union officials of the republic. A dissident group of Radical Party leaders who had thrown in their lot with Perón organized the "Renovated Radical Party," while a third group composed of miscellaneous elements announced their support for him on a so-called Independent ticket.

The opposition to Perón formed the Unión Democrática Nacional which consisted formally of the Radical, Socialist, Progressive Democratic, and Communist parties, and also had the backing of the Conservative Party. They nominated two old-line Radical politicians, José P. Tamborini and Enrique Mosca, for the posts of president and vice president, respectively.

The campaign was hectic. Both candidates were shot at several times. Although the opposition was allowed little use of the government-regimented radio, it controlled most of the country's newspapers. The opposition felt that they would win if the polling on election day were calm and honest. Although these were the conditions on election day, Perón won.

ORGANIZED LABOR UNDER PERÓN • On June 4, 1946, Perón was inaugurated constitutional President of the nation. During the succeeding years, he and his wife set about destroying the independence of the trade union movement. María Eva Duarte de Perón was the principal figure in bringing this about. She set up her headquarters in the Secretariat of Labor building and from there molded the trade union movement to her and her husband's will. Through repeated purges of the unions she removed those leaders who had thought that they were using Perón instead of the other way around. Ceaselessly active, Evita for six years kept constantly on the alert to oust any unionist of independent inclinations, while at the same time seeking to convince the workers that all blessings flowed from the Peróns.

THE LEY DE ASOCIACIONES PROFESIONALES • One of the most important measures used by the Perón regime to destroy the independence of the labor movement was the Ley de Asociaciones Profesionales. The significance of this measure was twofold. First of all, it officially put the power of the state behind recognized trade unions and implicitly obliged the employers to deal with them. In the second place, and equally important, the law for the first time made it essential for a union to acquire legal recognition before it could function effectively. Before 1945, unions wanting some kind of legal status registered as mere civil associations—on a par with a Rotary Club or charitable society. Many unions sought no kind of legal recognition whatever.

This law started off by defining a *"sindicato* or professional association" as a group "formed by manual or intellectual workers of the same profession or industry, or in similar or connected professions or industries, constituted for the defense of their professional interests." The decree then went on to say that these associations "can be freely established without necessity of previous authorization, always provided their objectives are not contrary to the morality, laws, and fundamental institutions of the nation."

Four types of workers' organizations are noted in the law. The first is the union having *personería gremial.* The second type is a union with *personería jurídica,* or mere registration as a civil association, a category reserved largely for unions which have for one reason or another lost their *personería gremial.*

Third, there are "professional associations inscribed but without *personería gremial.*" These organizations are registered in special files in the Ministry of Labor and "can act freely and can carry out . . . all those functions which are not expressly reserved to *sindicatos* with *personería gremial.*" In some instances, where no *sindicatos* with *personería gremial* exist in the area of their jurisdiction, these groups can function as if they had such a status.

Finally, there are the workers' organizations which have no kind of government recognition whatsoever. These, as we have already noted, cannot function as normal trade unions. They cannot bargain with the employers, they cannot represent the workers in negotiations with the governmental authorities, and they cannot conduct any of the activities usually associated with a trade union.

The unions which possess the prized *personería gremial* are, under law, the only organizations which enjoy the following rights:

1) To defend and represent the interest of the workers in dealings with the employers and the state;

2) To defend and represent the workers before the social security authorities, the courts, and all other governmental bodies;

3) To have representation in governmental organizations regulating labor relations;

4) To participate in collective bargaining, negotiating and modifying collective agreements, contributing to the enforcement of labor legislation;

5) To collaborate with the state as technical consultative bodies in the study and the solution of problems of their profession;

6) To participate in political activities, in conformity with election laws;

7) To conduct their meetings and assemblies in closed halls without previous permission (though they must receive permission to hold open-air meetings);

8) To have exclusive use of their names, all others being prohibited from using titles which might lead to confusion;

9) To determine the suspension and renewal of work;

10) To establish sanctions in case of violation of their statutes and trade union decisions;

11) To require employers, with previous authorization from the ministry, to install the check-off;

12) To be exempt from all taxes;
13) To have preference in employment insofar as the state and all firms having contracts with or concessions from the state are concerned.

The law provides certain minimum requirements for a union to gain *personería gremial*. These include having a minimum number of members and having statutes which provide adequate means for protection of the organization's property and collecting dues, and which set forth the officers, name, headquarters, objective, frequency of meetings and financial reports, as well as sanctions on members and means of modification of the statutes and dissolution of the organization.

Presumably the organization which represented the majority of the workers in a given trade or industry was to receive recognition and be granted *personería gremial*. In fact, the Peronista government used this decree on various occasions to destroy an existing union politically hostile to the regime in favor of a new group, which was Peronista.

One of the most notorious instances of this was the case of the shoemakers' union. The Sindicato Obrero de la Industria del Calzado had been the dominant union in the industry since its establishment in 1917, and for many years previous to the Revolution of 1943, had negotiated contracts with the employers' organization in the trade. However, when the union applied for *personería jurídica* it was unable to get action from the Secretaría de Trabajo y Previsión, and soon afterward a rival organization was founded, the Unión de Obreros de Calzado, headed by elements expelled from the *sindicato*. This new group was immediately given *personería gremial,* though it had practically no members at the time.

When the Sindicato Obrero de la Industria del Calzado

in March 1946 issued a proposal for a new collective agreement, it was notified by the Secretaría that since it did not have *personería gremial* it was not qualified to conduct these negotiations. The employers were forced to deal instead with the new Peronista union. Although the older organization kept going for some time, it was ultimately driven underground and its leaders into exile.

The law sets forth conditions under which a union can lose its *personería gremial* and be succeeded by a rival group, although needless to say, these conditions were not observed in the case of anti-Peronista unions. According to the law it is possible for a rival union to be granted *personería gremial* "when the number of dues-paying members of the rival union during a continuous period of at least six months immediately previous to the request for recognition is superior to that of the recognized union; the latter then losing its recognition if it ceases to be sufficiently representative, although the authorities must also take into consideration the previously recognized union's contribution to the defense of its members' interests in deciding whether to strip it of recognition." Furthermore, in order for recognition to be transferred from one union to another such action must have the approval of the union losing *personería gremial,* "even if its membership is smaller" than that of its rival.

Many unions were squeezed out of existence by use of the Ley de Asociaciones Profesionales. Included were organizations of textile workers, shoe workers, hotel and restaurant workers, printers, clothing workers, shipbuilders, and maritime workers.

THE PURGE OF THE UNIONS · Evita went even further than this. She sought to destroy labor leaders who, even though they were supporters of Perón, had been union officials before the Perón regime. Between 1946 and 1951, there was a thorough purge of nearly all those leaders who helped put Perón in power during the 1943–1946 period.

Cipriano Reyes, leader of the packing-house workers, was one of the first victims. He was vice president of the Partido Laborista and was elected deputy in the February 1946 elections. When Perón announced the merger of the three groups which had backed him into a single government party (first named the Partido Unico de la Revolución Nacional and later changed to Partido Peronista), Reyes opposed this maneuver. He fought the President for two years, then after his term in Congress had expired, Reyes was put in jail where he remained until the overthrow of Perón more than seven years later.

Virtually all the old-time labor leaders were ousted in less spectacular ways and were replaced by individuals who owed their posts to Perón rather than to union members. The purge was completed in the middle of 1951 when the leadership of La Fraternidad was forced at gun point to resign by a group of self-appointed union officials.

An important part of Evita's work was assuring the workers that all their grievances would be channeled through and resolved by the Perón government. This was her "philanthropic" activity. One or two days a week Evita held court in the Secretariat of Labor building and received anyone with a problem. The President's wife became a combination marriage counselor, pediatrician, public defender, and Tammany Hall ward leader on those days. Ministers and other officials were in attendance, and would frequently be dispatched to set right some complaint. Few of those who visited Evita went away without the gift of a few hundred pesos.

The Eva Perón Foundation, which was a monopoly of all charity in the republic, carried out a similar function on a grander scale. In addition to building hospitals, children's homes, and similar institutions, it gave handouts to needy people and those stricken by some disaster. The foundation, though it received large "gifts" from unions, employers, and visiting foreign dignitaries, and large appropriations from Congress, never had to present any accounting of its funds. There is little doubt that much of the "charity" was given to the leading figures in the Perón regime most closely associated with Evita.

The result of all of this was that by the time of Perón's overthrow, most of the labor movement was a tool of the dictator. The top leadership consisted of unquestioning servants of the regime and their selection was made in the Ministry of Labor or in the Casa Rosada (presidential palace) not in the congresses of the unions which merely rubber-stamped the government's choices. There was no democracy in the middle and upper levels of the trade union movement—in the CGT, its provincial and city "delegations," or in the national and regional leadership of the industrial unions.

The only level on which a modicum of democracy was preserved was in the election of shop stewards and factory or workshop committees. Here the government allowed the workers in many unions to choose their representatives. However, in cases where these officials showed too much activity which the government interpreted as endangering its welfare, the CGT or the national leadership of an individual union would oust the offending unionists.

This degree of union democracy undoubtedly served two purposes as far as the Perón regime was concerned. In the first place, it kept it aware of discontent among its followers. In the second place, it served as an escape valve for the workers themselves, giving them some feeling of having a say in their organizations.

13

ANGEL PERELMAN

MY FIRST CONTACT WITH PERÓN

Angel Perelman, a leftist metal worker, had been disillusioned by what he considered the treasonable role of the Communist leadership in the metal workers' strike of 1942 and was not in accord with the views of the leadership of the Socialist Party, with which he was affiliated. In April 1943 he decided to break with the old-line leadership of his union and form a new one. After the June 4, 1943, revolution and Perón's assumption of direction of the Secretariat of Labor and Social Welfare, the leaders of the rebel metal workers became aware that other union leaders were receiving help from the secretariat's new chief. In mid-1944 Perelman proposed to a meeting of the union's leaders that they go to Perón for help, but his proposal was rejected 15 to 2. Nevertheless, Perelman and his supporters sought and secured an interview with Perón.

Translated from Angel Perelman, *Como hicimos el 17 de Octubre* (Buenos Aires: Editorial Coyoacán, 1961), pp. 44–46.

He received us with complete cordiality and explained his views to us in general terms, which, in regard to the future of the union, coincided with our own. We decided to go ahead with the organization of the union and to await the most favorable occasion for mobilizing the metal workers. This was not long in coming because the inflation continued its course and the union found itself without support.

Once the resistance of the other directors was overcome, we arranged with the Secretariat of Labor to convoke a meeting at which Perón would speak to the metal workers. The date fixed, we calculated that we could fill the assembly hall of the Deliberating Council, where the Secretariat of Labor and Social Welfare was located.

We had no resources for publicizing this meeting. Until noon of the day of the gathering, we were still sticking together some posters announcing the convocation. It was a great surprise when, by the time of the meeting, the meeting hall was completely filled, and an enormous multitude of nearly 20,000 metal workers was concentrated outside in the Diagonal Roca. The shops they came from were identified by improvised placards and reflected the enormous repercussion the growth of industry was having on the working class at that time. . . .

Colonel Perón, in one of the salient parts of his discourse, told us that he was gratified to see the metal workers enter the house of the workers and that he had assumed that, since they were one of the last unions to come together there, they must be very well paid. But he added that, as a result of the remarks of the comrade who had preceded him on the platform, it appeared that this was not so, and consequently he was urging the metal workers to form a powerful union to defend their rights and the country's sovereignty. At this moment a metal worker

interrupted to shout: "Thus speaks a *criollo!*" [1] Banners
and posters fluttered approval of the metal worker's re-
mark. We went out of that meeting with the conviction that
the metal workers' union would soon be transformed into
a very powerful labor organization. And in effect it was;
from a membership of 1,500 we transformed that union
"of form" into the present Union of Metal Workers
(UOM) with 300,000 workers in the fold. So profound
was the need for the country to defend its political independence and economic sovereignty, and for the working
class to organize at last its unions on a grand scale, that,
faced by the treason of the parties of the left, this need
had to be embodied in a military man who had come from
the ranks of the Army.

.   .   .

And we came to constitute then that ideological tendency
known by many people as the "national left." In our union
activities at the end of 1944 we witnessed unbelievable
happenings: labor laws neglected in another era were being
carried out; one did not need recourse to the courts for the
granting of vacations; such other labor dispensations as
the recognition of factory delegates, guarantees against
being discharged, etc., were immediately and rigorously
enforced. The nature of internal relations between the
owners and the workers in the factories was completely
changed. The internal democratization imposed by the
metal workers' union resulted in factory delegates con-
stituting the axis of the entire organization and in the direct
expression of the will of the workers in each establishment.
The owners were as disconcerted as the workers were as-
tounded and happy. The Secretariat of Labor and Social
Welfare was converted into an agency for the organization,

[1] *Criollo:* a term designating one as thoroughly Argentine. [Ed.]

development, and support of the workers. It did not function as a state regulator for the top level of the unions;
it acted as a state ally of the working class. Such were the
practical results that constituted the basis for the political
shift of the Argentine masses and that were manifested
in the streets on October 17, 1945.

14

EVA PERÓN

OCTOBER 17, 1945

In the Peronist calendar October 17, 1945, outranks all other dates in significance. It was on that date that Juan Perón returned to the balcony of the Casa Rosada, the presidential palace, to reassure the descamisados *(the shirtless ones) that their efforts had indeed secured his return from the imprisonment that had followed his removal from power a few days earlier. For a subjective view of that crucial period in Perón's career, we turn to his intimate associate "Evita" (then María Eva Duarte), a little-known radio actress before the 1943 revolution brought her into contact with important military figures, including Perón. She played an important role in Perón's return to power, and a few days later they were married, first in a secret civil ceremony and later in a public church wedding.*

Translated from Eva Perón, *La razón de mi vida* (Buenos Aires: Ediciones Peuser, 1951), pp. 41–45. Although much of this volume was probably ghost-written by one of the Peróns' staff of publicists, the portion excerpted here reflects the emotional force of Evita's personality.

The fire [of revolution] continued to move us forward. The "common fellows" of the comfortable and tranquil oligarchy began to think that it was necessary to put an end to the incendiary [Perón] and that this would extinguish the fire.

Finally they decided to carry out their plans.

This marked the last hour of the Argentine oligarchy. Then came the dawn!

So for nearly eight days they had Perón in their hands! [1]

I was not in prison with him. But the memory of those eight days still causes me pain; and more, much more, than if I had been able to spend them in his company, sharing his anguish.

On parting he enjoined me to be tranquil. I confess that I never saw him so magnificent as then in his serenity. I recall that an Ambassador, a friend, came to offer him the help of a foreign nation. In few words and with a simple gesture, Perón resolved to remain in his Fatherland, in order to confront everything and everyone among his own people.

From the time Perón left until the people recovered the Fatherland for him—and for me!—my days were feverish and sorrowful *jornadas*.[2] I flung myself into the streets looking for friends who could still do something for him. So I went from door to door. In that arduous and incessant walking I felt my heart glowing from the flame of his fire that consumed me absolutely.

I never felt—I say it truthfully—so minute, so small as in those eight memorable days.

I walked along through the neighborhoods of the great

---

[1] October 9 to October 17, 1945, when Perón was first stripped of his offices (Vice President, Minister of War, and Secretary of Labor and Social Welfare) and then imprisoned. [Ed.]

[2] A *jornada* is an act of a Spanish play. The reference probably derives from Evita's past as a bit actress. [Ed.]

city. As a result, I know every type of heart that palpitates under the sky of my Fatherland.

As I went downward from the neighborhoods of the proud and rich to those of the poor and humble, doors were opened more generously and with more cordiality.

In the upper class neighborhoods I felt only cold and calculating hearts, the "prudent" hearts of "ordinary men" incapable of thinking or doing anything out of the ordinary; hearts that made one nauseous, disgusted, and ashamed of contact with them.

That was the worst aspect of my Calvary in the great city! The cowardice of men who were able to do something and did not do it, washing their hands like Pilates, pained me more than the barbarous blows given me when a group of cowards denounced me, shouting: "That's Evita!"

On the other hand, those blows made me well. With each one I seemed to die, but, nevertheless, at each blow I felt myself revive. That baptism of sorrow, which purified me of all doubt and cowardice, was rather harsh but at the same time ineffable [in its effect].

.   .   .

That week of October 1945 is a landscape of many shadows and lights. It would be better not to approach it too closely—better that we see it another time from farther away. This does not prevent me, nevertheless, from saying with absolute frankness, and as a preliminary to a time when I can write about it in detail, that the light came only from the people.

15

MARÍA FLORES

ANOTHER VIEW OF THE EVENTS OF OCTOBER

One could not expect Eva Perón to recall the events of October 1945 in any way except emotionally and subjectively. There is, however, another feminine reporter's views as to what caused Perón's removal and how his opponents failed to prevent his return. María Flores is the pen name of Mary Main, a porteña *and a long-time resident of Buenos Aires. The following selection is representative of her more objective approach to a controversial subject. We pick up the story with the ending of World War II and the Argentine reaction to the defeat of the Axis.*

The Argentines do not take readily to rebellion; those who live in the rich provinces around the capital are in the majority too comfortable and well fed; those who are very poor are also very ignorant and live in places so remote, very often, that what goes on in the government seems to

From María Flores, *The Woman with the Whip: Eva Perón* (Garden City, N.Y.: Doubleday, 1952), pp. 71–83. Reprinted by permission of the author.

have no relation to their lives. Yet the unrest in the country was increasing. The *porteño,* to whom a loss of dignity can be more important than a loss of liberty, had been disgusted by the government's philandering with the Axis—the civilian sympathies lay more with England and with France with whom Argentina had long held trade and cultural ties; and now the porteño was further humiliated to find that Argentina had, as Winston Churchill put it, "chosen to dally with evil and not only with evil but with the losing side." He was not even allowed to rejoice in Allied victory, for when Paris was liberated—and Paris has always been the spiritual home of the cultured Argentine— the crowd of three hundred thousand who gathered to celebrate were dispersed by the police; when Berlin fell all celebrations were forbidden and the groups that dared gather to cheer were attacked by hooligans under the protection of the police. A last-minute declaration of war by the government, who had finally been persuaded that Germany would lose, only served to humiliate the porteños more.

When Japan surrendered the crowds burst into the streets to celebrate and in the clash with the police that followed two students were killed and their deaths set off a series of strikes among students and university professors all over the country. In Buenos Aires eight hundred students, boys and girls, barricaded themselves inside the university. The police surrounded the building and opened fire and at last invaded the building with tear gas, the students defending themselves with tables and chairs. The young men were dragged off to the dreaded Special Section of the police and the girls were taken off to San Miguel prison, which is usually reserved for prostitutes, while libelous stories about them were circulated by the government-controlled press.

There was in command of the Buenos Aires police force

at this time a Colonel Filomeno Velazco; he had been given the post by Perón, and the two were at the time close friends. Eva eyed this friendship with some mistrust although it was not of Velazco's methods she disapproved—these were not corrected when she finally got him out of office—but of the man himself, for he was not ready enough to follow her lead. He had already become notorious for his arbitrary arrests—his minions, like those of the Gestapo, would arrive in the middle of the night to drag their victims off to jail—and for his sadistic methods of torture.

In September 1945 a great march of protest against the government was staged, and General Rawson,[1] who had loudly advocated cooperation with the Allies, harangued the crowd jubilantly as they passed beneath his balcony on the way to Congress. He received only a mild rebuke for this so that he was not deterred from carrying forward a plot he had concerted with a fellow officer who was in command of the garrison in the provincial city of Córdoba. But a week later, when they were ready to march on Buenos Aires, he and his fellow conspirators were abruptly arrested and put in jail.

The Army had not for a moment been hoodwinked by Perón's genial smile and disavowals of personal ambition. When he had taken on the office of Secretary of Labor it had seemed a thankless one, but they had watched with growing uneasiness as he welded labor into a weapon to be used against them; and still more uneasily they watched the machinations of the colonel's lady, who seemed less and less content with her successes in radio and with the fortune she was making on the side—and this they would have been prepared to allow her as a perquisite—and more

---

[1] A pro-Allied leader of the June 4, 1943, Revolution, who had been briefly provisional president after the ouster of the Castillo government. [Ed.]

and more inclined to interfere in government affairs and to advise the Vice President as to whom this office should be given or who dismissed from that. Moreover, it was noted that it was to her friends and to her relatives, rather than Perón's, that these offices were given.

Eva's mother, the perennial Doña Juana, had made a new friend, one Niccolini, a post office employee. Eva had used her influence on Perón to give Niccolini the directorship of Posts and Telegraph, a position that carried with it considerable influence since under it came the control of radio and film industry and all public means of communication. Eva had had a finger in this pie from the start, for her erstwhile friend Colonel Imbert had occupied that post—it had, indeed, been his chief attraction. But now that her stepfather-by-courtesy had taken over Colonel Imbert's office, Eva moved into an office alongside of his. It was evident who really had control in the offices of Posts and Telegraph.

This flagrant misuse of her privileges was more than the G.O.U. could tolerate. It was evident by now that Perón, for all his assurances that he had no presidential ambition, meant to run in the elections, which must be held soon if there were not to be a civil war; he was already courting one political party and then another and unblushingly changing from Labor to Conservative overnight. If he were elected there would be no holding Eva at all. And since the people were demanding a reform and would not be satisfied without a political shake-up of some sort, it seemed to the officers under the command of General Avalos in Campo de Mayo a good moment to throw Juan Domingo—and Eva with him, incidentally—to the wolves.

They presented their ultimatum and Perón, always more ready to be prudent than bold, accepted it. He was, since the disturbances of the last month or two, not quite so sure if those four million workers with their clubs were behind or in front of him, and he must have persuaded Eva that a temporary retirement was politic.

On October 10, 1945, it was announced that Colonel Perón had resigned the offices of Vice President, Minister of War, and Secretary of Labor and Social Welfare.

. . .

On the morning of October 12, 1945, when the first young green of spring hazed the dark branches of the acacia trees, a crowd began to gather in Plaza San Martín. The Plaza stands at the fashionable end of Calle Florida on the *barranca* above the port, the site of the old slave market in colonial days. On one side the august edifice of the Plaza Hotel turns a huffy shoulder on a parvenu sky-scraper of apartments and on the other stand the massively baroque mansions that until lately had been the *palacios* of the oligarchy. One of these buildings, whose wrought iron and gilded gates are at least two stories high, was now the Círculo Militar—the military officers' club. In front of it someone had chalked:

To the gallows with Perón!

The crowds that were gathering below its seignorial windows were not the sort of people that, in any city, would easily be led out into the streets to demonstrate; there were certainly some students among them but the majority were lawyers, businessmen, housewives, writers, doctors, and artisans. But now their temper was aroused and their shouting grew louder and angrier as they demanded free elections, an end to tyranny, and the head of Perón. The police, who were mustered in the narrow streets leading to the Plaza, threatened to dismiss the crowd with force, but a young officer, dashing melodramatically out onto the balcony of the club, cried out that he and his fellow officers were ready to lead the crowd against the police if they should interfere.

"*Viva! Viva!* Down with Perón!" yelled the crowd.

Later, when perhaps as many as fifty thousand porteños were gathered there, Admiral Vernengo Lima, the new Minister of Marine, came out onto the balcony to promise in the name of the President—"We have no president!" interrupted the people. "Out with Farrell! Down with Perón!"—that a new cabinet—"A civilian cabinet!" shouted the people—a civilian cabinet should be formed at once and that those to blame for the situation should be punished, Perón first of all.

"Death to Perón! Death to Perón!"

The crowds were still gathered there when dusk had fallen, waiting for news of the new cabinet and of Perón's arrest, when a trumpet call was sounded and a moment later the police opened fire on the people and charged. The men and women who scrambled for shelter in doorways, under the stone benches of the Plaza and behind the acacia trees, and the young doctor shot through the back while kneeling to help a wounded man—they had their answer then, the true answer of an army in power.

But it had not been Perón this time who had given the order to fire. Perón's friend Velazco was no longer head of the police and Perón and Eva were fugitives. His brother officers were only too ready to make a scapegoat out of him and the police had sought him, first in the apartment in Calle Posadas and then in Doña Juana's house in Junín. But neither he nor Eva was to be found.

. . .

They must have slipped away sometime on the night of October 11, driving out of the dark city, taking a back street so that they would not have to pass the gates of the presidential residence, north toward the river resort of Tigre at the mouth of the delta of the Río de la Plata. There are a thousand and more islands in the delta, separated by a thousand and more narrow waterways that are hidden under weeping willow trees and tangles of honeysuckle. At Tigre they took a launch and set off along one of the wider channels, their wash curling up the muddy banks behind and sucking the reeds and water hyacinths into dipping, swaying curtsies.

Their destination was the small resort of Tres Bocas where they had stayed for weekends in the early happier days of their intimacy. It must have seemed the perfect sanctuary to them now with the wide channel that led on from it to the open waters of the Paraná and the friendly-seeming coast of Uruguay on the horizon beyond. But the river police had had word that they were hiding there—certainly all their old haunts were watched—and set a guard on the channel and sent word of their whereabouts to the capital. On the evening of the twelfth, when the police were firing on the crowd in Plaza San Martín, Perón was arrested and, with Eva, brought back to the apartment in Calle Posadas.

There was evidence then of a fundamental weakness in Perón's character; he trembled when he was arrested and on the trip back into the city complained rather peevishly that he had a touch of pleurisy. It was not, he conveyed, at all good for his health to be under arrest. Later that night he was taken aboard a gunboat and put off on the prison island of Martín García, from whence he wrote letters to his old friend Farrell, complaining again of his pleurisy and of the rain that came in through the windows. But he was, in fact, in not any such uncomfortable circumstances as the workers and students whom his friend Velazco had sent to Villa Devoto prison after beating them up in the Special Section of the police.

Law and tradition in Argentina give the political prisoner a choice between exile and imprisonment—there is no death sentence even for the murderer.[2] And even now

---

[2] In late 1951, after an unsuccessful military revolt, Perón secured a revision of the military code which made rebellion against the government punishable by death. [Ed.]

[1952] in Perón's totalitarian state he prefers to ruin his political enemies financially and then allow them to escape into exile, and it is only those who present a real threat to his supremacy or who are too poor to be punished otherwise and too obscure to be avenged who are imprisoned and ill treated. It is significant that now, when Perón was separated from Eva, he wrote asking to be allowed to go into exile. One cannot imagine that he would ever have weakened to such an extent had she been at his side. It was then, in that moment of weakness, that she gained her hold.

It was during those few days when Perón was imprisoned and the Army itself was without any strong leadership—General Avalos who led the faction against Perón was no *Lider*—that the tragic weakness of the democratic opposition was most apparent. They [the opposition leaders] had at that moment a great part of the country behind them and had they been capable of any unified action they could have re-established a constitutional government. But that great curse of the Argentine character, to which they themselves refer with such pride as their *dignidad de hombre,* their "manly dignity," would not allow one Radical to give way to another Radical, much less to a Socialist, in any detail of policy or choice of minister, so that they were incapable of deciding on a popular and democratic cabinet. When the Supreme Court, which in Argentina takes over the executive power if for any reason both president and vice president are out of office, did at last present a list of ministers, it was as unpopular as it was conservative and the people, again disillusioned in their democratic leadership, were ready to make do with Farrell, who was too much of a nonentity to be personally unpopular.

But while Perón sat in his room—he was not put in a cell—on Martín García and grumbled about the weather, and the opposition quibbled over points of leadership, Eva showed neither weakness nor hesitation. She had wept and stormed with fury when they had taken her lover off, but no sooner was he gone than she began to fly around among their erstwhile friends, shrieking at them, bullying them, cajoling them and threatening them, demanding his release.

.   .   .

Eva was not without financial resources or without friends at this time—there were many who stood to lose all if Perón were lost. It is said that she and Perón took with them fifty thousand dollars in cash when they fled to Tres Bocas; certainly they would not have gone with empty pockets and, if it were so, the money must have been with Eva, for Perón would not have taken it with him to jail. What is certain is that, of the ten million dollars collected for the victims of San Juan a year and a half before, some six million had already disappeared. This was said to have been spent in finding homes for orphans but of the hundreds of children left parentless or homeless only one hundred and thirty-one had been helped. Even with the lavish notions of charity Eva later proved to have, it is impossible that six million dollars were spent on a hundred-odd small children, and since from that time Eva and Perón seemed to have possession of a magic crock of gold, it is not surprising that they were so often accused of misappropriation of funds.

.   .   .

But wherever the money came from, Eva did not stint the spending of it now or the spending of her own amazing energy. One can imagine the promises she made to any who would help her and how scornfully those promises were often received—and how that scorn has been regretted since. But some who listened to her promises had even more reason for regret. Her feud with Juan Bramuglia, almost the only able and honest man in the Perón regime, was born in those days when he lagged in helping her to get Perón out of prison; yet Bramuglia lasted longer in office than Cipriano Reyes who acted for Perón so promptly and energetically and found himself, just three years later, in jail.

It was Cipriano Reyes perhaps more than anyone else who was instrumental in rescuing Perón. Reyes was a leader in the labor movement; he had organized the meat packers' unions in the tough slum districts that lie south of the Riochuelo, a smokestack-banked stream that runs into the city's southern docks. As Secretary of Labor Perón had supported the meat packers' strike and the two men had become close friends, Reyes visiting the apartment in Calle Posadas frequently and informally. Now it was he who helped Eva make preparations for a demonstration of workingmen.

By October 16, groups of workers had begun to drift into the city. The opposition claimed that these ruffians were no workers; the syndicalized unions—the General Confederation of Labor—had not yet risen in support of Perón; the meat packers were among the roughest and most disorderly of workers; but it is not unreasonable to believe that many sober workmen, who owed their better wages to Perón, were ready to rally with very little encouragement to his support. The rowdies paraded up and down the narrow streets shouting, "Viva Perón!" while the police, uncertain now of how the business would turn out, stood around with their thumbs in their belts, and the porteños who had gathered in Plaza San Martín only four days before, stayed at home behind shuttered windows—*they* knew they could expect no protection from the police.

By this time the military themselves had done an about-face which, by the celerity and neatness with which it

was executed, said much for the efficiency of their German training. General Avalos, who had been foremost in
forcing Perón's resignation and who had taken over the
Ministry of War, now announced that Colonel Perón had
not been under arrest at all but had been taken to Martín
García under protective custody since there were undis-
ciplined elements loose in the city that had threatened
his life.

Perón, still complaining about his health—and he did
present rather an old-womanish picture at this time—had
been moved from Martín García to the Military Hospital
in Buenos Aires, where Eva flew to embrace him in her
emotional style. But however sincere were her tears of
relief on seeing him again, one can fancy that there was
a shade of difference in her manner towards him since
they had said good-by, a difference that may have been
scarcely perceptible but was most profound.

Hard on Eva's heels came General Avalos and a troop
of other officers all anxious to butter their bread on both
sides.

By October 17, the General Confederation of Labor
had declared itself for Perón; a day's stoppage of work
throughout the country was announced and great crowds
of "shirtless ones," as Perón's followers were from this
day called, began to gather under the balconies of the Casa
Rosada. Later the rally was spoken of as a spontaneous
demonstration of the "shirtless ones," although they had
been brought in in trucks from the shanty towns of the
southern suburbs, carrying banners and flags and portraits
of Perón which could not have been assembled, much less
manufactured, overnight. They streamed over the bridges
of the Riochuelo—in her book Eva says they swam, but
since there are bridges and it was winter and the stream,
which drains the meat packing district, is peculiarly foul

it seems an unlikely gesture on the part of any sober man
however carried away by enthusiasm—up along the cob-
bled dockside avenue and gathered in a great unruly,
vociferous, odorous throng under the balconies of the Casa
Rosada. All through the day the crowd increased and
each moment grew more unquiet, disturbed by rumors
that Perón would speak, that there had been a counterplot,
that Perón was free and would in a moment appear.

"Perón! We want Perón! Perón!"

.   .   .

Near midnight, when it seemed that the violence of
the crowd could be contained no longer, Farrell and Perón
stepped out on the balcony. A great roar greeted them.
They embraced, clasping each other around the shoulders
and kissing first on one cheek and then on the other, and
the crowd bellowed itself hoarse.

"Here," said Farrell, "is the man we all love—Juan
Perón!"

"Perón! Perón! We want Perón! Where did they put
you, Perón?"

It was a dramatic moment, even if much of the drama
were synthetic, and Perón was not the man to miss a
teardrop of emotional appeal. He embraced his beloved
"shirtless ones," he said; he understood their suffering
because they had suffered as his poor little old mother had
been suffering. He was resigning from the Army now
because he wanted to be part of the sweating, suffering
masses. Melodramatically he snatched off his sword belt
and gave it to Farrell. The two men embraced. The crowd
roared. But now, said Perón with tears in his eyes, his
"shirtless ones" must disperse quietly to their homes because there were women in the crowd who might be
injured, and he himself was worn out and tired—but before they dispersed let them stand there a moment longer
so that he might feast his eyes on them.

16

ARTHUR P. WHITAKER

THE ELECTION OF
FEBRUARY 24, 1946
''Braden or Perón": Second Phase

Perón's triumph in October 1945 restored his de
facto *powers, and the national elections of February
24, 1946, gave him a clear mandate to carry out
his program as constitutional President of Argentina. This excellent monograph by Professor Arthur
P. Whitaker provides a succinct discussion of the
election campaign and its results.*

Though the crucially important national election of February 1946 and the campaign preceding it were conducted
under a military dictatorship devoted to Perón's candidacy, they were featured on the part of the government
by a sustained effort to give them the appearance of a
free expression of public opinion. On the part of the op-

Reprinted by permission of the publishers from Arthur P. Whitaker,
The United States and Argentina (Cambridge, Mass.: Harvard Uni-
versity Press), Copyright, 1954 by the President and Fellows of
Harvard College (pp. 145–150).

position, they were featured by disunity and poor judgment in the early stages and by overconfidence at the end.

On October 30, 1945, the government rescinded a decree of December 1943 dissolving all political parties, and it also suspended the enforcement of a recently adopted Organic Statute for Political Parties, which might have handicapped the old-line parties by the novelty of its provisions. These parties, all of which were opposed to Perón, were accordingly permitted to reorganize themselves along familiar lines. They were then given a considerable measure of freedom in conducting their campaigns through the mails and public meetings as well as by press and radio. For the first and last time in Argentine history, provision was made for the equal treatment of all parties by the radio broadcasting stations. To be sure, law was one thing and enforcement another, and on January 31, 1946, the opposition parties published a manifesto denouncing "the climate of intimidation and violence" which the Peronistas had given the campaign.

There was a remarkably long delay in the nomination of the presidential candidates, Perón's being made on December 14 and that of the opposition standard-bearer, José Tamborini, two weeks later. In Perón's case the delay was not significant since his candidacy was a foregone conclusion and the announcement of it a mere formality. In the end, he was supported by three parties, all new. Two of these were labor parties and the third, a Radical splinter group. The last-named contributed his running mate, J. Hortensio Quijano, lawyer, banker, and Minister of Interior in 1945, and its support enabled Perón to keep the opposition from monopolizing the mantle of Irigoyen.

In Tamborini's case the delay was significant. He was the candidate of a coalition of most of the opposition parties— Radical, Socialist, Progressive Democratic, and Communist—formed in November 1945 under the name of Democratic Union. So sharp were the traditional rivalries among these parties, however, that they found it difficult to coalesce even in the face of the threat from their common enemy, Perón. Even after the coalition was formed they lost a precious six weeks in haggling over the candidate and the platform. At the end of that time they came up with a worthy but colorless candidate and a negative platform. Tamborini was a sixty-year-old physician who had been deputy and senator at various times, and a member of Alvear's cabinet in the 1920's. Nothing in his record or personality could approach Perón's popular appeal. His coalition's platform was no help, for it amounted to a demand for a return to normality, which the Argentine masses did not want.

They did want a social revolution, and that was what Perón promised to give them. In point of personality, too, he had an enormous advantage over Tamborini. Some idea of Perón's magnetic appeal to those who did not detest him for his policies can be obtained from the following description of him by a hostile correspondent of *The New York Times* in July 1945, when his fate still hung in the balance:

> Colonel Perón is a strong, vigorous man of medium height, dark-haired, clean-shaven, with an aquiline nose and ruddy complexion. He is close to 50, but considerably younger in appearance, and looks very smart and handsome in his uniform. He is endowed with great personal charm and speaks well and convincingly, both in private conversation and in public. His energy is unbounded and one can see at a glance that he is one of those men who know what they want and are ready to fight to obtain it. All these things fit him admirably for the task he has set himself of having himself elected the next President of Argentina. . . .

Yet for some strange reason the leaders of the Democratic Union seem to have been confident of victory, provided the government and the Army kept their promise of a free and honest election. In the very same manifesto of January 31 in which they complained of the "climate of intimidation and violence" created by the Peronistas, the leaders of the Democratic Union attributed this to their opponents' realization that they faced "the certainty of a crushing defeat." "In a fair election," continued the manifesto, "the rout of the Nazi candidate [Perón] will be crushing, definitive." On the eve of the election the Democratic Union leaders still held this optimistic view, and on February 7 one of them, Julio A. Noble (a leader of the democratic Acción Argentina group in 1940–1943), charged that the Peronistas were planning to seize the government by force because they knew that they were doomed to defeat in the election.

These confident prognostications turned out to be badly in error, and yet they were made by veterans in Argentine political life. Had the democratic leaders lost touch with the Argentine voters? Or could it be that they were right until the eleventh-hour headlining of the issue of Yankee imperialism enabled Perón to turn an incipient rout into victory?

Perón's exploitation of this issue was facilitated by the diplomatic campaign conducted against him from Washington, to which former Ambassador Spruille Braden had returned to become Assistant Secretary of State. Two weeks before the Argentine election, the campaign reached its climax with the publication of the State Department's "Blue Book on Argentina." [1] This 131-page booklet was the work of Assistant Secretary of State Braden and his staff. It gave what it called "incontrovertible evidence" (much of it drawn from recently captured German docu-

---

[1] Popularly so called. The actual title was *Consultation among the American Republics with Respect to the Argentine Situation. Memorandum of the United States Government.*

ments) that "the present Argentine Government and many of its high officials were so seriously compromised with the [Nazi-Fascist] enemy that trust and confidence could not be reposed in that government." Perón himself was prominent among the Argentines against whom such evidence was presented. Consequently the Blue Book's publication on the eve of the Argentine election stamped it as an obvious effort to defeat Perón.

Though we have no sure means of measuring its effect on Argentine public opinion, the evidence indicates that the Blue Book gained Perón more votes than it cost him, for it was a fresh and flagrant example of that Yankee intervention in Latin America which Argentines had long taken the lead in opposing. Also, Braden's responsibility for it gave it the air of another shot in the feud he had begun with Perón the preceding year. The latter was now able to make more telling use than ever before of a line of propaganda that he had been following since the beginning of the campaign, which was that the choice before the Argentine voters was not "Tamborini or Perón" but "Braden or Perón."

Above all, however, Perón's popular appeal was aided by what he called his struggle for social justice, though his opponents called it reckless demagoguery. The government came to his aid by decreeing, on December 20, 1945, the general pay increase which he had initiated just before he was forced out in October. The increase was a substantial one; ranging from 13 to 33 per cent, it applied to all workers and white-collar employees. And of course Perón, though no longer in office, received the credit for it. The main employer group, the Argentine Industrial Union, voted to ignore the decree; but the government's threats of heavy penalties soon brought compliance. In the end, the employers' resistance only increased the average *descami-*

sado's conviction that he would never be able to better his lot without Perón to protect him.

When the election was held on February 24, 1946, under Army supervision, the popular vote was close enough to give it the air of a real contest—a free and honest one; but Perón's majority was large enough to make the victory clear-cut. Of the 2,734,386 votes cast, he received 1,527,-231, or 56 per cent of the total, to 1,207,155, or 44 per cent, for Tamborini. This made Perón's margin of victory larger than that in most presidential elections in the United States since the Civil War. As often happens in the United States, whose electoral college had been closely copied by the framers of Argentina's Constitution, the electoral vote was much more one-sided: Perón 304, Tamborini 72. Perón carried all but four provinces (Córdoba and Corrientes in the north, San Juan and San Luís in the west). In Congress, his supporters won two thirds of the seats in the Chamber of Deputies and an even larger proportion in the Senate.

From all the evidence, the election appears to have been free and honest, as the government had promised. Just after the polls closed, the opposition leaders themselves, including Tamborini, described it as a model of democratic rectitude and the best election ever held in the history of Argentina; and, at that time, they did not complain that their pre-election campaign had been seriously hampered by the harassment to which they had been subjected. To be sure, that was before the votes were counted, and when they still believed their pre-election forecasts of a crushing defeat for Perón. After the votes had been counted and, contrary to all their expectations, Perón had won, they changed to complaint, but the change was too long delayed, too great, and too obviously not disinterested to carry conviction.

As for the representative character of the election, the number of voters in proportion to total population was much the largest in the history of the country; it was about 50 per cent larger than the average in the most democratic of the previous elections (those of 1916, 1922, and 1928), and the margin was of course even greater than in the case of all other previous elections.

Consequently, there seems to be no blinking the fact that Perón was the choice of a substantial majority of the Argentine people in 1946. Also, we should note that this was a personal triumph for him. He did not owe it to a party; there was no united Peronista party, but only three splinter parties, all new, which received more help from him than they gave in return. And he was not imposed by the Army, for it discharged its obligation as nonpartisan guarantor of the purity of the election of 1946 with a zeal for that task which may have been related to the lack of zeal of many of the officers for the demagogic Perón.

17

ANÍBAL O. OLIVIERI

WHY I FOLLOWED PERÓN

Admiral Aníbal O. Olivieri was the Secretary of the Navy when the abortive coup of June 1955 occurred. As a result of his known differences with Perón, over the latter's treatment of the Roman Catholic Church, and his close contacts with the naval leaders of the coup, Olivieri was arrested and was still in prison when Perón was overthrown in September 1955. A career naval officer, a rightist nationalist, and a practicing Catholic, he reveals why he had decided, in 1945, to abandon his apolitical attitude and support Perón.

I never liked to call myself a Peronist, insofar as doing so might imply an active political role, which I have not practiced, or the following of a political leader.

. . .

I have never participated in the conduct of internal political problems, nor have I sought out contact with political circles. Not even as a [cabinet] minister was I

Translated from Aníbal O. Olivieri, *Dos veces rebelde* (Buenos Aires: Ediciones Sigla, 1958), pp. 23–27.

affiliated with the Peronist Party. I have never been acquainted with a basic party unit nor have I ever entered
the headquarters of the presidency of the Peronist Party.
Although it may be difficult to believe, I did not even
know where it was located.

But all this only pertains to the forms. As in everything,
the important thing is that which one does regarding the
essential aspects of things. And in this respect I say that
I have been a sincere and enthusiastic partisan of the initial
plan of General Perón.

I concurred with his initial focus on some fundamental
problems, particularly those having to do with the fortunes of the people and the independence of the republic
from foreign economic servitude.

My personal experience in the military happenings of
September 6, 1930, and the subsequent political calami-
ties, served to keep me at some distance from the scene
of events between June 4, 1943, and the middle of 1945.

At that time I knew Colonel Perón only by name. But
by then it was no longer possible for any Argentine to
remain neutral or absent from the conflict involving far-
reaching national interests.

The moment had arrived when remaining neutral in
politics was equivalent to feigning ignorance of serious
civic obligations. The situation was tense, but the reasons
for it were easy to see. Part of the Argentines were clus-
tered around parties and politicians who were sinking to
their death. . . . The greater part of the Argentine people had stopped believing in them. Millions of citizens,
including the labor mass of the country, were being drawn
together by their awareness of how they had been deceived.

Labor was bereft of leadership and disowned. It was
awaiting someone who would fill the great vacuum [in
leadership].

Politicians had failed to produce the social formulas

the people were awaiting with more patience than a decoy bird. The Argentine republic was one of the most backward countries in Latin America in social welfare and labor legislation—at least in effectiveness.

In all the great crises that nations face, a providential savior always appears who owes a great deal to those who made possible and necessary his rise.

In our situation the appearance of a colonel, then unknown outside the Army, excited first the attention and then the adhesion of millions of his fellow citizens. And what was most extraordinary: a man of arms succeeded in being believed by the laboring masses.

.   .   .

Perón was the hope of the disenchanted ones confronted with the "do-nothing" politicians who had preceded him. If only consolidated political parties had existed. If only politicians had not fallen in disgrace through their own incapacity for giving their policy the content and efficacy which the life of civilized peoples has, then there would have been no occasion for an unknown man, without a national background, and even less repute among the masses of labor, to conquer irremediably in the open elections that carried him to the presidency of the republic.

I came to know Colonel Perón personally in July of 1945 when he was Provisional Vice President of the Nation and Minister of War. . . .

Colonel Perón created a good impression with me. He seemed to be an intelligent man, with interesting general views on the current political, economic, and social problems. He was personally *simpático* and cordial, although clearly vain.

.   .   .

October 17, 1945, is still too recent and its consequences too fresh to dwell upon it. Furthermore, I had nothing to do with the events that occurred.

I was just another Argentine among the many who witnessed those events and drew immediate conclusions. Colonel Perón would be constitutional president following the serious "political error" committed by those who had not perceived that he no longer was just a colonel but was also the hope of thousands of men. That day the people obtained citizenship and acquired a consciousness of its rights and of its weight in deciding great national problems. . . . Soon afterward the campaign began for the presidential elections on February 24, 1946.

By that time the intervention of a foreign diplomat in our internal problems was already more than visible.[1]

Painfully, I heard him one afternoon, over the radio, addressing the country from the elevated tribunal of the University of the Littoral. He spoke to us Argentines, harangued us as Sarmiento[2] would have. Much of the road I have traveled since then I owe to that gentleman.

I could not tolerate the unheard of affront to us. I decided to oppose that insulting interference, which so greatly wounded my feelings, with all the strength I could muster. It wounded my feelings just as much as it would have those of North Americans, Indonesians, or Frenchmen if a stranger were permitted a similar attack on the rights and respect free countries deserve. I decided to support Colonel Perón. I would have supported any other Argentine who adopted the position he did. If the other presidential candidates also would have rejected that interference, perhaps fate would have maintained me aloof from all the open struggle, but he [Perón] was the only one who did.

---

[1] Presumably Spruille Braden, U.S. Ambassador to Argentina before becoming Assistant Secretary for Latin America. For a more objective observer's opinion of Braden's role see document 16. [Ed.]

[2] Domingo F. Sarmiento (1811–1888), author of document 1, was president of Argentina (1868–1874) and spent his adult years establishing schools, writing and speaking out against what he considered the barbaric traits of the Argentines. [Ed.]

18

THE NATIONAL INVESTIGATIONS COMMITTEE OF THE ARGENTINE NATION

LA SEÑORA
Perón's Collaborator

In his consolidation of power Perón had an effective collaborator—María Eva Duarte, whom he married shortly after the events of October 17, 1945. "Evita" or "La Señora" was Perón's direct link to the descamisados, *who provided him popular support, and to their wives and daughters who secured suffrage as a result of the Peróns' efforts. The National Investigations Committee, established by the Provisional Government that assumed power after Perón's ouster, provides a useful analysis of her role in the Perón partnership.*

After several years of indoctrinating the masses and exerting himself in organizing his party, the dictator became aware that he had not succeeded in either effort. "A political force is not organized in five years," he said in his lectures on leadership, "because the task of persuasion, of

Translated from La Nación Argentina, Comisión Nacional de Investigaciones, *Libro Negro de la segunda tiranía* (Buenos Aires, 1958).

education, of infiltration of the doctrine into the spirit of men cannot be achieved in so short a time. There is even less chance if the men coming to Peronism have come from different places, from different directions, with different tendencies and different orientations. We must ensure," he concluded, "that they go away forgetting old beliefs and doctrines and assimilating new ones. This is the work of generations." For that reason he put his trust in children and teen-agers. . . .

As a beginning step he began to train women. Traditionally, the Argentine woman had remained aloof from politics, which, as with military matters and the priesthood, she considered the special province of men. In this regard world opinion had changed since the first English "suffragists" claimed their right to participate in civic contests. These ideas had penetrated all countries, including our own, so that the concession of suffrage to Argentine women could not be postponed. The dictator took advantage of this. "If with the men's vote we have won by an enormous margin," he said on the eve of his second election, "with the women's vote we will win by a great deal more."

From the beginning of his public life he had at his side an unusual woman, different from nearly all other native Argentine women. She lacked formal training, but not political intuition; she was impetuous, domineering, and spectacular. Her early years had been difficult, until the disaster[1] brought her into close contact with the ambitious Colonel who linked himself with her. Thus began a collaboration unparalleled in history, though there are a few cases somewhat similar, among them Juan Manuel de Rosas and his wife Doña Encarnación Ezcurra.[2]

---

[1] The earthquake that, in January 1944, devastated the city of San Juan, in western Argentina; Perón and Evita both participated in a national campaign for funds to aid the stricken area. [Ed.]

[2] Rosas was the dictator who exercised virtually absolute control over Buenos Aires and much of the rest of Argentina from 1835

It is hard to determine precisely what each one contributed to their joint dictatorship. She accepted ideas, but she added passion and courage. The dictator simulated many things, whereas she scarcely ever did. She was a fiery little thing—indomitable, aggressive, spontaneous, at times barely feminine. Nature had endowed her with agreeable physical features, which she accentuated when good fortune permitted her to sport brilliant jewels and splendid gowns. In that way she compensated for her own unforgettable wretchedness and frustrations as an unnoticed actress without a future.[3] But this has little interest for what we are dealing with here. We must emphasize, rather, the adoration and, at the same time, the revulsion this woman aroused in our country during the six or seven years of the dictatorship. At one moment she seemed triumphant over all her enemies—when the CGT launched her name as a possible member of the presidential ticket —but that lasted only a few days. Then her "renunciation" was produced, imposed by factors that are not yet public knowledge.[4] As a result of her early death, the country was spared graver disturbances in the final period of the tyranny.

---

to 1851. He had resigned as Governor of Buenos Aires Province in 1832, because the legislature would not grant him greater powers. While he was away campaigning against the Indians on the frontier, his wife, Doña Encarnación, manipulated provincial politics to Rosas' advantage, making it impossible for his successor to govern. As a result Rosas was recalled to take over with virtually unrestricted powers. [Ed.]

[3] Refers to Eva Duarte's career as a bit player in the Argentine cinema and her more prominent role in Argentine radio soap operas. [Ed.]

[4] In 1951 an obedient CGT (General Confederation of Labor) conducted an all-out campaign to secure Evita the second place on a Perón-Perón ticket for the presidential election of 1951. In a dramatic scene Evita finally withdrew on the grounds that she was "too young" to be eligible. Most observers credit her withdrawal to military pressure on President Perón. If Evita had succeeded to the presidency, on the death or absence from the country of Perón, she would have been Commander in Chief of the Argentine Armed Forces. This was a possibility that even the most compliant Argentine officer did not find appealing. [Ed.]

Eva Perón was the most extraordinary propaganda instrument the dictator had. Her jurisdiction over internal affairs, her decisiveness in difficult moments, her inexhaustible activity, and also her disdain for all conventional ways of doing things in social or political affairs served her well in subduing stubborn wills, maintaining lasting contact with the popular classes, organizing the feminine branch of the "movement," stirring up the multitudes, creating and fostering animosities, and above all exalting his [Perón's] name and his work everywhere and at all times. Her mission was not that of persuading but of promoting action, kindling passions, carrying out acts of vengeance. She was most likely sincere, because her scanty acting ability would not have permitted her to simulate so easily sentiments she did not have.

The dictator let "La Señora" go her own way. He knew that her sudden and unexpected attacks on their enemies reassured the common people more than his own discourses on indoctrination, that she reached the heart of the humble ones more than he did. He did not silence her words of delirious admiration for his person because they served him with the public. "Perón is a meteor burning with the desire to enlighten his century," she used to tell the most ingenuous ones, "he is not a politician, he is a leader, he is a genius, he is a teacher, he is a guide, no longer just of the Argentines, but of all men of good will. Our leader," she declared, "has come to fulfill in this difficult hour of world history the dreams and hopes of all peoples of all times and their inclinations for all the centuries. We do not wish to compare Perón with anyone. Perón has his own light. He is too great, and our leader can no longer be molested by the shadow of any sparrow." She lacked any sense of the absurd, so peculiar to the Argentines, and she was without modesty, although she repeatedly affected it.

19

GEORGE I. BLANKSTEN

THE PERONIZATION OF
THE EDUCATIONAL SYSTEM

When Perón came to power the Argentine public school system was considered one of Latin America's finest educational systems. Under Perón the national government's control over the country's schools was considerably tightened and they were brought into the service of the Perón dictatorship. George I. Blanksten, Professor of Political Science at Northwestern University, who lived in Argentina during the Perón era, describes the background and the process of Peronization in the following selection from his penetrating study of the Perón regime. Professor Blanksten is also the author of numerous articles on Latin America and a particularly useful study of Ecuadoran politics, Ecuador: Constitutions and Caudillos.[1]

From George I. Blanksten, *Perón's Argentina* (Chicago: University of Chicago Press, 1953), pp. 186–198, *passim.* Reprinted by permission of the author.

[1] George I. Blanksten, *Ecuador: Constitutions and Caudillos* (Berkeley, Calif.: University of California Press, 1951).

The Argentine school system, long regarded as one of the most successful in Latin America, was among the first victims of the revolution of 1943. . . . Long before the coming of Perón, the monopoly of public education by the national government had become settled practice; and the military men who came to power in 1943 found that the nation's public schools were already in their hands.

They made use of this situation to inject a curious combination of nationalism, militarism, and religiosity into the curricula of Argentine schools. In August of 1944, Alberto Baldrich, then the regime's educational administrator, asserted that the country's institutions of learning "must be absolutely Argentine. We must not allow ourselves to be corrupted by foreign ideas." And Perón himself has contributed to a strange nationalism in pedagogy. "Argentine students must be taught by Argentine methods," the president has said. "We do not need to resort to Pestalozzi or any other of the great pedagogues. . . . We must create everything for ourselves." What were the educational theories that the men of the "new Argentina" created for themselves? Hear one-time Education Minister Oscar Ivanissevich, speaking in 1948: "We will teach first that children learn to live, afterward that they should learn to know. That they should know less and want more. That they should know less and think more. That they should know less and feel more. That they should have more time for well-conducted animal spirits. . . . We will not place in the fertile soil of their intelligence more seed than their natural capacity can nourish effectively. We will fight with all our might against parasitic . . . intellectualism." How have these precepts been implemented? A few illustrations may suffice. In September of 1946, the *Peronista* Senators Alberto Teisaire, Vicente Saadi, and Sosa Loyola introduced in the congress a bill requiring that only one textbook be used for each course taught in Argentine secondary schools. The measure as finally passed provided that the book selected for each course would be approved and printed by the national government. Moreover, the nation's schoolrooms are used for the proselytization of projects supported by the regime. A case in point: during 1948 and the early part of 1949, when *Peronistas* were preparing the country to receive a new constitution, all public school teachers were directed to imbue their students with a desire for constitutional reform.

Militarism, a basic component of the revolution of 1943, soon worked its way into the schools. A decree published on September 27, 1943, directed all Argentine primary school teachers to "take advantage of every opportunity to exalt the sentiment of the fatherland . . . [and] to give to military glory and deeds of arms the preferred place which they deserve." Implementation of this decree and others like it proceeded apace in the first years of the "new Argentina." By the time that Perón was inaugurated as president in 1946, the country's military schools were organized so as to teach "the spirit of sacrifice," "the wealth of our soil," "the wealth of our language," and "the work and action of the heroes of our country."

But perhaps foremost among the early educational measures of the "new Argentina" was the celebrated Decree No. 18,411 [2] of December 31, 1943. This decree resumed compulsory religious instruction in Argentine public schools. In so doing, the measure reversed a long-standing Argentine solution of the characteristically Latin-American problem of the relationship of the Roman Catholic Church to public education. The Church played a major part in the Argentine educational arrangement until Domingo Faustino Sarmiento, the remarkable "schoolmaster-president," entered the *Casa Rosada* in 1868. He inspired a host of

[2] Law No. 12,978 of April 17, 1947, placed this decree on a statutory basis.

projects for educational reform. One of them did not become law until a decade after Sarmiento left the presidency. This measure, enacted by the congress in 1884, during the administration of President Julio A. Roca, provided for what Sarmiento had called "religious neutrality" in the public schools. The law, buttressed by enforcing legislation passed in 1888 and 1904, established secular education in Argentina based on the proposition of a separation of Church and state so far as the public schools were concerned.

This separation remained a controlling educational principle until the revolution of 1943. In that year, Argentine public policy with respect to this matter reverted to a pre-1884 position with the promulgation of the decree of December 31. The text of this significant measure is perhaps worth quoting here:

> In all public schools . . . instruction in the Catholic religion will be imparted as a regular section of the respective courses of study.
>
> Respecting liberty of conscience, exempted from this requirement are those students whose parents manifest express opposition because of affiliation with another religion. These students will be given moral instruction.

Official proponents of this decree pointed out that the president and vice president of the nation were required by the constitution to be Roman Catholics, and that compulsory religious instruction would have the effect in future years of rendering a greater proportion of the nation's population eligible for these offices. "The official school without religion is anti-democratic and unconstitutional," it was said. "It does not train the child for the supreme honor to which every Argentine may aspire, that is, to become president of the nation."

Perhaps more immediately important was the tendency

of the decree to encourage a somewhat political alliance between the "new Argentina" and the Roman Catholic Church. In a message to General Ramírez, who was nominal president at the time the compulsory religious education decree was promulgated, Monseñor Capello, the Cardinal of Buenos Aires, declared: "The patriotism shown by Your Excellency in fulfilling one of the deepest hopes and greatest ambitions of the Argentine people has recuperated for them the morality of our country's great destinies, the path of which was shown by the great thinkers and heroes who forged its nationality." And, in a message to Perón himself, none other than Pope Pius XII said, "We are pleased by this recognition of the rights of the Church in the field of Christian education." . . .

Argentine teachers and professors who did not agree with the educational and other policies of the post-1943 regime were, of course, dismissed from their posts. The mass exodus of Argentina's educators, begun in 1943, was still under way at the time these lines were written. This has been a spectacular tragedy: Argentina, whose scholars and teachers once set high standards for the Americas, has witnessed a large-scale departure of her more competent contributors to most fields of knowledge and thought. This has been an especially acute condition with respect to the social sciences—much research in these fields was branded after 1950 as "espionage"—but other fields have suffered as well. Certainly very few of the students who heard the last words—"And now I have delivered my last lecture. . . . The next must come from a colonel"—of the dismissed distinguished medical scholar, Dr. Bernardo A. Houssay, will soon forget that occasion. . . .

Making the country's six universities fit the Procrustean bed of the "new Argentina" has not been an easy task, even for Perón. It was one thing to dismiss intransigent administrators and faculty members; it was quite another problem to bring the 62,700 students of the Universities of Córdoba, Buenos Aires, the Littoral, La Plata, Tucumán, and Cuyo to heel. For the truth is that Argentine university students never were very docile, not even in the years before Perón. "The Argentine university, traditionally, is a miniature battleground of national politics," one observer has written. "Students strike, riot, and stage political demonstrations on the slightest provocation." This has been the traditional pattern of Argentine student behavior. Hear a *cordobés* recalling his student days at the University of Córdoba: the students' readiness to launch a political strike "becomes a passion that invades and confuses everything. I myself remember many postponed examinations; many study hours disturbed; countless meetings, speeches, discussions; strikes—a whole year lost in them—elections that ended with gunfire. . . ." Against the background of such a tradition it could not be expected that the "new Argentina" could be saddled on the nation's university students without a fight.

The revolution of 1943 was greeted by a mood of frank hostility and rebellion on the part of most of the students attending the country's six universities. They had gone on strike and conducted political demonstrations for causes much lighter than the coming of Perón; and in 1943 the students again prepared to do battle. The Argentine University Federation, with which students on all six campuses were affiliated, launched a general strike in October of 1943 in protest against the wholesale dismissal of their professors. The government responded by closing all of the universities on October 27. The schools were reopened a few days later, and the Argentine University Federation was ordered dissolved. The federation, however, had not learned the lesson of obedience. It continued to operate as a species of committee of co-ordination and correspondence for the six universities, and in July of 1945 it directed its affiliates to wear black in mourning for the "loss of public freedom and rights." A month later, the student federation joined with 208 professors in formally requesting the Supreme Court of Justice to withdraw its recognition of the military regime as a *de facto* government. And on September 30, 1945, the Argentine Student Federation called another general student strike.

The turmoil following this strike call was memorable. Argentines who were university students in 1945 still talk excitedly about those stirring "October days." They were curious and hectic days; they were in a sense heroic days, days in which the attention of the entire Western Hemisphere was drawn to the struggle of Argentina's university students against their military rulers. On many previous occasions, the students had barricaded themselves in university buildings, it is true; but those had been isolated, local affairs involving small numbers of students. The ordeal of October of 1945 was different: no fewer than *30,000* students rose in opposition against the regime! They stubbornly resisted the Federal Police; they threw marbles under the hooves of the horses of the mounted representatives of the "new Argentina." And they barricaded themselves in the buildings of the universities while the Federal Police milled about outside. The first to barricade themselves were the students at the University of La Plata, who shut themselves in on October 2; the example was soon followed at Buenos Aires and at other schools. While the frustrated Federal Police laid siege to the barricaded students and endeavored to cut off their communications and their sources of food, water, and electricity, the sit-down strikers drew the eyes of the Western Hemisphere to themselves and to the regime against which they struggled. The resourceful besieged students established loud-speaker systems, through which they broadcast encouragement to the sympathetic sectors of the populace

beyond the academic walls; the strikers organized systems
of communication and supply; they established a press.
"Argentine youth is united both within and without the
occupied buildings," the beleaguered students at the University of Buenos Aires proclaimed through their amplifiers
and their press, "and solemnly declares that it will fight for
constitutional normality with the one weapon available
to an unarmed people—civil disobedience." At the University of La Plata the situation was more desperate but
no less gallant. "We have converted our island into a
bastion, and we will stand guard in it for the republic until
the *Mazorca*[3] overcomes us," asserted Aquiles Martínez
Civelli, the acting president of the University of La Plata,
who was barricaded with his students. "We number 230.
Our arms: a recording of the National Anthem, a micro-
phone, and some loudspeakers. . . . We number 230. . . .
We are all proud."

But it was a losing battle. The Federal Police forced
their way into one university and then another; by
October 9 the last of the six universities was subdued. The
affair, though hopeless from the students' side from the
outset, was an epic in university annals: it created a
tradition, it built an *esprit de corps*. Though the Federal
Police eventually forced the buildings and arrested the
students and some of their professors, the "October days"
served in large part to kindle a spirit of resistance among
the students which was still very much alive when the
present writer visited the Universities of Buenos Aires, La
Plata, and Córdoba in 1950 and 1951. The casualties of
the "October days" may not impress some: at the University of Buenos Aires, 2 students were killed, and 1,445
men and 149 women students were jailed, together with
6 of their professors. Also imprisoned at Buenos Aires were

---

[3] The Mazorca was the secret police and terrorist instrument of
the Rosas dictatorship.

39 "agitators"—that is, persons who were not students or professors but who were nevertheless involved in the fray. The figures for each of the remaining five universities were smaller than those for the University of Buenos Aires; the over-all total number of imprisoned students came to approximately 2,000.

.   .   .

The "October days" of 1945 marked the apogee of university resistance to the "new Argentina." Thereafter organized opposition weakened, although the spirit of rebellion remained alive. But with the crumbling of organized academic resistance, the regime moved to consolidate its conquest of the universities. "Interventors," charged with the management of academic administration, were installed on all six campuses in May of 1946; later that year, it was decreed that all students who refused or failed to take their examinations would be suspended from school for the ensuing two years.

The Perón regime's basic measure for the control of the institutions of higher learning is the "University Law," which went into force on October 4, 1947. That legislation undertook the administrative reorganization of the universities and set forth a *Peronista* statement of what the proper function of a university should be within the context of the "new Argentina." The law provided that thenceforth the rectors (roughly equivalent to presidents) of the six universities would be appointed for three-year terms by the president of the nation. The duties of the rectors would be to serve as the legal representatives of their respective institutions, to appoint their administrative and academic personnel, and to direct the over-all administration of their respective universities. Moreover, the "University Law" of 1947 established a National University Council, composed of the six rectors and the minister of justice and public instruction, the last-named a member of Perón's cabinet.

The task of the National University Council, according to the law, would be to maintain liaison between the government and the universities and to "co-ordinate" the curricula and the administrations of the six campuses.

.   .   .

Two aspects of the role of educational institutions in Perón's system are significant. In the first place, it is true that education is now thoroughly controlled by the government, and that the schools now lie at the political service of the "new Argentina." The teachers and professors must be politically acceptable to the regime, the curricula preach the glory of Perón and the late Evita, research—especially in the social sciences—has been tightly curbed, and liberty of teaching and investigation does not exist. But on the other hand, while the quality of instruction and research has declined seriously since the revolution of 1943, what education the schools are still permitted to impart is open to a much greater percentage of the population than was true before the coming of Perón.

All Argentine public schools—be they primary, secondary or universities—are now tuition-free. In 1951 alone, 401 new primary schools were opened, 984,297 children were enrolled in the elementary schools, and 281,954 students were in the secondary, normal, and technical schools. "I can declare with legitimate pride," Perón said in 1951, "that my government has constructed more schools in five years than the total erected in the one hundred preceding years."

III

IN RETROSPECT

In this section three authors, writing after Perón was overthrown (September 1955), look backward—more in sorrow than in anger—in an attempt to explain his rise to power and the consequences for Argentina.

20

H. A. MURENA

THE NATURE OF THE
ARGENTINE CRISIS

The problem of Peronism prompted considerable introspection by Argentine intellectuals in the post-Perón period. H. A. Murena, a young writer, stresses the lack of an Argentine community spirit in the following selection which first appeared in Argentina's outstanding literary review Sur.

For how long has Argentina been in a state of crisis? From its foundation? If so, there was, nevertheless, during the nineteenth century an "animal" instinct, if I may use that expression, which carried the country onward in spite of itself. And there was also, at the end of the last century and at the beginning of the present, the illusion that a community had taken form. . . . Now, for the last few decades, for the last thirty years, we are witnessing the

From Lewis Hanke, *Modern Latin America: Continent in Ferment:* Vol. II, *South America* (pp. 160–161), Copyright 1959, D. Van Nostrand Company, Inc., Princeton, N.J. Reprinted by permission of the publisher. This selection first appeared in *Sur,* No. 248 (Buenos Aires, 1957), pp. 1–16, *passim.*

crisis of the crisis. What has become of that "animal" instinct, which was doubtless the source of the famous optimism of the cattlemen? In some way it grew tired, it disappeared, although it is still breathing its last, unconvincing moos.

The only force which could have taken its place, the community spirit, was never formed. The proof: that the country is sunk in paralysis. The sick one has fallen on his bed at last. Wherever I look, at the statistics, the way of life, or international prestige, I see the same. Of course, the world situation has changed. There is also the universal crisis: many tell me that the Argentine crisis is but part of the universal. But I cannot help thinking of Brazil: this country has faced general problems, but also others which are not universal but which are almost identical to the problems of Argentina. Nevertheless, it is not paralyzed. What is more, it has managed to pass to the head of the Latin American nations.

Argentina often hits the front page of foreign newspapers. Thanks to our military coups d'état . . . we have revealed ourselves to be just what we used to boast that we were not: South Americans. Since 1930 military coups —triumphant, defeated, or abortive—exceed three dozen in number. . . .

. . . Under the name of various political parties the forces of the oligarchy had the power in their hands for a long time. They did what they did: much of it good, much bad . . . the oligarchy was one of the forces which molded *Peronismo*. It refused to listen to half the country, it mocked half the nation by ignoring it. Not out of avarice, as some suppose, but out of a pride which wore the mask of a beneficent "patriarchalism." . . .

The crisis is not an economic problem. How could that be the case in a country which enjoys one of the highest standards of living in the world? There are economic problems, but the problem is not economic . . . the crisis is not a social problem. It is not the problem of any particular class, which has been inflicted upon the whole nation. It is a problem of all the classes, because all of them have failed to meet it, and all of them have contributed to it. It is, as a result, a common problem. A problem of the community, I am tempted to say. But I know I ought not to, for I know also that the problem is precisely the lack of *community*. . . .

There is no community in Argentina. We do not form a body, though we may form a conglomeration. We behave as if each one were unique and as if he were alone, with the unfortunate consequences which result when that is the situation. The hand knoweth not what the head thinketh, the mouth ignoreth the stomach, et cetera. . . . When a situation cannot be resolved within the framework of the community, then there must be a revolution in order to modify that framework. Party struggles and revolution are the resources which assure the community of life. Instead of life, Argentina has rancorous, factious chaos, periodically illuminated by coups d'état. It is not an organism of which all feel themselves a part. Each organ believes itself the whole, and functions as if it were more important than the whole. Is there any more succinct definition of sickness? Who is to blame? No one. Everyone.

. . . The demonism which periodically erupts in Argentine life does not feed on trivialities. In the final analysis, it is a form of religiosity and the spirit of religion will always resist the consolations of compromise, which in the long run is nothing more than the exaltation of the mundane. Will this absolutist impulse triumph in the end? That is to say, will this community grown sickly with the yearning to become, this community at whose ultimate ideal stands God, will it be purged, will it finally come into being?

21

MARIO AMADEO

YESTERDAY, TODAY, AND TOMORROW

Perón's appeal to the Argentine nationalist right was felt by Mario Amadeo, who first met the Colonel shortly after the June 4 revolution took place. At that time Dr. Amadeo was Director of Political Affairs in the Argentine Ministry of Foreign Relations. Unlike many of his fellow nationalists who fell under the spell of the dynamic Perón—and later repented—Dr. Amadeo did not succumb, leaving the Argentine Foreign Service early in 1945. After a period of reading and meditation he taught at the University of Buenos Aires, the Argentine Naval War School, and as a guest lecturer at the University of Santander in Spain. By mid-1953 his differences with the Perón regime had been publicized and his return from Spain, in November 1954, coincided with Perón's open attack on the Catholic Church. Dr. Amadeo then joined the forces planning Perón's

From Mario Amadeo, *Ayer, hoy, mañana* (Buenos Aires: Ediciones Gure, 1956), pp. 89–97, *passim*. Translated and printed by permission of the author.

overthrow and became Minister of Foreign Affairs (and Religion) during the provisional presidency of Perón's successor, General Eduardo Lonardi. When Lonardi was replaced by another general, Pedro Aramburu, on November 13, 1955, Amadeo also went and was subsequently imprisoned for some ten days. The following selection represents his reflections on Peronism and the Argentine crisis during the last days of 1955 and early 1956. Later, under President Arturo Frondizi, Dr. Amadeo was named Argentine Ambassador to the United Nations, a post he filled with distinction.

The reconstruction of the country, an essential objective of the revolution, involves a series of complex, visceral problems. Those problems, which assumed prominence at the very moment the regime was changed, are still awaiting an adequate solution.[1] Undoubtedly, they should be preoccupying the government that has the primary responsibility for facing up to them. But they also affect the nation's citizens, who share with the political authority responsibility for solving them.

The gravest and most urgent of those problems is the liquidation of the Peronist remains. Note well that we do not use the word "liquidation" in the sense of violent destruction; as when we say, for example, the Russian Communists have "liquidated" the supporters of Beria or of Malenkov. Such a meaning would involve choosing a solution that, we hasten to say, is not the best one. No; when we refer to the liquidation of Peronism we mean the assimilation of that great sector of the Argentine population that gave its name to the fallen regime, to which,

---

[1] Perón was overthrown in September 1955. Amadeo's essay was published in April 1956, during the provisional presidency of General Pedro Aramburu. [Ed.]

despite its mistakes and its failures, that group continues to be loyal. That mass sector is touchy and resentful. It looks askance at the movement that brought down its idol, and it takes refuge in an irrational and blind faith that soon they [the Peronists] will return to being what they were before [his fall]. Their motto and their war cry is: "Perón will return."

Well then; this position of uncompromising hostility must be overcome so that this mass sector may join spiritually in a task that is the patrimony and duty of all Argentines. Our country has been through an experience similar to that resulting from a war—a lost war. This is evident in the economic field, but so is it on the moral level. Unloosed rancors, unsatisfied aspirations, that indefinable state of uneasiness that accompanies defeat— these are the sentiments we can perceive in many of our compatriots and neighbors, the Argentines of 1956.

When a country finds itself in this situation, the first requisite for moving forward on the right road is to forge the compact unity of all the nation.

.   .   .

The success or failure of the attempt to unite the country depends, in good measure, on how one interprets the Peronist interval. There exists, in that regard, various versions, and it would be useful to review them systematically.

Thus the usual opinion among the socially conservative sectors is that Peronism was nothing but a nightmare, an evil period. Those sectors speak of "magnetic influence," of "collective suggestion," of "deformation of the conscience," and of other anomalies that reduce the problem to a question of pathological psychology. Those sectors consider that the Argentine populace have suffered a sickness, and that it is merely a question of submitting it to a vigorous cure. Once the period of treatment is over, everything will return to be what it was before; nothing will be left behind from the episode other than those vestiges a robust person would have from a case of the grippe or of the measles.

Others, in that same sector, are less simplistic, even though they perhaps are no less mistaken. These people agree that Peronism has been a more serious development than the first group claims and that it really has deeply stirred popular opinion. But they consider that Peronism has achieved that effect either through venality and corruption or by appealing exclusively to the lowest instincts of the common people. These people see nothing good or positive in the defeated movement. Peronism is the fruit of ignorance, as is superstition or quackery. This view has a binding effect only among the most primitive and uncivil sectors of the community. For them the question is settled with a little dose of re-education and a great dose of "beating." From the viewpoint of the anti-Peronists of the right, to "de-Peronize" is equivalent to "getting rid of rats."

For the anti-Peronists of our liberal left—the left composed of those intellectuals who today give direction to the revolution—the question is explained in terms of that sea where all rivers converge—Nazism. Perón and the Peronists were totalitarian Nazis who wished to impose on Argentina the system of Hitler and Mussolini. According to this viewpoint the ex-President was a doctrinaire thinker who, during his stay in Italy, had studied feverishly accelerated courses in the corporative system and had passionately resolved to apply that system in the *anima vili* of this innocent and democratic country. Consequently, these gentlemen cannot understand any other design but one in which all that is Peronist must be Nazi and all that is Nazi, Peronist. . . . For this sector, to "de-Peronize" is the same as to "de-Nazify."

Finally, there is another left—the anti-liberal and Marxist left; it finds fault only with the person of the Peronist chief and sees in that movement a form—crude and primitive but effective—of their fight against imperialism. As a result it was a little difficult for the men of this persuasion to explain how the petroleum contract with Standard Oil was a battle against imperialism, but contradictions do not terrify a Marxist.[2] These individuals are disposed to go beyond Perón in their social reforms because they perceive that his shortcoming was not in having been too radical in his procedures but in not having been radical enough. This sector, in which the Trotskyite variety of Communists are the leaders of the outcry, implicitly proclaims the formula "Perón plus X" and intends to take charge of the proletariat left now unattached by the absence of the "leader."

.   .   .

For my part, I cannot accept the Peronist phenomenon as being exclusively a mark of inferiority, or a vestige of primitivism, or even less, the artificial adoption of an ideology foreign to our idiosyncrasy. I consider that Peronism is a very complex and very important phenomenon and that one must differentiate between its positive and negative elements.

In the first place, I consider that Peronism has brought together, through failure, two transformations (some would say two revolutions) of diverse origin and destiny: an ideological and political transformation and a social renovation. Both were latent in the country, on June 4, 1943, and the sortie by the Army could have hastened the process but not provoked it. The country was living within discredited and outgrown socio-political structures,

---

[2] In his last year in office, Perón signed a contract with a subsidiary of Standard Oil of California to permit the exploitation of Argentine petroleum reserves under terms that were unacceptable to many Argentines. Even his own handpicked Peronist Party congressional leaders balked at supporting the contract. [Ed.]

and was struggling to free itself of them. The June Revolution—purely military though it was in origin—brought about the propitious occasion that allowed the change to take place. Since everything was in crisis—ideas, institutions, parties, and men—everything tumbled down.

What, then, is the meaning and extent of these transformations, which Perón took over and put forward as the banners of the movement that carried him to power? In regard to the ideological and political transformation we will say little here. . . . It is enough, at this time, to note that the country no longer allows the existence of doctrines and institutional forms within which a disruption of the national order was fomented. It is possible that the political currents then reigning in the various European countries contributed by giving substance and style to that internal unrest; but it would be erroneous to attribute it exclusively to a process of contagion. To demonstrate that the institutional mechanism was no longer functioning normally, we only have to recall that in 1930, for the first time in seventy years, a revolutionary movement triumphed, and that the free vote established in 1912 had to be "corrected" by fraud. And finally, in order not to continue multiplying examples indefinitely, let us note that a great mass of the population, perhaps the majority, had definitely isolated itself from contact with the political parties. When a country's people isolates itself from civic life, it is either because it finds itself in the last stages of decadence, or because it is on the eve of a fundamental change. I believe that we were finding ourselves in the latter and not the former of those two situations.

The country was also longing for a great social renovation. In that respect it is necessary to admit that, at the time of the 1943 revolt, Argentina was one of the most backward countries of Latin America. And let it be clearly understood that we do not say this because we believe that the proletariat here was poorer or in more wretched circumstances than in other places or that it had less legislation for its aid and protection. On the contrary, the living conditions of the Argentine worker—rural or urban—were relatively humane and infinitely better than those of the majority of his Latin American counterparts. Compare, for example, the situation of a peon from one of our large farms with that of a Bolivian miner of that same epoch. If the housing of the Argentine worker was—and continues to be—defective, his level of nutrition was not a little superior to that of the middle class of any European country. As for social security laws, even if they were deficient and incomplete, they still formed a body of legislation that, in general, was respected.

The Argentine social problem was not so much one of a miserable and hungry proletariat as that of a nonexistent proletariat. It is very true that the tardy appearance of our working classes on the public scene was due, in part, to the lack of great industry and, in part, to the fact that until not many years ago those classes, in the urban sector, were composed of foreigners. But by 1943 the facts of the problem had already changed. World War II and the consequent economic isolation had given considerable impetus to industrial development so that several million urban workers were dependent on it. And as for the nationality problem, it had been resolved by the passage of time. The foreign grandparents and parents had been replaced by their native children and grandchildren, and their descendants became involved in the country's problems with the same interest and, from then on, with the same rights as the native, long-established traditional families. Some time the singular patriotism characteristic of the sons of the immigrants in this country must be analyzed.

The Marxist parties attempted to mobilize these forces

before Perón, but they did not succeed, except in a very partial and fragmentary way. They did not succeed because, in the first place, they were employing ideological rather than emotional or temperamental concepts. In the second place, those ideological concepts, insofar as they were intelligible, met with the incoercible resistance of our workers against letting themselves be won over by extreme positions. It is a commonplace to say that Socialism can never pass over the Riochuelo,[3] and it will always be a mystery for the European from an industrial country that the only place where a conservative caudillo repeatedly triumphed without using fraud was in Avellanada, which had the largest agglomeration of workers in the republic.

Until 1945, therefore, the Argentine proletariat could not—even though desiring to do so—feel a sense of solidarity with the national destiny. No one had concerned himself with speaking its language, with understanding its innermost desires, or with contacting it directly. Lost in the past was the memory of Yrigoyen (who, strictly speaking, was not a proletariat caudillo). Governed by strangers, it was inevitable that the Argentine working class would wholeheartedly follow a caudillo who seemed to express its sentiments clearly. Ideological transformation and social renovation, therefore, were being postulated by the historical conditions of the country at the end of the first third of the century. It would not have been impossible to consummate them in an orderly manner since the great wealth of the country and the peaceful disposition of its inhabitants were helping in the process.

The great and perhaps the only genius of Perón was in taking notice of the latent existence of these transformations and, putting himself at their head, utilizing the

---

[3] The Riochuelo is the stream separating the city of Buenos Aires proper from the working districts of the neighboring province of Buenos Aires. [Ed.]

state powers the June Revolution had conferred on him
and those that, soon afterward, he could snatch away
from his comrades in arms. If he succeeded in doing it,
it is undoubtedly because he possessed some of the gifts
that denote a leader. He was speaking in clear, precise,
and forceful language, designed for the multitude's simplistic attitude. And he knew how to say exactly what the
mass of people wanted him to say. In this restricted sense,
one could accept the interpretation that Peronism was a
phenomenon of collective magnetization. But while this
interpretation assumes that only Perón could create such a
phenomenon, in our judgment he was merely the catalytic
agent or unifying element of a movement that was obeying
deeper motives than just his personal influence.

This is where that element of chance intervenes so that
history is not a series of fatal deeds linked by the principle
of causation but—like all that is human—possesses that
ingredient of free choice that makes it impossible to guarantee its course. The free factor, in this case, was the personality of the man who put himself at the forefront of those
transformations and impressed his stamp on them. His
absolute lack of discrimination between good and evil,
his total lack of the talents of a statesman, his monstrous
and growing egocentricity, ought to provoke—as they did
provoke—the tergiversation and the adulteration of a
profound and legitimate desire for change. Thus it was
that the ideological renovation was diluted in the puerile
and stammering "Justicialist doctrine"; the political transformation into a constitutional reform that, although it
does not have the diabolical outlines that now are assigned
to it, turned out in the final analysis to be timid and
lacking in technical skill. And the social renovation, even
though the most effective and lasting work of the regime,
dissipated itself in demagogic pyrotechnics. For that
reason the Peronist adventure was, above all else, a great

opportunity lost. And in the life of nations, as in the life of men, opportunity usually does not knock twice.

Perón, who as we have seen was much more the *medium* than the leader of the masses, exacerbated a problem that we share with all Hispanic America and that forms the crisis of this drama: *the divorce of the people from the governing classes.*[4]

---

[4] For another Argentine view of the problems of Peronism see Ernesto Sábato, *El otro rostro del Peronismo* (Buenos Aires, 1956), which was written in answer to Amadeo's essay. [Ed.]

22

GEORGE PENDLE

THE PAST BEHIND
THE PRESENT

*For a view of Perón and Peronism against an histori-
cal backdrop, we turn again to the English historian,
George Pendle. In the following selection he examines Argentine history, before and after Perón,
and rejects the view that Peronism was only a malignant growth obstructing the course of Argentine
democracy.*

To anyone unfamiliar with Argentina's history it may seem
strange that although seven years have passed since the
overthrow of President Perón, Argentina has still not
become the orthodox parliamentary democracy which, it
was said, Perón alone prevented her from being. After so
many years, and after so much purging of *Peronismo,*
Argentina's ruling class themselves still blame Perón for

From George Pendle, "Argentina, the Past behind the Present,"
International Affairs, 38, No. 4 (London, October 1962), 494–500,
passim. Printed by permission of the author.

the country's present-day political and economic troubles.[1] For them, the Perón regime was a malignant growth. The truth is, of course, that Argentine history is a continuous process and that both Perón and present-day events have followed naturally from the past.

.   .   .

In 1930 Ortega y Gasset said of the immigrants to Argentina that they were 'men lacking in all interior discipline, men uprooted from their native European societies, where they had lived, without realizing it, morally disciplined by a sort of stabilized and integral collective life'. Emigrating, they broke away from that collective life and became unattached individuals. This characteristic has survived. A young Argentine author, H. A. Murena, writes: 'We behave as if each one of us were unique and as if he were alone.' Dr. Marcelo T. de Alvear, a former President of the Republic, remarked of his compatriots: 'Contradicting one's friends or enemies is routine.' In spite of the relatively advanced state of the national economy, and in spite of the endeavours of earnest men such as Dr. Raúl Prebisch and Señor Alvaro Alsogaray to persuade the people to cooperate, this proud nation continues to be (in Murena's words) a conglomeration rather than a community.[2]

The absence of a 'stabilized and integral collective life' in Argentina is partly the consequence of the country's extraordinary geographical diversity—sub-tropical luxuriance in the north; Andean deserts, and oases, in the west;

---

[1] See, for example, Dr. Federico Pinedo—a highly respected member of the ruling class who made a brief comeback as Minister of Economy in 1962—quoted in the *Review of the River Plate* (Buenos Aires, 19 April 1962).

[2] The quotations in this paragraph are from Lewis Hanke, *South America* (Princeton, N.J.: Van Nostrand, 1959).

temperate, fertile plains in the centre; the windswept south—and the great distances that separate the chief groups of population.

Argentina has been divided by history no less than by geography. In colonial times the Spaniards, whose main base in South America was on the Pacific coast at Lima, generally approached the area now named Argentina from that side of the Andes; and they established their principal settlements in the Andean foothills and marginal mountain ranges, where they founded Salta, Tucumán, Santiago del Estero, Mendoza, Córdoba. To the east, across the vast pampa, on the muddy estuary of the Río de la Plata, Buenos Aires was no more than a sad little outpost of the Empire. Thus geographical separation was confirmed by the pattern of settlement.

.   .   .

Again and again liberal-minded men sincerely tried to set up representative government of the British or North American kind, but when a more or less democratic régime was established it almost invariably evolved into a dictatorship or was overthrown by a coup d'état. It would not be an exaggeration to say that the conflict between imported democratic ideas and the local tradition of personal leadership—*caudillismo*—has been the central theme of political development in Argentina, as in other South American republics. Parkinson has even suggested that 'it is to South America that we must look, in the first instance, for dictatorship introduced and perpetuated as an admitted necessity; defended by thinkers of integrity and seen by historians as a positive good. . . . All modern dictatorship owes its inspiration to Simón Bolívar.' [3]

.   .   .

Under Irigoyen the Radicals wasted their opportunity,

[3] C. Northcote Parkinson, *The Evolution of Political Thought* (London: University of London Press, 1958), p. 251.

and they were replaced in 1930–1931 by a military-Conservative alliance. In fact the Radicals—the name was a misnomer—had discovered that they did not really desire any drastic alteration in the economic system. Consequently they, almost as much as the Conservatives, failed to gain the support of the urban working class, who were rapidly growing in strength and could not indefinitely be denied participation in public affairs. Nor were the workers greatly attracted to Socialism, which they were inclined to regard as a foreign creed. When the stream of immigration was cut off after the economic crisis of 1930 the workers became more and more Argentine in outlook and ready to follow a *caudillo* who would appeal to their nationalist sentiments and who would offer to improve their standard of living—an improvement which they were unable to achieve by parliamentary means.

The army [officers], too, were increasingly dissatisfied with the Conservatives, into whose hands the government had passed again. A group of younger officers, in particular, were determined that Argentina should be transformed into a modern industrialized state, and they realized that the conservative oligarchy were obstructing that transformation. So the military coup d'état which occurred in 1943 not only removed the Conservatives but prepared the way for a new era.

In the next two years, however, the senior officers grew alarmed by the activities of one of their colleagues, Colonel Juan Perón, who, as Secretary of Labour and Social Welfare, was gaining extraordinary popularity among the working class by promoting their interests with great zeal and publicity. In 1945, in an attempt to halt this process, Perón's military critics compelled him to resign from the government. Perón defiantly appealed to the workers for support. He was then placed under arrest. Working-class riots followed, and the trade union leaders

—feverishly assisted by the young radio performer Eva Duarte, who, like Perón himself, was of humble social origin—organized large-scale demonstrations. To appease the crowds, Perón was released.

.   .   .

As President of Argentina Perón raised the standard of living of the workers. He encouraged the expansion of urban industry—not only in Buenos Aires, but also in provincial towns such as Córdoba. He would have developed the southern oil fields if he had remained longer in power.

In making these and other contributions to social and economic progress, however, and in his manoeuvres to maintain himself in power, Perón aggravated the fragmentation which for so many years had been characteristic of Argentine society. By playing one sector of the community against another—politicians, landowners, businessmen, workers—he weakened the opposition but increased internal disunity.

Perón's military successors likewise, by repressing and ostracizing the *Peronistas,* made it impossible for an 'integral collective life' to come into being. The Aramburu government dedicated itself to the purging of the country of every trace of *Peronismo.* Those who had been connected with that régime were dismissed from the federal and provincial administrations, and from universities, law courts, and embassies abroad. Military *interventores* were placed in charge of the trade unions, and the *Peronista* Party was outlawed. The workers retaliated with strikes and sabotage. Employers (as the Buenos Aires correspondent of *The Times* wrote) now treated the workers with deliberate lack of consideration, their attitude being: 'Well, you fellows: you have had your day. Now it is our turn.'

As the *Peronistas*—comprising about one third of the electorate—were not permitted to nominate their own candidates for the general elections in 1958, they voted for the faction of the Radical Party that was headed by Dr. Arturo Frondizi, who had indicated that he would give them a fair deal if he were elected. With the *Peronistas'* assistance Frondizi won an overwhelming victory, and in spite of the protests of some members of the military hierarchy General Aramburu allowed him to be inaugurated in the presidency.

Frondizi had declared that he would govern, not for any one party, but for the whole nation, and it was evident that he intended to bring the *Peronistas* back into the community. Soon after assuming office he ordered a general increase in wages, granted an amnesty to those who were in prison or exile for political offences, and enabled *Peronistas* to re-enter the public service. The military leaders objected to these concessions, and during the next three years they repeatedly compelled the president to dismiss from official posts those whom they suspected of having *Peronista* sympathies. Nevertheless, at the congressional and provincial elections in March 1962 Frondizi rather rashly allowed the *Peronistas* to vote for their own candidates. This was doubtless another attempt to close the rift in the community; at the same time Frondizi probably judged that the *Peronistas,* having been proscribed for six years, would no longer vote as a bloc. In the event, the *Peronistas* won more than half of the available seats in the Chamber of Deputies and the majority of the available provincial governorships. Thereupon the leaders of the armed forces, fearing that Frondizi would permit the revival of *Peronismo* to continue, deposed him, imprisoned him, and ordered the annulment of the elections. The generals and admirals now had no clear policy for the nation. Their one aim was to keep the *Peronista* workers out of politics, to drive them back to where they properly belonged—to the meat-packing plants, the textile factories, etc., whence Perón had so irresponsibly brought them forth.

.   .   .

In deposing Frondizi, as when overthrowing Perón, the military were serving the interests of the upper class (now consisting not only of the landowners, but also of industrialists, bankers, and merchants). It is true that the majority of the military officers today are of *petit bourgeois* origin, but they (and their wives) saw a career in the armed forces as means to social advancement. During the 1930's and 1940's they were pampered by military governments, and in the social upsurge of the Perón era they gained prestige and quite comfortable prosperity. After the revolution which overthrew Perón in September 1955, officers with *Peronista* left-wing tendencies were placed in retirement, and the disputes which subsequently occurred within the armed forces arose mainly from disagreement on the measures to be adopted for preserving order and the traditional social structure.

In Argentina, as in other Latin American countries, the desire of the present military hierarchy, as of the civilian oligarchy, is that the capitalist system shall be perpetuated, and that whatever modifications may have to be made to adjust it to modern conditions shall cause the least possible inconvenience to the privileged members of the community.

.   .   .

Conditions are constantly changing, but to a considerable extent we can find in the past the explanation of why the Argentines behave as they do today. During the nineteenth century, as we have observed, they acquired the habit of *not* cooperating with one another. *Caudillo* was against *caudillo,* the capital city against the provinces. Landowners who amassed vast wealth soon became (with some notable exceptions) absentee owners, inhabiting quite another world from that of their *peones*. When foreign settlers arrived, they were allowed to live their own lives in their own way; and while their children were taught at school to sing the Argentine national anthem and to honour the national heroes, they learned also to be Argentine individualists, each one of them a *'Señor Yo'*, a 'Mister I'. Military officers—featherbedded heirs of the soldiers who marched across the Andes with San Martín—today still pay lip service to parliamentary democracy but take it for granted that government by decree is the only practical method of preserving order.

Of course, many of the characteristics and conditions described in the present article are by no means peculiar to Argentina. A combination of *all* of them does not exist, however, in any other country. Critics—foreigners, and Argentines too—contend that the Argentine way of conducting affairs is deplorable. Nevertheless, it is in this way that Argentina became, and still manages to remain, the most highly developed nation in Latin America.

Most foreigners—and, indeed, most Argentines whom one meets abroad—know little of Argentina outside Buenos Aires and the nearby holiday resorts. But Buenos Aires is a deceptive city. In appearance, and in its way of life, it is the most European of all Latin America's major cities, so one is apt to forget that it only exists by reason of the very *un*-European hinterland, which it dominates but which, since the pastures and grainfields provide the city's wealth, does, in a sense, dominate the city in return.

Buenos Aires is swept by a wind that comes from the desolate south; a wind that has passed over the dreary adobe villages of the remote regions and over the rich *pampa;* a wind which, meeting the warm air currents from the north, creates violent storms upon the capital. Likewise, Buenos Aires, in spite of its European aspect, is affected by powerful social and political pressures that are provincial, disturbing and, above all, South American. This is nothing new. It has always been so.

A Bibliographical Note

The literature on the Argentine past that was the prelude to Peronism is so extensive that one should first note the more useful historiographical guides to the material. Rómulo D. Carbia's *Historia crítica de la historiografía argentina* (La Plata, 1925; definitive edition, Buenos Aires, 1940) is still the most complete historiographical study of the pre-World War I periods of Argentine history. Ricardo Caillet-Bois' "La historiografía," in *Historia de la literatura argentina* (Buenos Aires, 1960), Vol. VI, pp. 19–198, not only covers the more recent period, it also is more objective and is better organized. Joseph R. Barager's "The Historiography of the Río de la Plata Area since 1830," in *The Hispanic American Historical Review*, Vol. XXXIX (1959), pp. 588–642, concentrates on Argentina and discusses the effect of the Perón era on the study and writing of Argentine history.

Clifton B. Kroeber examines the revisionist view of the dictator Juan Manuel Rosas in "Rosas and the Revision of Argentine History, 1880–1955," *Inter-American Review of Bibliography*, Vol. X (1960), pp. 3–25. Kroeber's is a scholarly, detached point of view. José P. Barreiro's *El espíritu de Mayo y el revisionismo histórico* (Buenos Aires, 1955), on the other hand, reflects the views of a liberal opposed to both the Rosistas and the Perón dictatorship. Fritz L. Hoffmann provides a helpful guide to the works published during and after the Perón decade, particularly those by Argentines, in "Perón and After," Part I, *The Hispanic American Historical Review*, Vol. XXXVI (1956), pp. 510–528, and Part II (conclusion), *ibid.*, Vol. XXXIX (1959), pp. 212–233. José Luis Romero illuminates the major trends in Argentine history, although individual works are not singled out, in his "Guía histórica para el Río de la Plata," published in *Ensayos sobre la historia del Nuevo Mundo* (Mexico, 1951). Finally, James R. Scobie's *Argentina* (document 5) has an extensive, well-annotated bibliography, which covers a wide range of Argentine subjects.

In addition to the works from which selections have been taken, particularly documents 2, 3, 4, 5, 8, 12, 16, and 19, the following are among the most useful studies, in English, of the Argentine nation before 1943: Miron Burgin, *Economic Aspects of Argentine Federalism* (Cambridge, Mass., 1946); H. S. Ferns, *Britain and Argentina in the Nineteenth Century* (Oxford, 1960); C. H. Haring, *Argentina and the United States* (Boston, 1941); John J. Kennedy, *Catholicism, Nationalism and Democracy in Argentina* (Notre Dame, 1958); F. A. Kirkpatrick, *A History of the Argentine Republic* (Cambridge, England, 1931); Thomas F. McGann, *Argentina: the Divided Land* (Princeton, N.J., 1966); Harold F. Peterson, *Argentina and the United States, 1810–1960* (New York, 1963); Ysabel F. Rennie, *The Argentine Republic* (New York, 1945); Domingo F. Sarmiento, *Life in the Argentine Republic in the Days of the Tyrants; or, Civilization and Barbarism,* translated by Mrs. Horace Mann (New York, 1868 and 1961); and Carl C. Taylor, *Rural Life in Argentina* (Baton Rouge, 1948).

The literature in Spanish on the post-1810 period is enormous. A basic source, for which every student of Argentine national history should be grateful, is Emilio Ravignani's painstaking editing of the monumental *Asambleas constituyentes argentinas* (6 vols.; Buenos Aires, 1937–1939), which provides ready access to the issues debated by some of Argentina's most distinguished political figures. The last five volumes of the ten-volume *Historia de la Nación Argentina—desde los orígines hasta la organización definitiva en 1862* (Buenos Aires, 1936–1950), edited by Ricardo Levene for the Academia Nacional de la Historia, provides studies in depth of the 1810–1862 period, including developments at the provincial level, that are still useful although many of the chapters have been outdated by subsequent research. The Academia has undertaken publication of a multi-volume history of the 1862–1930 period, *Historia argentina contemporánea.* The first two volumes, *Historia de las presidencias,* with individual chapters on each of the administrations from 1862 to 1930, were recently published (Buenos Aires, 1965). Enrique de Gandía's *Historia de la república argentina en el siglo XIX* (Buenos Aires, 1940) is perhaps the most informative single volume on political development; and Alejandro E. Bunge's *La economía argentina* (4 vols.; Buenos Aires, 1928–1930), is still valuable for its analysis of the Argentine economy in the post-World War I era.

There is still no major study of the Rosas period that could be called objective, and one of the few essays that meets that requirement is Emilio Ravignani's *Inferencias sobre Juan Manuel de Rosas y otros ensayos* (Buenos Aires, 1945). The case against the dictator, considered by many observers as the precursor of Perón, is ably presented in Antonio Dellepiane, *Rosas* (Buenos Aires, 1950; 2d ed., 1956), and Ernesto H. Celesia, *Rosas: Aportes para su historia* (Buenos Aires, 1954). For the pro-Rosas view the most scholarly studies are by Ernesto Quesada, *La época de Rosas* (Buenos Aires, 1898 and subsequent editions), and Carlos Ibarguren, *Juan Manuel de Rosas: Su vida, su tiempo, su drama* (Buenos Aires, 1930 and various other editions).

There are some excellent biographical studies of other leading nineteenth-century figures, including: Alberto Palcos' *Echeverría y la democracia argentina* (Buenos Aires, 1941); Ricardo Piccirilli's *Rivadavia y su tiempo* (2d ed., 3 vols.; Buenos Aires, 1960); Abel Chanetón's *Historia de Vélez Sársfield* (2d ed., 2 vols.; Buenos Aires, 1938); Luis B. Calderón's *Urquiza: Síntesis histórica de su época, su actuación y su obra* (2d ed.; Paraná, 1951); Jorge Meyer's *Alberdi y su tiempo* (Buenos Aires, 1963); Agustín P. Rivero Astengo's *Juárez Celman, 1844–1909* (Buenos Aires, 1944); and José S. Campobassi's *Sarmiento y Mitre: Hombres de Mayo y Caseros* (Buenos Aires, 1962).

There is a great profusion of studies of the controversial Sarmiento. Ricardo Rojas' *El profeta de la pampa. Vida de Sarmiento* (Buenos Aires, 1945); Allison W. Bunkley, *The Life of Sarmiento* (Princeton, N.J.: 1952); and Alberto Palcos' *Sarmiento: La vida, la obra, las ideas, el genio*

(Buenos Aires, 1929 and subsequent editions) are generally sympathetic in their interpretation; Manuel Gálvez's *Vida de Sarmiento, el hombre de autoridad* (Buenos Aires, 1945) and Leopoldo Lugones' *Historia de Sarmiento* (Buenos Aires, 1911 and later editions) are critical and reflect the authors' antiliberal outlook. Paul Groussac's *Los que pasaban: José Manuel Estrada, Pedro Goyena, Nicolás Avellaneda, Carlos Pellegrini, Roque Sáenz Peña* (2d ed.; Buenos Aires, 1939) provides a leading Argentine intellectual's views of some of the important figures of the latter part of the century.

For the intellectual currents of the period the monumental effort by Ricardo Rojas, *Historia de la literatura argentina* (4 vols.; Buenos Aires, 1917–1922 and subsequent editions), is still valuable but should be supplemented by the *Historia de la literatura argentina* (6 vols.; Buenos Aires, 1958–1959), edited by Rafael A. Arrieta. Bernardo Canal Feijoo's *Constitución y revolución* (Mexico, D.F., and Buenos Aires, 1955) provides a thorough analysis of the ideas of Juan Bautista Alberdi, one of the most important nineteenth-century figures. The works of José Ingenieros, particularly *Sociología argentina* (Buenos Aires, 1915) and *La evolución de las ideas argentinas* (2 vols.; Buenos Aires, 1918–1920), have gone through numerous editions, are still as provocative as ever, and are recommended reading for the serious student of the Argentine past. Alejandro Korn, *Las influencias filosóficas en la evolución nacional* (Buenos Aires, 1936), and Juan C. Torchía Estrada, *La filosofía en la Argentina* (Washington, D.C., 1961), are two thoughtful surveys of how philosophical ideas affected Argentine society. Ezequiel Martínez Estrada has examined Argentine society in *Radiografía de la pampa* (2 vols.; Buenos Aires, 1933), *Cabeza de Goliat: Microscopía de Buenos Aires* (Buenos Aires, 1940), and *Muerte y transfiguración de Martín Fierro* (Mexico, D.F., 1948)—all of which have gone through subsequent editions. Gino Germani's *Estructura social en la Argentina* (Buenos Aires, 1955) is a trailblazer as an attempt of a trained sociologist to analyze the nation's social structure.

The 1890 revolution has been treated in two older monographs, Mariano de Vedia y Mitre's *La revolución del 90* (Buenos Aires, 1929) and Juan Balestra's *El Noventa: Una evolución política argentina* (Buenos Aires, 1934), and by several individual scholars in the initial issue of the *Revista de Historia* (Buenos Aires, 1957), which concentrated on "La crisis del 90." For the period after 1890 one has to rely largely on biographical studies and general surveys since official documents in the Argentine Archives are closely held—after 1862—and those pertaining to the present century are even less accessible to the native as well as the visiting scholar. Consequently, many of the biographies of individuals prominent in the post-1890 period must be used with care. A case in point is the subjective nature of two biographies of Hipólito Yrigoyen: Manuel Gálvez's *Vida de Hipólito Yrigoyen, el hombre de misterio* (Buenos Aires, 1939) and Félix Luna's *Yrigoyen, el templario de la libertad* (Buenos Aires, 1954). There is also little in the way of critical analysis of the revolution of 1930—an exception is the treatment by the contributors in the third issue of the *Revista de Historia* (Buenos Aires, 1957), which concentrates on "La crisis del 1930." José M. Sarobe's *Memorias sobre la revolución del 6 de septiembre de 1930* (Buenos Aires, 1962) is a valuable source. The definitive monograph on that bench mark in Argentine history, however, has not yet appeared.

For the important 1930–1943 years there are the political memoirs such as Ramón Colomba's *El Congreso que yo he visto: 1934–1943* (Buenos Aires, 1951); Enrique Dickmann's *Recuerdos de un militante socialista* (Buenos Aires, 1949); Federico Pinedo's *En tiempos de la República* (5 vols.; Buenos Aires, 1946–1948); and Nicolás Repetto's *Mi paso por la política*, Vol. I, *De Roca a Yrigoyen* (Buenos Aires, 1956), and Vol. II, *De Uriburu a Perón* (Buenos Aires, 1957). These are valuable sources—albeit of the "selected" variety—and should be used with care, as should the political party histories such as Rodolfo Puiggrós' *Historia crítica de los partidos políticos argentinos* (Buenos Aires, 1956) and Francisco Scilingo's

Decadencia de los partidos en la Argentina (Buenos Aires, 1945). This is also true of Gabriel del Mazo's three-volume study of the Radical Civic Union, published as *El radicalismo: Ensayo sobre su historia y doctrina* (Buenos Aires, 1951), *El radicalismo: Notas sobre su historia y doctrina, 1922–1952* (Buenos Aires, 1955), and *El radicalismo: El movimiento de intransigencia y renovación, 1945–1957* (Buenos Aires, 1957).

For the Radical Party, Peter G. Snow provides an objective and well-balanced treatment in his *Argentine Radicalism: The History and Doctrine of the Radical Civic Union* (Iowa City, 1965). Another North American, Francis Herron, relates his impressions of Argentine society, at the close of this period, in *Letters from the Argentine* (New York, 1943). Felix J. Weil analyzes the country's economic problems, on the eve of Perón, in his *Argentine Riddle* (New York, 1944). The most useful studies in English of the 1930–1943 period are Ysabel F. Rennie's *The Argentine Republic* (New York, 1945), and Arthur P. Whitaker's *The United States and Argentina* (Cambridge, Mass., 1954) and *Argentina* (Englewood Cliffs, N.J., 1964). An Argentine symposium, edited by Jorge A. Paita, *Argentina, 1930–1960* (Buenos Aires, 1961), puts the period in the perspective of the decade and a half that followed.

The problem of Perón, his rise to power, and his regime have been the subjects of a veritable flood of publications, of which only a trickle even pretend to be objective in their approach. Since so few Argentines—Germani (document 6) is a notable exception—have been able to examine Perón or Peronism from a detached viewpoint, the views of non-Argentines assume particular importance in the literature on the Perón period. In addition to the works of non-Argentines from which selections in the text have been taken, the following studies by foreigners of the Perón period are particularly noteworthy: Robert J. Alexander, *The Perón Era* (New York, 1951), for its discussion of Perón and labor; George I. Blanksten, *Perón's Argentina* (Chicago, 1953), for the clearest exposition of *justicialismo,* the Peronist ideology; the works of a Chilean,

Alejandro Magnet, *Nuestros vecinos justicialistas* (Santiago de Chile, 1953) and *Nuestros vecinos argentinos* (Santiago de Chile, 1956); Arthur P. Whitaker, *Nationalism in Latin America* (Gainesville, 1962); and Whitaker and David C. Jordan, *Nationalism in Contemporary Latin America* (New York, 1966), for the role of nationalism before, during, and after the Perón period.

Fritz L. Hoffmann's two review articles in *The Hispanic American Historical Review* (November 1956 and May 1959), cited above, provide a carefully annotated guide to the flood of controversial publications from Perón's fellow countrymen. There is little effort on the part of most of their authors to examine the conditions that enabled Perón to come to power and hold it for a decade. For example, the former Radical Party Deputy, Silvio Santander, in his *Técnica de una traición: Juan Perón y Eva Perón, agentes del nazismo en la Argentina* (Montevideo, 1953), depends heavily on documents of dubious authenticity and is more a political tract than the result of serious research. (Professor Hoffmann's apparent acceptance of the authenticity of Santander's theses constitutes one of the few cases in which this writer finds himself differing with the reviewer's views.)

In the main, those Argentine political figures who were strongly anti-Axis in World War II—the Socialists, Radicals, and Communists—tend to portray the Perón regime as the result of the influence of European Fascism and Nazism. On the other hand, in *Perón and la crisis argentina* (Buenos Aires, 1956), Julio Irazusta, an ardent Anglophobe and rightist nationalist, condemns Perón for having sold out to the British after World War II.

The Trotskyites, and other Communists who reject the Moscow line, take a more sympathetic view of Perón, seeing him as an anti-imperialist, preparing the way for the rise of the proletariat to power. Jorge Abelardo Ramos, *América Latina: Un país* (Buenos Aires, 1949) and *Revolución y contrarevolución en Argentina: Las masas en nuestra historia* (Buenos Aires, 1957), Jorge Enea Spilimbergo, *Nacionalismo oligárquico y nacionalismo revolucionario* (Buenos Aires, 1958), and Arturo Jauretche, *Los profetas del odio* (Buenos Aires, 1957), are examples of the reaction of extreme leftist nationalists to Perón. Alberto Methol Ferré's *La izquierda nacional en la Argentina* (Buenos Aires, n.d.) discusses the views of these and other left-wing nationalists *re* Perón in some detail.

While the definitive monograph on the Perón regime has not yet appeared, the works of Gino Germani, *Estructura social de la Argentina* (Buenos Aires, 1955) and *Política y sociedad en una época de transición* (Buenos Aires, 1962), are the sort of building blocks upon which such a monograph will eventually be based. The recent collaboration by Germani, Torcuato S. Di Tella, Jorge Graciarena, and others in *Argentina, sociedad de masas* (Buenos Aires, 1965), José Luis de Imaz, *Los que mandan* (Buenos Aires, 1964), and José Manuel Saravia (h.), *Argentina 1959* (Buenos Aires, 1959) are other studies by Argentines that provide useful information on the society and institutions that produced Perón. Tomás Roberto Fillol attempts to explain the Argentine economy's failure to "take off" in his *Social Factors in Economic Development: The Argentine Case* (Cambridge, Mass., 1961). Arthur P. Whitaker analyzes the factors leading to Perón's overthrow in *Argentine Upheaval* (New York, 1956).

Samuel L. Baily, *Labor, Nationalism and Politics in Argentina* (New Brunswick, N.J., 1967), which appeared after the manuscript for this book was completed, provides an excellent analysis of Perón's impact on the Argentine labor movement and labor's reasons for supporting him. The author's extensive bibliography will also prove extremely useful to students of Argentine labor and its history.

A Note on the Type

The text of this book was set on the Linotype in a face called TIMES ROMAN, designed by Stanley Morison for *The Times* (London), and first introduced by that newspaper in 1932.

Among typographers and designers of the twentieth century, Stanley Morison has been a strong forming influence, as typographical advisor to the English Monotype Corporation, as a director of two distinguished English publishing houses, and as a writer of sensibility, erudition, and keen practical sense.

Composed, printed, and bound by
The Colonial Press, Inc., Clinton, Massachusetts

Designed by
LEON BOLOGNESE